Mutual Growth in the Psychotherapeutic Relationship: Reciprocal Resilience

Mutual Growth in the Psychotherapeutic Relationship: Reciprocal Resilience is an essential, innovative guide for mental health professionals who listen repeatedly to stories of devastation and trauma.

Moving beyond traditions that consider the clinician as existing only for the patient and not as an individual, this breakthrough model explores the possibility of mutual resilience-building and personal benefit developing between therapists and their patients. The first section of the book situates Reciprocal Resilience in the context of evolving resilience studies. The second section provides lively, demonstrative clinical anecdotes from therapists themselves, organized into chapters focused on enhancing their positive strategies for coping and growth while functioning under duress.

This book presents a framework for teaching and supervising psychotherapists that can enrich clinician well-being, while recognizing the therapeutic relationship as the key for enabling patients' emotional growth. It challenges mental health practitioners to share their own experiences, presenting a research model syntonic with how clinicians think and work daily in their professional practice. It offers a pioneering approach, finding inspiration in even the darkest moments for therapists and patients alike.

Patricia Harte Bratt is a psychoanalyst and psychotherapist practicing in Livingston, NJ and New York City. She is a director of the Academy of Clinical and Applied Psychoanalysis (ACAP) and the Boston Graduate School of Psychoanalysis-NJ, and president of the National Association for Advancement of Psychoanalysis (NAAP) and the NJ Certified Psychoanalysts Advisory Committee.

"Can therapists benefit from listening to traumatic stories, from being the holding container for clients' feelings? With theoretical and historical backdrop, stories unfold, in therapists' own words, introducing the concept of Reciprocal Resilience: the emotional loop between client and therapist that sustains each in the process. Patricia Bratt's commentaries bring to life the psychic struggles clinicians face, opening unexpected perspective on the therapeutic relationship. Stories reveal contexts where coping skills, resilience correlates used to manage earlier life issues, re-emerge in the co-created emotional field in therapy. In this pioneering work, she describes a method, easy to adopt in treatment or in supervision. It makes use of the nuances of the therapeutic relationship, enhancing early defenses, and promotes reciprocal resilience and psychic growth for both parties. *Mutual Growth* is a generative and generous book."

Donna Bassin, PhD, faculty at NYU and maintains a private practice in New York City. Her documentary, *The Mourning After*, was the winner of the 2017 Gradiva award

"Patricia Bratt's book opens up a new clinical vista for our consideration. This pertains to the mutual interplay of psychic growth between the patient and the therapist as their work progresses. Bringing Bion's notion of the 'container' and Winnicott's concept of 'survival' to bear upon the modern relational paradigm of the therapeutic process, Bratt formulates the novel concept of 'Reciprocal Resilience'. She elucidates its overlaps with resilience, adaptive countertransference, and altruism. The neglected dimension of the therapist's well-being is thus brought into a sharp focus, adding an important tool to our therapeutic armamentarium!"

Salman Akhtar, MD, Professor, Thomas Jefferson University, and Supervising and Training Analyst, Psychoanalytic Center of Philadelphia

"It may be an odd idea that treating our most traumatized clients can lead to growth and resilience on the part of the therapist while helping the client develop better coping skills. Instinctively, Pat understands the mutual benefits of therapy for both. In a theoretical and clinically alive book, this symbiotic interaction leading to 'Reciprocal Resilience' is deftly presented. Fascinating, moving stories in therapists' own words highlight 'the interactive, emotional loop between client and therapist'. 'Tales of resilience' demonstrate ways therapists' work is growth enhancing. The book presents a framework for teaching and supervising psychotherapists that can enrich clinician well-being, while recognizing the therapeutic relationship as the key for enabling patients' emotional growth. Making use of the concept of Reciprocal Resilience, it presents a trail-blazing approach easily incorporated in clinical practice."

Vicki Semel, PsyD is President and supervising faculty of the Academy of Clinical and Applied Psychoanalysis (ACAP). She maintains a private practice in Livingston, NJ and New York City

Mutual Growth in the Psychotherapeutic Relationship

Reciprocal Resilience

Patricia Harte Bratt

Routledge
Taylor & Francis Group

LONDON AND NEW YORK

First published 2019
by Routledge
2 Park Square, Milton Park, Abingdon, Oxon OX14 4RN

and by Routledge
52 Vanderbilt Avenue, New York, NY 10017

Routledge is an imprint of the Taylor & Francis Group, an informa business

© 2019 Patricia Harte Bratt

British Library Cataloguing-in-Publication Data
A catalogue record for this book is available from the British Library

Library of Congress Cataloging-in-Publication Data
Names: Bratt, Patricia Harte, author.
Title: Mutual growth in the psychotherapeutic relationship: reciprocal resilience / By Patricia Harte Bratt.
Description: Milton Park, Abingdon, Oxon; New York, NY: Routledge, 2019. | Includes bibliographical references and index.
Identifiers: LCCN 2018045201 (print) | LCCN 2018045665 (ebook) | ISBN 9780429433153 (eBook) | ISBN 9781138360426 (hardback) | ISBN 9781138360433 (pbk.) | ISBN 9780429433153 (ebk)
Subjects: | MESH: Psychotherapeutic Processes | Resilience, Psychological | Professional-Patient Relations
Classification: LCC RC480 (ebook) | LCC RC480 (print) | NLM WM 420 | DDC 616.89/14—dc23
LC record available at https://lccn.loc.gov/2018045201

ISBN: 978-1-138-36042-6 (hbk)
ISBN: 978-1-138-36043-3 (pbk)
ISBN: 978-0-429-43315-3 (ebk)

Typeset in Times New Roman
by codeMantra

Printed and bound in Great Britain by
TJ International Ltd, Padstow, Cornwall

Mutual Growth in the Psychotherapeutic Relationship: Reciprocal Resilience is dedicated to the clinicians and their patients who willingly share the moments of their lives in a courageous way that helps each grow and become resilient. It is a testimony to the power of the therapeutic encounter and, while recognizing the value of clinician self-care, is more importantly an assertion that we care. We, the supervisors, faculties, therapists, and administrators who observe and walk with you through deep emotional waters, care about assuring your well-being, and continued sense of astonishment and satisfaction at the important role you play in the lives of so many.

Contents

List of tables

About the author

Patricia Harte Bratt, PsyaD, PhD, a psychoanalyst/psychotherapist with practices in Livingston, NJ and New York City, is a Director of the Academy of Clinical and Applied Psychoanalysis (ACAP) in Livingston, NJ, its Trauma and Resilience Program, Applied Psychoanalysis Division, and the Boston Graduate School of Psychoanalysis - NJ. She has designed staff development training programs to enhance skills and intervention strategies for professionals serving vulnerable members of our communities for many groups, such as the Department of Child Protection and Permanency, the Child Life Specialists Association, NJ Crisis Negotiators Association, and the International Neuropsychoanalytic Society. She is faculty and training supervisor at several psychoanalytic institutes, and has been graduate faculty at the Boston Graduate School of Psychoanalysis, Drew University, Centenary College, and Union College. Her areas of specialization include training clinicians to work with the full range of emotional disorders, clinical supervision, child treatment, couples therapy, and work with young adults on the spectrum and their families. She, and colleagues at ACAP, recently founded i*Strive,* a program for young adults high functioning on the spectrum, who age out of most services, but continue to thrive at *iStrive.* She served as a diagnostic psychologist and forensic consultant for the Passaic County Court system, Seton Hall Law Clinic, and the Brooklyn Center for Psychotherapy. Dr. Bratt is President of the National Association for the Advancement of Psychoanalysis (NAAP), and of the NJ State Advisory Board for Psychoanalysis since 2002. Her publications include, "The Impact of Strategic Emotional Communication on Memory and Identity Development," "Nurturing Emotionally Resilient Children," "Consulting the Patient: The Art of Being Together," "Fearless: Or Resistance to Resilience," and "Reciprocal Resilience: Surprising Benefits for Clinicians of Listening to Stories of Overwhelming Experiences."

Acknowledgements

A most special thanks goes to my dear friend Dr. Salman Akhtar. In his boundless generosity he encouraged publication of this work, shepherded its outline and title, and was available whenever I got stymied about how to proceed. Without his brilliant, helpful, and always humorous coaching, *Mutual Growth in the Psychotherapeutic Relationship: Reciprocal Resilience* would not have happened.

The superb minds, hearts, patience, and stamina of many colleagues in Boston, New Jersey and New York contributed to bringing this work to completion. Drs. Vicki Semel, Stephen Soldz, Ghislaine Boulanger, Jane Snyder, and Mary Massaro, from the Boston Graduate School of Psychoanalysis (BGSP), our branch campus in NJ, BGSP-NJ, and the Academy of Clinical and Applied Psychoanalysis (ACAP) in NJ, all had a hand in reviewing or shaping material along the way. What started as a quest to find ways to help increase therapists' emotional resilience and general well-being led to numerous talks, conferences, groups, a research project, and now this book.

Many mental health practitioners contributed to the development of the concept of Reciprocal Resilience through discussions of experiences of listening repeatedly to overwhelming stories from patients. Their willingness to share clinical and personal vignettes, despite the often painful emotions triggered, has been inspiring and profoundly moving. This is particularly true of those who participated in the extensive interviews described throughout *Mutual Growth in the Psychotherapeutic Relationship*. All stories, identities, and many details have been modified to protect privacy. So I cannot mention names here, but you know who you are, and it is important to acknowledge that I am honored and touched by the spunk, generosity of spirit, and courage you shared with me. Each time I go back to the interviews I learn something new about a person, another dimension. It has been a remarkable experience.

My family is an endlessly supportive cheering squad, for which I am always grateful. I want each to know how much I appreciate their bighearted, reinforcing belief anything can be accomplished. Of course, a special thanks to my son, Jonathan, always ready to help out, making it great fun at the same time, his passion to know and grow are an inspiration.

The team at T&F Routledge has been amazing. Starting with Russell George and Kate Hawes, who took over their new adoptee authors when Karnak was acquired. Elliott Morsia, the editor coordinating all of *Mutual Growth in the Psychotherapeutic Relationship* has been a readily available resource with boundless encouragement. Jamie Magyar skillfully coordinated artwork. While Sophie Dunbar was tasked with copyediting. Sophie saved me from untold embarrassments where I was certain I'd done a fantastic job. With her impeccable photographic mind and attention to detail, she rescued me from many citation gaffs and suggested creative alternatives in text and formatting. Many thanks to all at Routledge.

Introduction

Mutual Growth in the Psychotherapeutic Relationship: Reciprocal Resilience is about stories, storytellers, listeners, and the magic that can be drawn from even the darkest moments. A breakthrough concept, advocating for mental health professionals who listen repeatedly to stories of devastation and trauma, and for those training them, unfolds in the words of clinicians as they describe experiences helping fragile and mistreated individuals become whole. The book departs from the tradition of attending only to patients' well-being, where the clinician is not considered an individual in his or her own right, entitled to care, benefits, and sense of meaning or compensation. This blind spot in understanding the therapeutic alliance reduces clinicians to empty containers, void until filled by the patient, and re-drained in the clinical process. Countering that is the phenomenon of Reciprocal Resilience, the interactive emotional loop between client and clinician, or clinician and supervisor, offering psychic growth for each.

Part I, Theoretical Applications, outlines the emergence and importance of the concept of Reciprocal Resilience in the context of the growing field of resilience studies. The research project and method that led to identifying reciprocal benefits in the therapeutic loop is described. This naturalistic, interview approach, much in sync with clinicians' way of analytic thinking and practice, will hopefully inspire novice to seasoned professionals to engage in more research, and share their important observations with the professional community.

Part II, Clinical Applications, consists of "tales of resilience" chapters that recount, in their own words, the anguish, spunk, coping skills, and creativity of therapists working with difficult cases while challenging their own ghosts. They begin to describe previously unrecognized personal rewards from together confronting clients' struggles. We learn about life situations, early relationships, and personality styles influencing development of specific defense skills to navigate conflict. We see how they work, or do not, and strategies for enhancing those that can.

Mutual Growth in the Psychotherapeutic Relationship: Reciprocal Resilience demonstrates that beginning from within oneself, and increasing through the power of reciprocal connectedness, stories of overwhelming events can present shared opportunities for transformation. Clinicians, and those who train or supervise them, can quickly integrate the resilience building strategies described. The book offers a window into the remarkable adaptive skills therapists bring to their work, how they can be developed to increase resilience, and a model for teaching and supervising psychotherapists that boosts clinician well-being, minimizing burnout. It is especially important, in the context of mental health professions, to develop an understanding of the curative and generative capacity of Reciprocal Resilience. We need to quickly rethink our unspoken position regarding personal benefits and well-being of those in our field if we want to keep them with us, encourage new candidates, and finally, provide the best therapeutic experience and opportunity for psychic growth for both. Recently there has been much said about the need for clinician self-care. This book affirms *we care*. We who are the supervisors, teachers, therapists, administrators, and friends of mental health practitioners, who observe and walk with you through deep emotional waters, care about assuring your well-being, with a continued sense of astonishment and satisfaction at the important role you play in the lives of so many.

Prologue

Chapter 1

Concept of Reciprocal Resilience

A question of benefit

Mutual Growth in the Psychotherapeutic Relationship is about stories, story-tellers, and listeners. It explores the possibility of benefit to clinicians exposed to narrations of crushing experiences. It encompasses years studying emotional resilience, talking with numerous groups, and influences from clinical practice and teaching. Stories recounted reflect the anguish, courage, joy, and resilience of therapists working with difficult cases while battling their own ghosts. As I studied this phenomenon of the clinicians' experience of self, it became increasingly clear that their welfare is rarely considered. Their patients and clients are treated as more important throughout the therapeutic world. There, the therapist exists solely as a vehicle to increase patient welfare. Therapist well-being is rarely considered.

The perspective of therapists' personal reward breaks from a long-standing dictate in the field. Our tradition is to attend only to patients' issues. Tabachnick, Keith-Spiegel, and Pope (1991) found 59.6% of mental health clinicians surveyed acknowledged working when too distressed to be effective. "Principle A: Beneficence and Normalficience" of the General Principles of the American Psychological Association's (APA) *Ethical Principles of Psychologists And Code Of Conduct* (APA, 2017) states, "Psychologists strive to be aware of the possible effect of their own physical and mental health on their ability to help those with whom they work." In other words, it is the psychologist's mandate to be mindful of self-care in order to protect their patients. The psychologist is charged with maintaining a form of selfless self-care.

Harris, Martin, and Martin (2013), in their research on the relationship between psychological well-being and perceived wellness in graduate level counseling students, studied ninety-seven graduate students in counseling at a state university in Pennsylvania. "The study aimed at addressing a critical need, namely, to assess and address the wellness of masters-level counseling students by providing information on the psychological well-being and perceived wellness of such students" (Harris et al., 2013, p. 18).

The authors state research has shown there is a high incidence of personal emotional conflict among those considering careers as mental health professionals. This can negatively impact their clinical development in ways such as effectiveness, burnout, and job stress. The study's goal was to provide what was considered a useful screening tool for students, alerting them to psychological issues that might impede their development, and offering strategies for resolving them (Harris et al., 2013). It is one of the few recent ones centering on identifying clinician well-being. However, the concern for well-being remains about the therapist as a vehicle for the clients' welfare. In this scenario, while the focus is on the emotional health of the student, any impact beyond the clinical encounter is considered a fringe benefit or a hindrance.

Self-care among mental health professionals is a growing concern, described as an ethical imperative (Norcross, 2010). Barnett, Baker, Elman, and Schoener (2007). When exploring who becomes a therapist, present data indicates that 70% of female psychologists, and 33% of male psychologists, report incidents of abuse or molestation in early life. The percentages among mental health professionals are significantly higher than in other fields. With a large number of those entering the field having either a history of, or currently living in, dysfunctional environments, they are said to be more vulnerable to the negative effects of the job. Over-identification, regression, personal resonance with what they hear compromising judgment, a tendency to be the rescuer or the parent-surrogate, anxiety, depression, and hopelessness are just a few on the long list of negative impacts clinical work may have on the therapist whose self-care is neglected.

Akhtar and O'Neil give an example of the dynamics of one of the vulnerabilities mentioned above. Quoting Schmale (1964): "Hopelessness is ... a loss of ego autonomy due to one's own inability to provide oneself with gratification" (Akhtar & O'Neil, 2015, p. 10). This is contrasted with helplessness, described as loss of ego autonomy occurring through a recurrent history of failure to be cared for by an important figure in early life. Akhtar's discussion of hopelessness and hopefulness as the flip sides of a dynamic is relevant when considering therapist well-being and perception of it. According to Akhtar, the pathologically hopeless individual, or one who dips toward that periodically, is actually defending against unrealistic feelings of hope. They are using hopelessness as a mechanism to avoid changing or confronting the idealized view of hope they harbor and hide. As long as hope remains barricaded in the preconscious, ferociously defended by the expressed feelings of hopelessness, growth and adaptation are limited.

Akhtar and O'Neil offer a vignette where Akhtar intervenes, after unwaveringly listening for some time to a patient who has long criticized the analysis for not making him taller. It is hopeless just like everything else in life. The patient was asked, "The intensity with which you berate me about this issue makes me wonder if you really believe that analysis could or should lead you to become taller. Do you?".

The intervention was made well into the treatment, with a stable foundation in place to modulate the patient's response, if needed. He reluctantly agreed that he did believe analysis could make him taller. This marked the initial step in the patient's reconsideration of the hidden, idealized, irrational belief system around hope that his hopelessness denied. Height represented something more than itself. It was a symbolic communication of a conflict ultimately resolved through the transference relationship (Akhtar & O'Neil, 2015, p. 14). This type of potentially crippling hopefulness is what may underlie therapists' slumps into deep states of hopelessness. The hopelessness denies the hidden fragments of hopefulness, the tacit belief of themselves as the rescuer, which they are loathe to abandon. So they remain trapped in the version of themselves as a failure to protect the preconscious vision of the champion.

When therapist welfare is addressed it concerns 1) advice about self-care so that the job can be effectively accomplished, or 2) recovery from inevitable, negative effects of the work. The mental health professional is not discussed as an individual in her/his own right entitled to care, benefits, and a sense of meaning or compensation. Should they be different from any other professional? One fact has become clear: mental health professionals themselves have not been oriented toward considering any benefits to them their work might include. Positive, personal impact of work is not on the radar. The confluence of denial by society and the professions presents a gap in our ability to care for the caregiver, short-changing them. It creates a blind spot in understanding significant elements of the therapeutic alliance. This view renders the clinician an empty container, void until filled by the patient, and re-drained again in the therapeutic process.

We have a population of mental health professionals whom we trust to be mindful of the well-being of others. Health and professional satisfaction, as related to the clinician without reference to the clients, is ignored. There are several reasons this may have become the norm. The simplest is an unarticulated belief it is wrong to profit from another's crisis or bad fortune. An attitude of moral rectitude informs society's assumptions about those in the "helping professions." Self-sacrificing and committed to the good of others are traits frequently attributed to them. This issue is unaddressed in academia or analytic training institutes. With such silence on the topic one could wonder about an unspoken, unconscious societal collusion designed to insure the helping professional maintains productivity without seeking personal benefits. The motives of a mental health practitioner expecting personal gain beyond salary, as part of compensation, could be considered questionable.

Another reason for ignoring benefits is our natural inclination to focus first on threats (Dijksterhuis & Aarts, 2003). Humans are survivors attending immediately to challenges to that powerful life drive rather than relishing the good of the moment. Psychoanalysis started with examination of pathology. The field of medicine is no different in its origins. It is a difficult leap to try to put threats in perspective and instead look at growth and enhancement factors encountered in different situations, even if ignoring keys to well-being threatens survival. Our emotional sensors are hard-wired and respond instantly to a threat. They trigger signal anxiety, which activates a neurobiological response, setting in motion a series of hormonal and bodily reactions to assess the danger and plan for survival (Damasio, 1999; LeDoux, 2003).

The hyper-activation of psychic monitoring and signal anxiety results in behaviors such as the fight-flight-freeze and recently noticed fawn responses. Each has its own value in protecting the individual, if used in the appropriate circumstance. If not, disaster can ensue. What is interesting about these responses is their involuntary nature. The person is left with little opportunity to make an informed choice, given the cascading overstimulation the responses provoke. If one has been under threat in the past and escaped, it is likely the mechanism of escape used then will be redeployed. This can have a positive or negative effect in the moment, and long term. That is, if it works, it may remain an embedded, reflex response used in future events when another choice would be more beneficial. Or, if it does not work, when confronted with similar, future incidents the individual may experience the memory of failure. They might fear another failure, coupled with cognitive dissonance about a once believed effective response now considered questionable. This cycle could cause a freeze response in the face of threat.

A third reason to unconsciously ignore benefits may be the consensus of a culture that focuses on eliminating or reducing negative impacts. An incessant barrage of threatening news speeds its way across cyberspace, and impulse-driven overexposure on social media tears us in several directions. At once we want to stop the bombardment, and yet find ourselves gleefully addicted. On the job, pressed with the overwhelming experiences of others, and knowing it is never-ending, clinicians naturally find themselves putting out potential psychological fires rather than reflecting on the full experience of their work. Life is complex even when not threatening. It is as dangerous to get bogged down focusing on negative realities to the exclusion of positive aspects, as the opposite. One cannot ensure safety and well-being simply by believing or hoping it will be so if you are vigilant, or by always ignoring a part of the picture to maintain that danger surveillance. We need to find better ways to provide a balance for those, the containers, we charge and entrust with the care of our more fragile.

In the following chapters, I explore the question of possible benefits to clinicians from their work and outline an approach for increasing the experience of personal resilience. This is relevant for all professionals who listen to stories of hardship and devastation. The process described can have an immediate influence on the clinician's self-perception and be included as a regular component of training curricula. This model takes advantage of the power of unconscious motivation. It makes use of object-oriented interventions to protect ego functioning (Margolis, 1994), respects existing defenses, and appreciates the reciprocal nature of the therapeutic relationship. It incorporates development of therapist awareness of possible benefits from clinical encounters. The approach underscores the interactive, interpersonal field generated by therapist and patient, and by supervisor and clinician, as sources of mutuality. The therapeutic or supervisory relationship is identified as the tool for reciprocity and for resilience enrichment (Baranger, 2012; Bratt, 2012).

Reciprocal Resilience

I refer to the result of the dynamic listening-holding process in treatment as Reciprocal Resilience. This interactive loop can present a powerful resource for helping each party access and increase resilience: valuation and healthy adaptation to a perceived threat, followed by growth. It involves the empathic or emotionally mirroring response of the therapist to the undercurrent of feelings communicated by the client. This happens in the course of listening to the stories of traumatic experiences and communication with the patient; either silently through an accepting, holding attitude or through words mirroring, reflecting, or joining what is being told (Margolis, 1994). In this way the client feels a sheltering, supportive presence, and is freed to speak in a less censored way. Sharing in the resilience building process creates one component of the Reciprocal Resilience loop. The clinician remains ready to welcome and contain emotional communications from the patient. The willingness to filter painful feelings produces a safe environment in which the patient may tolerate reintroduction of once noxious feelings (Almond, 2003; Bion, 1970; Bratt, 2012; Brown, 2012).

This co-creative therapeutic loop is validating. It spurs increased emotional risk-taking and empathic capacity in the therapist. It is similar to Bion's "mother" premasticating toxic emotions projected by the infant, with both container and contained in reverie. Together they can sustain connectedness as the mother provides the holding environment, tolerating the disturbing feelings, until safely crunched to digestible portions the infant can absorb (Bion, 1963).

When the therapist is able to recognize the powerfully creative dynamic in the continuous reciprocal loop, confidence about ability to form positive adaptive strategies in the face of difficult challenges in therapy heightens. The therapist's ego as holding container can welcome feelings discharged by the patient. These once noxious elements flush through the buffering therapeutic holding environment, shedding toxicity. They return through the emotional exchange in the therapeutic relay as ego reinforcing for the patient. The ability to choose to be the container, coupled with a capacity for sorting what is self and other, offers psychic growth potential for the therapist. "In therapy, narratives and worlds are generated that are more than the sum of their parts, i.e., the internal and intersubjective worlds of the patient and analyst" (Grossmark, 2012, p. 292). A growing attention to the psychical entity co-created in the therapeutic relationship is developing synchronously with interest in the impact of that interaction on the therapist, as well as the traditional focus on the patient's experience (Katz, 2013).

Hernandez, Gangsei, & Engstrom (2007) looked at the possibility that clinicians may have a type of transformative experience during the course of working with trauma victims. This notion arose out of interviews with therapists involved in trauma remediation who remarked about not only the difficulties, but also the positive effects they noticed doing their work. They proposed a concept of Vicarious Resilience, which I am referring to as Reciprocal Resilience (Hernandez et al., 2007). The word reciprocal highlights the energy and emotional interaction within the dyad or group. This interaction may represent a potent resource in helping each party access and increase resilience potential.

It is through the therapist modeling a resilient and empathic stance, being open to risk, confident about adequate assessment and ability to identify positive adaptive strategies in the face of difficult challenges, that patients feel safe to reveal their story. A patient's narrative, in the full sense of words, attitudes, behaviors, and emotional communications guides the receptive therapist along the landscape of their psychic world. The situation can present both a treacherous route for the therapist, and a possible positive one (Bion, 1970; Bratt, 2012; Power, 2014). Unlike post-traumatic growth (Bonanno, 2004), which relates specifically to a victim's transformation post trauma, vicarious trauma and Reciprocal Resilience are indicators of the therapist's responses within the therapeutic engagement, as well as after.

The study of resilience is emerging as important in understanding and defining risk response and protective processes in relation to developmental adaptation, or emotional and functional restoration and growth post-crisis, or in the face of overwhelming experiences of everyday life situations. Much of resilience research, theoretical and clinical, has focused on the negative impacts on individuals who experience adverse events.

For example, the ACE (Adverse Childhood Experiences) Studies, originating from the Kaiser Permanente research (Felitti & Anda, 2009), developed from a pilot study of employees undergoing routine medical exams. Questions were asked related to life experiences, rather than medical data. Inquiries such as "Have you ever been physically abused?" and "Has anyone one in your family been imprisoned?" A series of other questions sought to find more about the challenged backgrounds of employees and their relationship to occupational functioning. An unexpected result from the introduction of the questions was a dramatic decrease in absenteeism and reported illnesses. This, even though there was no discussion or follow up on answers to the survey. In the third year the survey was discontinued, investigating it as a validity variable in the earlier findings. Absenteeism and medical claims increased. It appeared that the simple intervention of listening by another to details of adverse experiences correlated positively with an increase in adaptive functioning. It was also learned that those reporting more than three incidences of what was labeled as Adverse Childhood Experiences (ACE) were at much greater risk for illness, troubled lives, addiction, even early mortality.

Resilience has primarily been identified in relation to a response to a negative event: to adversity. One's level of resilience was not in question, nor was there a strategy for assessing it independent of negative events. As a result, more attention has been paid to understanding the effect and treatment of adverse stress responses, than on how to proactively build skills to weather life's crises. The ACE project underscores the predictive value of attention to ACEs. It also demonstrates opportunity for resilience enrichment through engagement with a listening other when no traumatic incident is occurring. It is among the first studies to report resilience increase without reference to a precipitating trauma, only to a brief shift in the traditional medical exam: an interpersonal exchange about the employees' personal-emotional background.

When studying the clinicians, responders, educators, all those who work with individuals and groups struggling with severe life situations, overwhelming events, or trauma, the focus has been on avoiding harmful effects, vicarious trauma responses or stress reactions. The consensus has been that these workers inevitably risk negative stress reactions, and the guiding goal is to provide tools for minimizing and/or reversing them so that they can continue their important work. There is no consideration about whether there may also be some benefits accrued to the clinician's personal and professional life.

As a clinical supervisor, and director of a psychoanalytic training institute, Academy of Clinical and Applied Psychoanalysis (ACAP) and our graduate degrees (BGSP-NJ), in partnership with Boston Center for Graduate Studies in Psychoanalysis (BGSP), I am interested in the growth of clinicians and promotion of their well-being. This requires knowledge of the conscious and unconscious experience of their work. One needs to understand their experience of its impact on personal life and clinical practice, ways they cope, and ideas of what helps or hinders. Fostering growth relies on building emotional resilience, an essential element for healthy ego and identity development.

It was striking in classes, seminars, and conferences, once the idea of benefits to clinicians surfaced in my thinking, to notice how minimal attention was paid to any positive aspects of participants' work. At first I thought this a product of a learning environment dedicated to teaching therapists about the complexities of the mind, relationships, healthy and pathological functioning, and ways to intervene when things go astray. Quickly I recognized that notions of positive experiences or benefits did not emerge because they simply are not in the worldview of the academic or mental health communities.

Many experiences brought me to question what helps mental health professionals not just survive, but thrive. Facing Everest-like challenges daily in work that is often unacknowledged and underpaid, what keeps them plugging away? I share two examples here that stimulated me to consider this conundrum.

I cannot take the elevator

This is a 9/11 story. I worked with the Hostage Negotiators Association, the FBI, and the police developing training programs to increase ability to manage exposure to overwhelming, dangerous assignments. When the Towers went down, I contacted these groups, and others, to help with disaster relief. At my institute, ACAP, we established a team from within our faculty. I trained our group, organizing times to meet with survivors or their families.

On 9/14, I arrived in New York City at Time Magazine for a session. Checking through security, I got directed to the 43rd floor. Walking to the elevator, standing with a crowd, I watched the floor indicator descend. My resolve did too. Close, tight spaces with too many people were always distressing.

At a debriefing the day before, security twice evacuated us from a building for bomb threats. I couldn't bear the idea of being stuck in an elevator. At Time I thought, "I'm taking the stairs. No elevators." An image flashed of people trying to escape the Towers, paralyzing and panicking me. What if the power died? What if people lost control, trampled everyone in the stairwell? I envisioned the editors, reporters, and photographers upstairs screening brutal photos from the attack. Several of them or their family members were in the buildings when the planes struck. How did they get to the office, ride an elevator, and return to routine?

I considered these questions as I got onto the elevator, and up to the 43rd. Who are they, what are their expectations of me? Will I be able to connect? A faint whisper from analytic training pierced my numbed anxiety, and provided an answer: be in the moment and the room. An analyst needs to close out the externals, be with the patient. This session required the same of me, with all the fears and feelings of horror, disbelief, and sadness. It was a humbling moment.

Later I realized that recognizing the journalists' commitment, and stepping outside myself, allowed me to get on the dreaded elevator. Apprehension about the stories I expected to emerge in the meeting receded. I could be a receptive container for them. They were inspirational without knowing. A seed was planted, encouraging me to wonder about possible benefits for clinicians in carrying out their work. Elevators are still not my favorite transportation, but hesitation getting on is rare since then.

Sit down. Breathe.

As director of ACAP's Applied Psychoanalysis Division, I organize speaking events, conferences, and projects not part of our regular curriculum.

We design programs to teach effective strategies for approaching difficult people and challenging incidents. The Department of Child Protection and Permanency (DCPP) provided one of our first and most consistent groups. Their cases are heart wrenching and frustrating. Many caseworkers are on call 24/7 for explosive situations. The sense of accomplishment, the pay, and the support never matches the intensity of the demands.

During these DCPP conferences, I noticed something surprising in supervising even the most distraught or self-attacking clinician. When I highlighted an exchange showing clinical ingenuity or skill, perspective on their role in the case shifted. One therapist, who was intensely critical of herself told me:

> I was so frustrated and frightened when he said he had a knife, I didn't know what to do. So I just said, "We're going to sit down, breathe, and wait this out a minute." And I did that, not sure he'd cooperate.

Hearing that, I commented, "Even under stress, your judgment could be trusted?" I made the intervention to explore her openness to another perspective, and introduce the notion of her own resourcefulness. Where did her sense of incompetence originate, from her history or the relentless demands of a near impossible job? My comment focused on an aspect of her functioning she never considered. She experienced it with a surprised giggle. It allowed her to approach the case from a new vantage with an idea that she had made a clinical appraisal resulting in an effective intervention.

This discovery of the significance of surprise as a primer for shifting perceptions developed as an important factor in my explorations of resilience building. Positive surprise has a pleasing and focusing effect. It opens the door for new connectedness and experiences. Once an idea comes into awareness under these circumstances, it is natural to begin seeing it in other instances (Langer, 1997). The interaction prompted me to consider planned resilience building and personal benefits gained while facing even the direst cases.

The clinician's dilemma

Mental health professionals spend a good portion of their day listening to the painful, disturbing, and often traumatic stories of the patients, clients, students, congregants, or staff members with whom they work. This is particularly true of mental health professionals working directly with patients. I began wondering what might be different ways to offer the interpersonal tools and understanding of emotional dynamics developed in the Modern Psychoanalytic modality, in which I originally trained, to students, supervisees, and a broader scope of professionals.

My observation of professionals who work either in private practice or in agencies or institutions indicates they routinely do not receive the support or training necessary to sustain high levels of functioning when repetitively exposed to the overwhelming life situations of their clients. They are vulnerable to countertransference responses, emotional induction that is triggered in reaction to the intense communications from patients. This is most true when the story or situation resonates with the therapists' own unresolved past or current experiences.

In the study I describe in the following chapters, one interviewee broke down crying, racked with guilt and remorse. On the job he was assigned to work with a dying man who reminded him of his Pop. He had been unable to be with his beloved grandfather until the end was imminent. Pop was unconscious when he arrived, and he wept at not having gone to him sooner. The feelings aroused by the elderly patient on his job were intolerable, so he left. There is more to the dynamics of this story and the young man's psychic life, but the vignette demonstrates clinicians' vulnerability to regress in the face of induced feelings, even when not part of a cataclysmic event. Therapists need ongoing support, validation, and opportunities to talk and cope successfully with feelings aroused in their work. Just as important, they need a window opened on the subject of what benefits they may get from the same work, coupled with the difficult feelings.

Many clinicians, particularly those working in agencies and institutions, serve the most abused and neglected in our communities. They work with individuals whose lives often include either persistent experience of life-threatening mistreatment or catastrophic events. A domino effect can result from the lack of attention to the well-being of the clinicians. High stress-inducing or overwhelming cases confront those working in such environments daily. They are generally underpaid, often little respected, and can feel inept and demoralized in their work. They may identify the client presenting the devastating situation as the source of their own feelings of inadequacy or hopelessness, and start to personalize, blame the client, and lose empathic capacity. They may feel their hands are tied with bureaucratic demands, and gradually lose their ability to create options or solutions.

This intensely dissatisfying state conflicts with therapists' sense of themselves as dedicated professionals. It can create an overpowering cognitive dissonance, where all responses seem wrong, and stress reactions such as the fight-flight-freeze triad take hold. The client/patient/student/staff member becomes the adversary and possibly the victim in this scenario. Resentment grows in the client, promoting more resistant, difficult or withdrawing behaviors. The client feels at the mercy of the system and drops out. The supervisor on the case feels the staff member is not being cooperative, did not listen to instructions, or is just incompetent. Multiple experiences like this can create a sense of both worthlessness and superiority in the supervisor, interfering with effective communication with staff. The clinician feels attacked or abandoned on both sides, and the client can experience it as another episode of neglect or mistreatment.

A nasty encounter

One supervisee mentioned a nasty, unsettling encounter with her supervisor at work. This took place in a residential treatment center for adolescents. The clients, a group of boys, were promised a treat for dessert at lunch. The delivery was delayed. Teasing and bullying broke out in the lunchroom, frustration levels and disappointment increased. Naturally the youngsters believed they had been tricked or misled "again and again." The therapist felt powerless to lower the emotional temperature. She offered other dessert alternatives. She tried initiating fantasy games while they waited. Her own voice began rising in frustration and anxiety that the situation was getting out of control, and someone might get hurt. There was supposed to be an attendant in the lunchroom with the group, but he had stepped away to track down the delivery truck. Two boys began wrestling on the floor, and at that point the supervisor marched in, drawn by hearing the shouts even down the hall in her office. All participants were given "demerits," and dessert was out of the question, if it ever arrived.

Later, in the supervisor's office, the therapist was reamed out for not managing the situation better. She should not have allowed the attendant to leave, and she should know by now the strategies one uses in those circumstances to help the boys remain calm. She could have told them to just move on to the next period and she would let them know about the dessert as soon as she heard. The therapist later learned that the supervisor, herself, was supposed to order the treats for the week, and had forgotten to do so.

So there are the clients who feel betrayed and punished; there is the therapist whose confidence is crushed, and who feels unsupported by her supervisor; and there is the supervisor who acts punitively to mask her own embarrassment. All of this is the impact of a negligent bureaucratic culture at the facility that fosters negative incidents that could be avoided. In an environment where the well-being of both clients and clinicians is considered, the young therapist could have been advised beforehand about the missing dessert, and prepared properly by the supervisor for an encounter with the group. This unempathic cycle begins at the top of the administration and trickles down, as we see. It takes a concerted effort on the part of each professional to recognize that and make choices about how to manage their immediate work environment: staff, clients, and facility. Even with the most insensitive administration, choices can be made to improve morale in the immediate environment, and positively impact clinical staff and their clients.

Stepping back, recognizing choices

The scenario I describe above could happen in multiple settings, from social service agencies to a Fortune 500 company's HR department. In the private office environment, therapists who work listening therapeutically to patients whose experiences may include the kind of severe abuse and/

or deprivation mentioned above, or those who have suffered long-term developmental abuse, medical trauma, loss of loved ones, or catastrophic community/environmental disasters, might themselves undergo the kinds of responses one has with overwhelming experiences. That is, these clinicians are also vulnerable to feelings of hopelessness, frustration, self-doubt, inability to think clearly, vicarious trauma, and ultimately to burnout.

A therapist, Jeremy, told me the other day that he realizes he is just not a good therapist. He has been in private practice for several years and works as a consultant for the family court system doing custody evaluations in divorce cases. Jeremy described his inability to think of anything to say when parents demanded answers to their problems from him. His mind goes blank, he cannot think of a question or even repeat what the patient said. It is even worse with the court cases where he feels dragged down by the bottomless fighting and manipulations of warring parents whose children are helplessly caught and injured in the melee. "Hopeless, all hopeless," he said, "I have to quit, get out. I haven't been able to help one person in all these years."

Jeremy's despondency became a bit dramatic with the statement about never having helped anyone. That raises a flag, but does not diminish the despair this dedicated and talented clinician was experiencing. I, too, felt helpless and hopeless that anything I said would matter. We sat together, the mantle of heavy feelings surrounding us. I began to wonder what Jeremy actually wanted or needed from me. Was it reassurance? Agreement? Did he need more than a space where his feelings could be held without being dismissed? I wondered why he needed to make the definitive statement about not helping one person, when objective reality would indicate it untrue. But it had a meaning and symbolism for Jeremy that I needed to accept before I could understand his whole communication.

"It's true." I said. "You're up against some of the worst cases. There's probably little, if anything that could be done. That's why so few people will do that work." He nodded in assent. "It's amazing you've stuck it out this long. I should have insisted you quit ages ago. I knew those were hopeless cases," I said. Jeremy looked up at me, confused. "You think I'd quit just because you said to?" he asked. "Doesn't matter. I should have said it anyway. I knew not one, single person in that jungle of a court system could be helped. How could they?" I responded. He looked perplexed, then thoughtful. "I'm not sure you're right. I'm thinking now of a couple of cases that turned out much better because I worked with the family." So I responded, "You see, you're right back there saying something can be done, when we both know it's not true." He said:

OK, OK. You can have your opinion, but I can list several positive outcomes. Sure, most are lost causes, and I'm stuck with them if I want to be around for any of the ones where I can make a difference. And that does happen. I just hate that there are so many that can make you feel useless. And by the way, I resent the fact that you've been thinking I'm struggling at a dead end job and didn't speak up about it till now.

The session provided Jeremy with a safe haven where his feelings of despair could be held, acknowledged, and processed. My hypothesis about the communication was that he was angry with me for not helping him feel better about the work and his competence. It became clear he was the "one person" unconsciously referred to, whom he could not help to tolerate feelings of futility and despondency. He wanted reassurance that he was doing the right thing, that there is hope with hopeless cases.

I was in the same quandary as Jeremy, my mind a blank, suffused with the powerful feelings of his sadness about having to relinquish a fantasy, and his anger I had not helped him make things better. I knew it would be a disservice to spark false hope about the dreadful cases, that being able to appraise things more realistically would by itself strengthen Jeremy. I also knew we needed to mourn the loss of the rescue fantasy with the jeopardized children, and acknowledge my failure to rescue him from the feelings of failure and uselessness.

Hooray for Jeremy! He was able to assert his annoyance with me in the end, bringing these feelings where they belonged, in our relationship, and begin to consider a different appraisal of his work. This resilience building exchange where Jeremy was able to step back, become open to alternatives, recognize choices, acknowledge both positive and negative about his professional efficacy, and assert himself in our relationship was pivotal in his psychic growth. It was important for me, as well. Sitting in those long moments, weighed down with the awful feelings, and soundlessly committing to being in it with Jeremy, gave me an opportunity to focus on this young man in a way I had not been. I, too, was caught in the drama of his cases. His threat to end his career, which we could also look at as a transference communication about being dissatisfied and ending supervision, jolted me into shifting perspective on what I was hearing and study from a different angle. I appreciated Jeremy's effort, though symbolically disguised, to re-enlist me, to connect.

Reverberating from experiences like that with Jeremy and other supervisees, and patients in mind, I set out to explore the possibility of personal benefit to clinicians exposed to traumatic stories, and about what keeps them persisting in the face of unbearable tales. The following chapters share what I learned listening to these courageous, generous professionals who, for a brief time, allowed me to be part of their stories.

References

Akhtar, S., & O'Neil, M.K. (2015). *Hopelessness.* London: Karnac.

Almond, R. (2003). The holding function of theory. *Journal of the American Psychoanalytic Association, 51,* 131–153.

American Psychological Association. (2017). Ethical principles of psychologists and code of conduct (2002, Amended June 1, 2010 and January 1, 2017). Retrieved from http://www.apa.org/ethics/code/index.aspx.

Baranger, M. (2012). The intrapsychic and the intersubjective in contemporary psychoanalysis. *International Forum for Psychoanalysis,* 21, 130–135.

Barnett, J.E., Baker, E.K., Elman, N.S., & Schoener, G.R. (2007). In pursuit of wellness: The self-care imperative. *Professional Psychology: Research and Practice,* 38, 603–612.

Bion, W.R. (1963). *Elements of psycho-analysis.* London: Heinemann.

Bion, W.R (1970). *Attention and interpretation.* London: Tavistock.

Bonanno, G. A. (2004). Loss, trauma, and human resilience: Have we underestimated the human capacity to thrive after extremely aversive events? *The American Psychologist,* 59, 20–28.

Bratt, P. (2012). Consulting the patient: The art of being together: Perspectives on technique and therapeutic field. *Modern Psychoanalysis,* 37, 193–202.

Brown, L. J. (2012). Bion's discovery of alpha function: Thinking under fire on the battlefield and in the consulting room. *International Journal of Psychoanalysis,* 93(5), 1191–1214.

Damasio, A. (1999). *The feeling of what happens: Body and emotion in the making of consciousness.* New York, NY: Harcourt Brace.

Dijksterhuis, A., & Aarts, H. (2003). On wildebeests and humans: The preferential detection of negative stimuli. *Psychological Science,* 14, 14–18.

Felitti, V.J., & Anda, R.F. (2009). The relationship of adverse childhood experiences to adult health, well-being, social function, and healthcare. In: R. Lanius, E. Vermetten, & C. Pain (Eds.), *The hidden epidemic: The impact of early life trauma on health and disease* (pp. 77–87). Cambridge, UK: Cambridge University Press.

Grossmark, R. (2012). The flow of enactive engagement. *Contemporary Psychoanalysis,* 48: 287–300.

Harris, M., Martin, M., & Martin, D. (2013). The relationship between psychological well-being and perceived wellness in graduate-level counseling students. *Higher Learning Research Communications,* 3(2), 14–31.

Hernandez, P., Gangsei, D., & Engstrom, D. (2007). Vicarious resilience: A new concept in work with those who survive trauma. *Family Process,* 46(2), 229–41.

Katz, S.M. (2013). General psychoanalytic field theory: Its structure and applications to psychoanalytic perspectives. *Psychoanalytic Inquiry,* 33, 277–292.

Langer, E. (1997). *The power of mindful learning.* Cambridge, Ma: DeCapo Press.

LeDoux, J. (2003). *The synaptic self.* New York, NY: Penguin.

Margolis, B.D. (1994). The object-oriented question: A contribution to treatment technique. *Modern Psychoanalysis,* 19, 187–198.

Norcross, J. C. (2010). The therapeutic relationship. In: B. L. Duncan, S. D. Miller, B. E. Wampold & M. A. Hubble (Eds.), *The heart and soul of change: Delivering what works in therapy* (pp. 113–141). Washington, DC: American Psychological Association.

Power, D. (2014). Hoodwinked: The use of the analyst as autistic shape. Retrieved from: *http://www.frances-tustin-autism.org/eng/pal_pdfs/DolanPower.pdf.*

Schmale, A.H. (1964). A genetic view of affects with special reference to the genesis of helplessness and hopelessness. *Psychoanalytic Study of the Child,* 19, 287–310.

Tabachnick, B., Keith-Spiegel, K.G., Pope, P., & Kenneth, S. (1991). Ethics of teaching: Beliefs and behaviors of psychologists as educators. *American Psychologist,* 46(5), 506–515.

Part I

Theoretical foundations

Chapter 2

Seeking Reciprocal Resilience

This chapter provides an overview of a research process and the criteria for organizing and analyzing its interview material. The concept of research can be daunting for many clinical practitioners. Therapists are accustomed to being in the thick of action, more than stepping back to study, quantify, or record. Some fear the process stifles creative expression. Others are intimidated by the potential for domination by numbers and formulae. Most do not enter the field with intent to commit to professional writing or research. Quantitative research can seem the antithesis of the therapeutic skills they seek to perfect. In contrast, a different type of methodology, qualitative research, with all its flaws and drawbacks, can be conducted in a way to shed new light on the phenomena of the treatment process. And it is more in sync with the clinician's mentality.

My experience with the research project I am about to describe was one of the most emotionally significant, inspiring adventures in communication and psychic exploration of my professional life. It felt more like an extension and expression of therapeutic encounters than the depersonalizing and quantification one reflexively associates with the idea of research. I learned, I grew, I had fun. I discovered much about myself and those I work with that would not have surfaced with such clarity if not for the project. My hope is to encourage other mental health professionals to consider engaging in research about the therapeutic experience.

We in the mental health disciplines are really detectives, searching the vast psychic space co-shared in the therapeutic relationship. Many of you may be surprised to learn you are already involved in a form of research without that label. It is for this reason I share the rudiments of the project's methodology. You will see that this type of analytic, critical thinking is familiar, not alien. It is a matter of organizing thinking on paper differently than we do mentally with the same material. If you are lucky, it will strike a chord and stir you to create and share your own project so we can all learn more about our amazing psyche. But this aspect of the project may not move everyone. Feel free to skim on to Chapter Three if that is the case for you.

Let me now tell you about the project. It investigates how mental health professionals, whose therapeutic work involves repetitive listening to stressful, overwhelming or tragic stories, consciously and unconsciously describe ways they cope with these stressors and their own experience of personal resilience. It examines whether the therapist's experience may, in addition to documented negative effects, result in any positive personal or professional benefit. It explores whether a directed focus on aspects of emotional resilience the clinician currently possesses, and a reframing of the clinical experience to include recognition of benefits, may have a positive influence on the conscious or unconscious experience of resilience in professional or personal life.

I elected to study participant interviews through the lens of use of adaptive defenses and their resilience correlates. This approach would give access to both conscious and unconscious communications about the volunteers. Defenses employed repeatedly can help create a portrait of the individuals' sense of, and wishes for, their place in the world. Because the study is in part about the experience of resilience, the possibility that it can be enhanced, and understanding how therapists view the impact of their work, I focused on the Higher Adaptive Defenses. That is: altruism, sublimation, supression, anticipation, and humor. I tracked their occurrence, coupled with their resilience correlates, in the initial interview and then in a follow up one, and compared them as an amalgam of participant responses, and each respondent with him/herself.

A positive shift in use of adaptive defenses in talking about the experience of internal conflict, and of working with clients' painful or overwhelming stories, can imply an increase in the clinician's emotional resilience. Increased employment of more evolved defenses is an indication of an enhanced internal, and largely unconscious, assessment of one's ability to navigate conflict and problem-solve successfully. It implies that the individual experiences her/himself as more capable of managing adversity and channeling it into positive growth.

Sample and procedure

Selection criteria

There were four levels of criteria for selection of participants in the project. They were recruited from the list of registrants at a conference on trauma and resilience. The conference presented an opportunity to sample a range of professionals from diverse backgrounds and training, but primarily from mental health disciplines and education. Second, these professionals were likely to have exposure in their workplaces to repeatedly hearing stories of trauma and overwhelming experiences so could speak to questions about that. Third, participants were selected from conference registrants who both responded to the recruitment letter and were registered for the full three days. The three day criterion was to maximize the possibility that participants had similar time exposure to the topics during the conference. An additional selector was to attempt to have a mix among the subjects of those who had prior experience with this annual conference and those who did not. I intended to interview at least twelve subjects. Approximately thirty volunteered and were culled to meet the requirements. Sixteen were selected to insure that there would be at least twelve who completed both interviews.

Recruitment and demographics

Sixteen registrants in a three-day conference addressing some of the dangerous and/or positive effects of our wired, digital society, "Connecting: Emotional Resilience in a Digital World", participated as interviewees in this study. The conference was composed of multiple workshops and keynote presentations, and staffed by faculty working in a resilience-informed method of teaching. That is, instructors worked in an experiential mode, geared toward: participant involvement in defining the issues to be discussed; promotion of group interaction and problem solving; active listening to participant case presentations; awareness of group members as problem-solving resources; and acceptance of materials presented without challenging perceptions.

Those who became part of this research were informed that a study was being conducted to learn more about how they experience the impact of the work they do, particularly that of repeatedly listening to stories of life struggles. At the conference they were also exposed to stories and scenarios about issues such as cutting, suicide, abductions, traumatic medical issues, community disasters, internet bullying, date rape, stress, and dissociative disorders. Strategies for working with individuals presenting with these adverse life problems were presented in the general sessions and workshops over the three-day period.

Research subjects included four men and twelve women. Their ages ranged from mid-twenties to mid-sixties. All had some experience in mental health settings, but their years doing clinical work varied widely from a recent graduate of a Master's program to participants with more than twenty-five years of experience, and multiple advanced degrees in a variety of fields.

Eight of the sixteen participants had some previous experience of psychodynamic education. Of those, four had taken a course at some point, and the other four had been in several. Two of the sixteen were unable to participate in Interview II because of unforeseen personal or family issues: a disabling accident and a daughter whose condition required constant attention.

Regardless of the diversity in backgrounds, all participants currently work in clinical situations where they are exposed to stories of overwhelming experiences and/or trauma. Several participants were career changers who had moved from previous professions, such as Internet technology, to mental health. The initial, common observable denominators among participants, in addition to working in emotionally challenging settings and having some experience of personal therapy, were their interest in attending a conference geared toward trauma and resilience studies, and a willingness to help in a research project.

In the course of the interviews almost all of the participants spontaneously revealed that they had experienced some form of abuse, domestic violence, extreme family dysfunction, or chronic bullying during their lives. Eight overtly referred to experiencing forms of abuse on their jobs in the past. Of those, only two were in a mental health field at the time of the negative events. Their experiences were related to mistreatment by co-workers, not clients. The other six had abusive experiences in corporate, medical, or educational settings in relation to unreasonable administrations or managers.

Interviews

The original inquiry of this study included a focus on the possible impact of listening to stories of trauma and overwhelming experiences. It was proposed that a pre and post conference interview might be a way to explore the research participants' sense of their personal resilience before and after the resilience-oriented conference. As it happened, most interviewees expressed only mild interest in the topic or purpose of the research. They enjoyed the idea of being interviewed. They expressed a wish to be helpful, but were clearly intrigued by the notion of sharing, with an attentive listener, stories of their experiences of working or living in difficult situations.

As the interviews progressed it quickly became evident, through volunteers' communications and attitudes, that the interview itself was the foundation for resilience awareness building rather than the conference as primary intervention. Interviews prompted conscious, near conscious, or an unconscious sense of the experience of personal resilience. The conference provided the opportunity for subject recruitment and was the conduit through which the interview experiences were reinforced.

The first interview, then, was recognized as an intervention that primed individuals to be mindful of their own experiences and responses in relation to emotional resilience. A shift in my perspective on the research occurred with that. The focus remained understanding the impact of hearing traumatic stories on the experience of resilience for clinical listeners, and how it might be increased. However, the main vehicle for studying this became the two interviews and their comparison. This modification in perspective also increased attention on the relationship between interviewer and interviewee. I had worked with resilience building and had the experience that talking about it increases one's awareness and experience of it, but had not originally planned that the interviews serve that purpose.

Interviewees were as interested, if not more so, in talking about challenging situations in their own lives as well as those in professional situations. It would happen that someone was talking about an incident at work, switch to something personal, then go back to the work story. This type of associational thinking and communication, somewhat of a stream of consciousness, was possible because of the open-ended nature of the interviews. It became an avenue for understanding the countertransference experience of listening to stories echoing one's own past. While maintaining the structure of the guiding questions for interviewees, they were still able to take their time drifting to other associations and stories. If they were involved in any story I would prompt further exploration and deeper consideration by nodding, reflecting what they said, asking an exploratory question, or using another technique to indicate interest.

I conducted all interviews. They were recorded and transcribed with the interviewee's written consent. Recording devices were plainly visible and interviewees were given a few minutes to acclimate to them and the interview environment.

In the pre-conference interviews participants were asked ten questions (Table 2.1), among others that arose in the discussion. The original questions related to how they view themselves functioning in their work, how others might describe them, and some of their most memorable experiences of working with clients struggling with overwhelming or traumatic life events.

Table 2.1 First interview questions

1	Can you tell me a story about a situation at work that had a strong emotional impact on you?
2	How would you characterize the way you typically respond to difficult situations? How would people who know you well describe you? Can you tell me about some times in your work as a _____ when you noticed that?
3	Have there been times when it didn't feel that way? Can you tell me about one of them?
4	Are there people you've worked with who impressed you with their ability to handle tough situations? Can you tell me about one of them?
5	Can you tell me about two or three of your most difficult experiences at work?
6	Can you tell me about a case where you regret the outcome, or wish you had behaved differently?
7	Are there sometimes things that help you to deal better with these tough situations? Can you tell me more?
8	Does working with a challenging population ever impact your personal life? How so?
9	Was there ever a time when you felt like you just couldn't continue with this work? Can you tell me about it?
10	Can you tell me a bit about what you expect from the conference?

While a set of questions was constructed for the interview, these were designed to be a guide rather than a rigid structure. The objective was to ask each interviewee the same, or similar, questions as well as to respond with new ones generated in the course of the interview. The goal was to conduct an interview in which participants would feel safe to speak spontaneously about their experiences. In turn, this would promote the emergence of patterns and communications, giving clues to unconscious reactions to listening to overwhelming and troubling stories, and about the individual's personal experience of resilience.

My approach during each interview was one of casual conversation, following up on participants' statements, or through verbal or nonverbal cues encouraging them to further discuss questions posed. When the interviews were completed and I said something like, "Thank you so much. This has been extremely interesting and helpful," several people were startled. They asked, "Isn't there going to be an interview?" or, "That's it already? I thought there were going to be formal questions," or, "Really? I've just been blabbering on. I thought you were helping me get comfortable for the hard part." Their reactions indicated that despite natural anxiety induced by the situation they had become engaged in the connection, and open to self-revealing. This approach made it possible to identify unconscious attitudes, reactions, and feelings. It encouraged free association and helped minimize censorship.

According to Galletta, "The [interview] questions are open-ended in order to create space for participants to narrate their experiences; however, the focus of the questions is very deliberate and carefully tied to your research topic" (Galletta, 2013, p. 47). Questions for this research were originally designed to guide the participant to reflect on what kinds of situations in their work life have a strong impact on them and how they respond. It was thought that this type of self-assessment is unlikely to be typical for interviewees, so it set the stage for them to begin to function in that reflective mode. Questions moved from describing difficult situations to considering what emotional, professional or interpersonal tools each has to cope with the challenging situation. From there they proceeded to an exploration of how this type of work might influence their personal lives, and finally to a question about the conference and expectations.

Study participants engaged in a second interview approximately two to three months after the conference to explore whether any observable shift in their conscious or unconscious experience or awareness of personal emotional resilience or ideas about themselves had occurred. Thirteen questions (Table 2.2) were slated in this second interview. They were geared toward eliciting responses about interviewees' ideas and experience of themselves in general, in contrast to their views of functioning in challenging situations. Participants were asked to relate how some other imaginary person might describe them, if being that way influenced their work, and questions about humor, community, and loneliness that came up in the earlier interviews. They were also asked to recount any memorable experiences from the conference, whether there had been any thoughts about the notion of resilience since the first interview, and ideas or suggestions regarding the conference.

Table 2.2 Second interview questions

1 Have you had any thoughts or feelings about what we discussed since we last spoke?
2 Last time we met I asked how you would describe yourself responding to difficult situations, and how others might describe you. Could you tell me more about that now? Give a couple of examples?
3 I'd like to get a sense of you as a person. How might someone who knows you very well, deeply, describe you?
4 Has being that kind of person impacted your ability to do the work you do?
5 The idea of a community, of having a place or group of people who can be supportive, share experiences – is that something you've thought about? Can you tell me a bit about what that might mean to you, if anything?
6 Sometimes professionals have a sense of being alone, or lonely, when they're with someone, listening to the other person's difficult stories. Does that ever happen to you? If yes, can you give me a couple of examples? If no, can you imagine why someone might feel that way?
7 There's been talk about emotional resilience, both when we met and at the conference. Has that come to mind? Have you thought about it at all since we talked? How? When?
8 If someone asked you what one or two goals you have, things you might like to accomplish in the work you do with people, what might you say? Can you tell me a story or two of when you've felt like that's happening? Or times when it's felt like an impossible task-goal?
9 How would you describe your feelings about the work you do, and your relationship with your clients/students/staff?
10 If someone asked you about going into your profession (old or new), what might you say are the pros? What could be the cons?
11 Have you noticed anything new or shifting in your experiences listening to clients/students/staff/family or at work since the conference? Could you tell me a story or two about that?
12 Can you tell me a story or two about your most memorable experiences at the conference (workshops, general sessions, or the social times)?
13 Was there something at the conference, or since then, that's felt like an important insight or revelation? Can you tell me a story about how it might impact or influence your work?

Originally there were five questions for the second interview. They were ones largely centered on the person's experiences at the conference. My observations from the first interviews highlighted some responses that seemed to repeat through the various participants' stories. These generated additional questions for second interview exploration. The new questions had to do with themes of community, loneliness, feelings, and perceptions of themselves in the world. Again the interview format was structured around the questions as guidelines with participants free to respond and/or divert as they wished.

Data analysis

I chose to follow a semi-structured, inductive, qualitative research method (Seidman, 2006; Thomas, 2006; Galletta, 2013). The data emerged freely from the content of the interviews and was analyzed from a psychodynamic perspective. I was interested in learning more about how interrelatedness in the therapeutic relationship consciously and unconsciously influences the experience of emotional resilience in the therapist. A longer-range goal was to use this new understanding as a springboard for improving clinicians' experience of personal resilience and professional satisfaction. I did not enter the research project with a hypothesis to prove but with a question to explore. According to Thomas:

> The primary purpose of the inductive approach is to allow research findings to emerge from the frequent, dominant, or significant themes inherent in raw data, without the restraints imposed by structured methodologies. In deductive analyses, such as those used in experimental and hypothesis testing research, key themes are often obscured, reframed, or left invisible because of the preconceptions in the data collection and data analysis procedures imposed by investigators.
>
> (Thomas, 2006, p. 238)

In this way the qualitative inductive approach is similar to the therapeutic process in which we watch, speculate, or hypothesize. We design an intervention, test it, and observe. We regroup and review, building additional hypotheses and interventions to test them.

The process of an inductive qualitative research format strives to explore a phenomenon through a generative method that can address the above-mentioned concerns, such as self-selection, positive outcome bias, and shifting research focus. It includes continual review and reassessment of data collected and integration of emerging questions or ideas into the fabric of the inquiry. The process of on-going data analysis permits a flexible focus on the shape, aim, and structure of the research (Thomas, 2006).

In the Generic Qualitative Research Method, using a semi-structured dynamic interview style, the researcher does not begin with a preconceived hypothesis to prove. The goal is to repeatedly compare and classify data into themes that can be attributed to the problem or question at hand. Eventually this results in what can be seen as probability statements. This method can generate a theory that in turn can be applied and tested through other methods (Beck & Perry, 2008). Like researchers, we clinicians strive to know nothing at the outset, to have no agenda other than to help the individual unpack the story of their life or current conflict.

In contrast to a strict Grounded Theory protocol (Glaser & Strauss, 1967), where one would not include any literature research prior to beginning the project, nor would interviews be taped, I used extensive literature review to integrate the concepts under study conceptually and historically. This put the research in context. Interviews were also taped in order to attain the optimum level of reliability of content. According to Beck and Perry, the advantage of the semi-structured interview is to permit "internal dynamics such as defenses, motives, and relationship patterns to unfold" (Beck & Perry, 2008). Taped and transcribed interviews allow for a more accurate record of the nuances of the interview content.

Some researchers contend that prior exposure to related literature and taping might contaminate the researcher's objectivity in collecting and studying the data (Glaser and Strauss, 1967). Others, including Thomas and James (2006) maintain that researchers cannot come to the project pristine or the project ideas would not have occurred to them. They hold that a review of the literature helps the researcher know more about current thinking about the problem, what has been studied, and what some controversies may be. Thomas and James consider a literature review an important part of the creative process involved in inductive research.

The 500+ pages of interviews for the study described here were transcribed and studied with respect to emerging themes of responses between participants. Within each respondent's protocols, development of associational patterns in connection with emotional resilience, and any common areas of resistance to openness were noted. Bernauer, Lichtman, Jacobs and Robertson (2013) present a description of qualitative data analysis as a form of critical thinking. One explores a problem or question by observing it and studies by gathering data about it. Data is organized and reorganized as it comes in and is broken down into components that can be grouped into classes of facts about which inferences may be drawn. This deconstruction may lead to development of new avenues of data to incorporate into studying the phenomenon. The final stage in critical thinking integrates the inferences from the threads of data constructing a perspective on the original problem.

In recent years there has been a move toward including more of the "fuzzy" data that can be collected in the research process. It is maintained that:

> Human beings and consequently their organizations and societies are in fact "fuzzy". Unless we are willing to reduce ourselves and our culture to linear or even curvilinear equations, then we might be better served by using a type of "fuzzy logic" that includes feelings, perceptions, and empathetic knowing in addition to more scientific approaches.
>
> (Bernauer et al., 2013, p. 6)

Bernauer et al. argue that the process of thinking critically about a question would best be served by including all the armamentarium available to the researcher including those abilities such as gut feeling, intuition, and reading between the lines. In other words, they conclude that some of the methods with which we routinely process and analyze data are subconscious and unarticulated, but nevertheless contribute to the formulation of understanding of the phenomenon under study.

Thomas also argues that a generic research methodology, one that does not require training in a specific methodological terminology or debates over protocol structure, provides a platform for the researcher who is interested in a pragmatic approach to analyzing data and reporting findings (Thomas, 2006). These are some of the considerations that led me to use the generic research model.

Galletta (2013), Thomas (2006), and Thomas and James (20013) suggested approaches to organizing the design, implementation, and subsequent organization of the research process, data collection and analysis in a generic qualitative study.

Further, Thomas (2006) states that coding or simple categorizing can be accomplished in many effective ways, from use of a computer program designed for coding complex data, to memoing by hand on cards. There is no single way to best organize data. The process depends on the researcher's cognitive/mental style, the size and complexity of the data, and the depth to which one wants to explore the data. The inclusion of recognition of meaning making from unconscious communications in a multi-modal approach to collecting data fits with a psychodynamic style of critical thinking and inductive data analysis.

These are the steps followed, as per the recommendations of Galletta (2013), Thomas (2006), Thomas and James (2013), and Seidman (2006) in my research, a General, Inductive, Semi-Structured Qualitative Study. You will see that aside from the mechanistic necessities of preserving a form of reliability and validity, and the end process of writing up and communicating what has been learned, the thought process is both analytic and intuitive, as well as intellectual. It is probably familiar with most therapists, resonating with how you function in daily work. What is not represented in this mini-guide, is the quality, depth, and emotional experiences of the actual interviews, and the material shared. That is for a later discussion. These are the guidelines I established:

1. **Define project, procedures, logistics** – After defining the parameters of the project and sources of data (interviews), develop an interview protocol that can be administered in a mainly identical process for each participant. Secure a time and place for interviews, recruit participants and obtain releases allowing use of their material, organize technology and transcription assistance, and schedule interviews. An IRB (Institutional

Review Board) process may need to be completed depending on the nature of the study – its potential impact on human subject participants. This is generally a simple process for which clear guidelines exist to complete the IRB request.

2. **Prepare interview files** – Arrange for transcription of interviews. It is important to have them available as the remaining ones proceed. Organize transcripts in easily readable fashion, order in a sequence relevant to context, label, make backups: hard copy and electronic.

3. **Read text multiple times** – Read each initial interview at least once, before reading any second interviews. Read each volunteer's full set of interviews from beginning to end. Note apparent themes or patterns, anything that may relate to the topic, e.g. devise color code to note spots to revisit. Then create file of preliminary observations of patterns and themes. Take a break from reading text, and return after some days to begin rereading. If audiotapes are available, it is useful to listen to them in the background as you go about ordinary tasks. Familiarizing oneself with the speech patterns and subtleties of participants' discussions is extremely helpful when reading the text. It is also useful to listen to the audio version while reading the text.

4. **Create categories, subcategories, define themes** – These represent codes that will be your identifiers for data placement, e.g. Interview I Altruism. Design system for quickly identifying similar items among the different participant files, e.g. color code and excerpt to a separate file that represents that code only (e.g. as above, Interview II Sublimation would be a category).

5. **Organize coded files** – There will be overlapping coding (your identifying symbols of a category), and uncoded text. Some data may fit in multiple categories, some remains uncoded because not immediately integral to the context. Never discard the uncoded; it may become useful later in the project. Place coded text that fulfills more than one category into the file folder for each, in multiple files – always identifying its exact origin. It will be decided later whether the data applies more to one category or another, or important as demonstrations of each.

6. **Continue multiple reviews of data** – Read and listen from different perspectives having the advantage of familiarity with the whole continuum of interviews (data). Raise additional questions; look for anomalies, or new relationships. Fine-tune category system.

7. **Extract meaning from patterns** – Pull together all of the patterns that are relevant to your original inquiry, and organize in a form, narrative and/or graphic, so it can be shared with others. Then organize the relationships found between factors observed that were unexpected, implications of them, and relationship to, or influence on, original inquiry.

A theoretical framework for conducting and studying interviews

I generally work from a Modern Psychoanalytic perspective, but also incorporated concepts from relational theory, self psychology, object relations, and attachment theory in framing the study of responses from interviewees. In Modern Psychoanalytic practice the patient is encouraged to speak freely and spontaneously. There are no directives about subject matter and the analyst typically remains quiet, especially in early encounters, unless requested by the patient.

In contrast, the research format required that I directly ask questions and give information about the project if asked. Aside from the previously established questions, I tended to encourage further exploration by nodding, reflecting what the interviewee was saying, or asking questions about the content of the story. Mainly I took an encouraging, attentive listening stance, and communications were of an exploratory or supportive nature. In most cases there was little need for me to talk.

George Vaillant's "hierarchy of defenses" (Vaillant, 2000) was used in this research as one tool for categorizing conscious and unconscious statements or communications in relation to resilient or non-resilient functioning. Vaillant's hierarchy consolidates defenses of emotionally resilient, healthy adaptive individuals. He says that healthy adaptive people tend to most frequently use the five Mature Adaptive Defenses: altruism, sublimation, suppression, humor, and anticipation to cope with life's difficulties and conflicts.

As the analysis of the data proceeded and categories were defined and filled in, more questions emerged that were integrated into the analysis. For example, was there a noticeable difference between participants who were familiar with me and those who were strangers? How many people reported they could not remember what was discussed in the first interview? Was there a change in attitude or behavior toward the interview process from the first interview to the second? How many interviewees spontaneously reported incidences of personal trauma during their own childhood?

In categorizing analysis of data for this research, traits and attitudes generally attributed to emotional resilience were listed with the qualities corresponding to each Mature Adaptive Defense. Interview transcripts were read and notated for evidence of demonstration of resilience traits, attitudes, ideas, and general defense patterns. Each interview was then reviewed, as described in the process (Steps 1-7) noted above, to assign the notated statements to its corresponding Mature Adaptive Defense. Following this, each individual's first and second interview was studied to determine whether there were any shifts in reported experience or new material surfacing in the second interview with that person. Response protocols were also studied in terms of the participant's age, years of experience, type of work, education, and experience with personal therapy or advanced clinical training.

In addition to identifying defense patterns I also looked at instances that might demonstrate the individual's unconscious desires, repetitions of unresolved conflict patterns, references to family dynamics, self-concept, patterns of personal trauma, and interpersonal relationship references. This was done to explore possible factors unconsciously influencing the interviewee's adaptive challenges and any connection to experience of personal resilience. It also helped infer whether elements of healthy resilience were operating unconsciously. That is, evidence for resilience traits functioning outside of the person's conscious awareness, for whatever adaptive/defensive reason, was considered.

Cognitive psychology has added to the study of the unconscious, in a manner differing from psychoanalytic study of it but influenced by Freud's theory, through research on topics such as automatic processing of information and decision-making (Hasher & Zack, 1984; Bargh & Morsella, 2008; Wilson, 2002; Kahneman, 2012). Malcolm Gladwell describes adaptive unconscious in *Blink*. It is faster, more fluid, can quickly process what is important from unimportant, and often leads to a clearly conceptualized decision that eludes conscious thought processes (Gladwell, 2005). These notions of the psychoanalytic concept of the unconscious and the cognitive studies of adaptive unconscious became increasingly important focal points as this research project progressed.

References

Bargh, J.A., & Morsella, E. (2008). The unconscious mind. *Perspectives in Psychological Science*, 3(1), 73–79.

Beck, S.M., & Perry, J.C. (2008). The definition and function of interview structure in psychiatric and psychotherapeutic interviews. *Psychiatry*. Spring, 71(1): 1–12.

Bernauer, J., Lichtman, M., Jacobs, C., & Robertson, S. (2013). Blending the old and the new: Qualitative data analysis as critical thinking and using NVivo with a generic approach. *The Qualitative Report*, 18(2), 1–10.

Galletta, A. (2013). Mastering the semi-structured interview and beyond. New York, NY: NYU Press.

Gladwell, M. (2005). *Blink: The power of thinking without thinking*. New York, NY: Little, Brown and Company.

Glaser, B., & Strauss, A. (1967). The discovery of grounded theory: Strategies for qualitative research. London: Weiderfeld and Nicolson.

Hasher, L., & Zacks, R. (1984). Automatic processing of fundamental information: The case of frequency of occurrence. *American Psychology*, 39(12), 1372–1388.

Kahneman, D. (2012). *Thinking, fast and slow*. New York, NY: Macmillan.

Seidman, I. (2006). *Interviewing as qualitative research*. New York, NY: Teachers College Press.

Thomas, D. (2006). A general inductive approach for analyzing qualitative evaluation data. *American Journal of Evaluation*, 27(2), 237–246.

Thomas, G., & James, D. (2013). Re-inventing grounded theory: Some questions about theory, ground and discovery. *British Educational Research Journal*, 32(6), 767–795.

Vaillant, G.E. (2000). Adaptive mental mechanisms: Their role in a positive psychology. *American Psychology*, 55(1), 89–98.

Wilson, T.D. (2002). Strangers to ourselves: Discovering the adaptive unconscious. Boston: Belknap Press.

Chapter 3

Resilience, countertransference, and induced feelings

Introduction

For the past thirty years increasing attention has been given to the study of resilience and resiliency. There continue to be differing camps with regard to a definition of resilience. The lines of disagreement fall into a nature vs. nurture discussion, with views on one side holding that resilience is genetic, or biologically driven, and the other maintaining that resilience is a dynamic process developing from the interaction of many factors (van Breda, 2001; Richardson, 2002; Tusaie & Dyer, 2004; Cichetti & Curtis, 2006; Martin-Breen & Anderies, 2011; Windle, 2011; Rutter, 2012). The earliest resilience studies centered almost exclusively on children exposed to adverse or traumatic life situations. The focus has expanded to include adaptation across the life span, but continues to be skewed toward addressing resilience in children. It is the possibility to intervene in the developmental resilience process before maladaptive defenses are embedded that inspires theoreticians and researchers to study factors influencing adaptation in childhood.

Another aspect of the differing camps is the question of whether, if resilience is an innate, fixed trait, it is possible for someone to develop it in the maturational process? Alternatively, if resilience is a matter of developing coping skills, is there a way to identify the skills without subjecting individuals to serious, adverse experiences? Can resilience only be identified in its relation to adverse experiences? If resilience is dynamic does that imply someone may be resilient at one point in life, under certain stressors, and not in another? How does stress exposure contribute to, or detract from, resilience? What are the most significant risk factors and the essential protective factors that influence individual resilience? These are among the significant questions addressed by resilience and resiliency researchers of the past few decades.

There is some confusion among terms and definitions, for example concepts like benefit finding, posttraumatic growth, and compassion satisfaction all relate to reciprocal resilience but are, in fact, descriptions of different phenomena arising from the experience of trauma or trauma work. A brief overview of thinking about other types of responses, negative reactions to experiencing or listening to accounts of overwhelming or traumatic situations will be helpful in setting the theoretical context of this book.

Current ideas about countertransference, the clinician's emotional response to the process of listening, are discussed in this chapter. Countertransference is an allied phenomenon in the Reciprocal Resilience process. It represents the clinician's individual response to the therapeutic situation, the client, and the content of the material in the session. It is the emotional, historical, and relational mindset the therapist brings to the therapeutic relationship: the lens through which the therapist processes the clinical encounter. A description of George Vaillant's categorization of adaptive defenses and their relationship to emotional resilience is also included in this chapter. Vaillant's approach to defining adaptive processes will provide a platform for examining interviewee transcripts in terms of their conscious and unconscious reflection of adaptive attitudes and functioning.

Resilience

The study of emotional resilience investigates how it is that some people are better equipped to rebound from overwhelming experiences, and then grow. There have been strong proponents of thought about the definition of resilience as a construct (Cicchetti & Garmezy, 1993; Cicchetti, 2007; Garmezy, 1971; Herrman et al., 2011; Leipold & Greve, 2009; Richardson, 2002; Rutter, 1987, 2012; Windle, 2011; Martin-Breen & Anderies, 2011). Several meta-studies attempt to clarify the differing positions, how they developed, and how to adequately assess the rigors of theories and their implementation (Fletcher & Sarkar, 2013; Martin-Breen & Anderies, 2011; Richardson, 2002; Tusaie & Dyer, 2004; van Breda, 2001).

Resiliency studies today are largely interdisciplinary, reflecting the idea Norman Garmezy proposed, in his groundbreaking work (Garmezy, 1970, 1971; Garmezy, Masten & Tellegen, 1984). In contrast to the idea of a fixed, constitutional trait (Anthony, 1974; Anthony & Cohler, 1987), Garmezy concluded that multiple factors influence a person's resilience, including constitution, environment, life events, and interpersonal supports.

In his studies of hospitalized schizophrenics, Garmezy observed two categories of patients: those who remained chronically in the hospital (process schizophrenia), and those who had breakdowns and recovered (reactive schizophrenia). More recent longitudinal studies have questioned that finding, suggesting that there is no clear evidence of discrete trends in the course of the illness (Docherty, St-Hilaire, Aakre, & Seghers, 2009; Bota, Munro, Nguyen & Preda, 2011). Garmezy's findings, however, indicated that those who recovered had clear patterns of "competency" in their lives, while the "process schizophrenics" did not (Rolf, 1999, p. 6). His early research, first with adults and then with children of parents with schizophrenia, indicated that factors of premorbid social competence correlated highly with subsequent patterns of pathology. The initial social competence variables identified were: age, intelligence, education, occupation, employment history, and marital status (Garmezy, 1970, p. 60). Recognition that social competence plays a crucial factor in adaptation to adversity led Garmezy to posit that interventions enhancing social competence might outweigh the adverse impact of exceptional life stressors.

The Minnesota Risk Research Project (Garmezy, 1991, 1993) studied children in environments where one would expect adverse life experiences to negatively impact development. The researchers began to hear stories of competently adaptive children who found ways to be in their environments despite adverse life conditions. This led to the idea that competence in the face of exceptional stressors, whether in crisis or chronic, is a function of resilience. Garmezy was particularly concerned with the summation of stressors: the cumulative toll taken by multiple or persistent adverse experiences. He thought that a focus on successful management of extreme, cumulative stressors, rather than on major catastrophic events, would yield more clues to the components and protective processes that promote stress resistant behavior (Garmezy, 1987).

In a reverse of traditional mental health research, paradigm resilience studies began to investigate the protective factors helping individuals manage risk factors and impact healthy adaptation. The thinking was that understanding gleaned from this approach could ultimately lead to prevention or mitigation of psychopathological conditions. As Garmezy and other investigators developed the study of protective factors, such as social competencies. Along with the original indicators of intelligence, education, personal relationships, school or employment performance, they included additional factors such as self-esteem, forward planning ability, social resources within and outside the family, and problem solving abilities. Resilience research began to question what might enable one person to not only adapt, but also excel in the face of persistent adverse experiences, and another to succumb and fail to adjust. It began to focus on the commonalities among those who successfully adapt rather than on the failure factors (Anthony, 1974; Garmezy, 1971, 1974; Masten et al., 1988; Rutter, 1987).

Garmezy and those who worked with him, and followed, have continually maintained that poverty is the most debilitating common factor among low-success adapters. Masten, who worked with Garmezy, became a proponent of "Ordinary Magic". "The great surprise of resilience research is the ordinariness of the phenomena. Resilience appears to be a common phenomenon that results in most cases from the operation of basic human adaptational systems" (Masten, 2001, p. 227). Masten maintains that although resilience is a basic, shared human capacity, the degree and length of exposure to adverse events may interfere with an individual's adaptive ability. She states this as the basis for recommending early intervention when risk factors are known in order to mitigate counter-adaptive development and promote resilience. The new resilience research continued to support the findings that there are common denominators among those who demonstrate resilient qualities and life skills in the face of adversity: positive family and social connections, cognitive skills and self-regulation, self-esteem, and a desire to be a positive part of a community (Masten, 2001).

From the 1970s onward, defining the concept of resilience and its components aroused significant controversy. Among the issues were variations and lack of consensus regarding definitions and use of terminology (Masten, 2001). Considering this deterrent, some investigators have attempted to integrate and formalize language and operationalizing concepts in the study of resiliency (Luthar & Cicchetti, 2000; van Breda, 2001; Martin-Breen & Anderies, 2011). There are differences in approaches to measuring resilience. Variations in research methodologies yield findings that are difficult to compare. Some researchers study resilience from the perspective of risk and competence, others explore protective factors.

There are questions about resilience as an internal, constitutional factor or as a trait dependent on external factors. This leads to another controversy within resilience studies and that is whether resilience is a static trait or a dynamic process. The terms ego resiliency and resilience are used interchangeably in the literature, but they actually have two different meanings. Ego resiliency refers to a relatively stable personality trait, while resilience refers to a dynamic process during and after adversity. Masten suggested that the term resilience be used when talking about positive adaptation in response to extreme hardship. The concern about use of the term "resiliency" is its implication as a fixed trait that would imply some people are natively resilient and others incapable of developing resilience (Masten, 1994).

Assessment of resilience can be clouded by the nature of the adverse experience recruiting resilience. Different defenses or skill sets may be required for resilience in the face of singular catastrophic events and prolonged exposure to adverse conditions (Luthar & Cicchetti, 2000; Tusaie & Dyer, 2004). The question also remains whether a distinction needs to be made between adequate resilience and a higher level of excellence in resilience. Like the concept of the good-enough mother, is good-enough resilience a sufficient benchmark? Should we, or can we, strive for superior levels of resilience to meet critical events? Another question is whether levels of risk can be accurately assessed from one individual and situation to another. Does everyone exposed to a risk situation experience it in the same way, with the same intensity? If not, how do we evaluate the individual's level of resilience?

Another controversial issue in resilience studies is that of "subjective perceptions of risk" in resilience research. Gordon and Song (1994) note that the meaning of a particular adverse event to the individual experiencing it can differ substantially from that of the resilience researcher. The researcher's life perspective may skew their perception of the individual's risk level (Bartlett, 1994; Luthar & Cicchetti, 2000). This aspect of the subjective skewing of the degree of adverse experience has led to the development of a variety of research methods to investigate resilience, but also to the difficulty of cross-referencing findings (Leipold & Greve, 2009; Luthar & Cicchetti, 2000). Findings from research on resilience may be unstable. Researchers note that qualities of resilience may vary within an individual from one incidence to another, making it difficult to form generalizations about the concept. At present there are two main foci: areas of competence and exposure to adverse experiences (Luthar & Cicchetti, 2000; Martin-Breen & Anderies, 2011; Fletcher & Sarkar, 2013).

Martin-Breen and Anderies completed an extensive review of the literature about resilience. They concluded that the history of resilience studies has been across disciplines including fields such as psychology, public health, sociology, engineering, and emergency management. Each discipline has built their knowledge base with language and concepts reflecting the specific aspects of resilience they investigate. Martin-Breen and Anderies advocate that this diversity in studying the phenomenon calls for an interdisciplinary systems approach to resilience studies, enabling cross-sharing in developing resilience building interventions (Martin-Breen & Anderies, 2011). They conceptualize resilience as an interactive process between the individual and the environment, with each adding its own contribution to the end result. Their method represents a postmodern approach to studying the phenomenon of resilience, looking at it across several interactive domains, rather than from a singular perspective (Kahneman, 2012).

> Resilience is then defined as an ongoing process of continual positive adaptive changes to adversity, which changes enable future, positive adaptive changes. Such definition assumes bidirectional interactions as well as recognition that the history, including previous adaptations, determine (positive) adaptive outcomes.
>
> (Martin-Breen & Anderies, 2011, p. 45)

This cross-referencing between fields as a means to understand a phenomenon was also described by Richardson as the "Third Wave" of resilience studies:

> The paradigm shift from a reductionistic, problem-oriented approach to nurturing strengths is a prevalent theme across academic disciplines and the helping professions. Resiliency and resilience have emerged as intriguing areas of inquiry that explore personal and interpersonal gifts and strengths that can be accessed to grow through adversity.
>
> (Richardson, 2002, p. 307)

In his metatheoretical study of resilience and resiliency, Richardson describes the three waves of resilience studies as evolving from the observation of individuals functioning under adverse conditions, rather than being grounded in a theory. The first wave developed from the question of what characteristics differentiate the person who will survive and thrive better under adverse conditions as opposed to those who will be unable to adapt. The search to identify the traits of, and protective factors needed, for those who can rebound was the mission of the first wave. Garmezy's longitudinal research revealed a consistent, stable group of correlates associated with healthy adaptation across diverse groups. Masten's studies corroborated Garmezy's and led to the development of what she called the "short list" of correlates of systems that interact to promote healthy adaptation to life. This included protective factors from individual personality traits, and family, societal, cultural and environmental influences (Wright, Masten, & Nurayan, 2013). Emmy Werner's pioneering longitudinal studies of children in Hawaii (Werner & Smith, 1992; Werner 1993) demonstrated that children who exhibited high levels of resilience in the early years tended to maintain that over time. Results from researchers such as Masten (2001), Egeland, Carlson, & Sroufe (1993), and Cowen et al. (1997) also indicate that resilient functioning is relatively stable across the lifespan.

The second wave of resilience inquiry focused on how resilient traits could be acquired or learned, and this marked the beginning of recognizing resilience as a process rather than a fixed trait (Richardson, Neiger, Jensen, & Kumfer, 1990). It was a search for identification of protective factors that fortify responses to risk situations. In the second wave researchers looked at life conditions that require restoration, some adaptive responses to life disruptions, and the concept of motivation was introduced into resiliency studies. During the second wave the notion of resilience as exemplifying more than simply bouncing back developed. Resilience was viewed as a process of growth in response to adversity. Research became about the complexity of the phenomenon and how different systems might impact it (Wright et al., 2013). This marked a shift from studying resilience in terms of the individual to that of exploring interactive systems. It became the inquiry of understanding what processes influence responses to adverse life experiences, what impacts ability to adapt under extreme stressors, and how those abilities can be promoted.

The third wave of investigation of resilience recognized that to activate the resiliency response energy was required, and this instigated exploration of the question of where that energy would come from and how one becomes motivated to expend the energy. In the third wave researchers became interested in developing methods for implementing interventions based on findings from the first two waves. Interventions were developed to promote competence in addition to minimizing or protecting against risk. There was a focus on "testing theories of change" (Wright et al., 2013, p. 29).

Current resilience studies grew from an eclectic perspective; a complex and ambiguous taking into account that there is more than one view. An emphasis on exploring characteristics of those who thrived, even in the most debilitating circumstances, emerged in order to identify what factors influence resilient development. Wright et al. describe a fourth wave in resilience research that considers resilient adaptation as a multi-level process integrating diverse influences that include genetic predisposition as well as personality, familial, and socio-environmental factors (Gottlieb, 2007; Masten, 2007; Wright et al., 2013).

An additional factor in considering resilience building was proposed by Rutter. He posited that exposure to adverse experiences may have a "steeling effect" that promotes resilience development (Rutter, 2012, p. 337). That is, exposure to traumatic or overwhelming circumstances or material may have either a strengthening consequence or it may increase vulnerability. This accords with findings of researchers such as Garmezy (1985), Masten (2007), Luthar & Chichetti (2000), and Herrman et al., (2011), who maintain that early positive familial and/or caregiver relationships are among the strongest predictors of future resilience and adaptive functioning. Those with early positive attachments are more likely to develop increased resilience when facing multiple experiences of hardship. There can be a growth and building factor, as well as negative stress responses, when confronted with adversity. Positive, interactive relationships provide the foundation of resilience.

Countertransference

Akhtar delineates four models of "analytic listening" that encompass the understanding of transference and countertransference embraced by each model (Akhtar, 2013). The models of Empathic Listening, listening from the patient's perspective, and Intersubjective Listening, the co-creation of the emotional field between therapist and patient, most closely reflect the countertransference process that occurs when considering Reciprocal Resilience. These induced feelings, countertransference, may be objective or subjective (Spotnitz, 1995; Geltner, 2013; Anthony & Cohler, 1987). If the feelings experienced are likely to trigger similar reactions in most people, it is considered an objective countertransference.

Until Winnicott (1949) spoke of the analyst being induced with feelings generated primarily by the patient's stories and repetitions, the classical attitude toward countertransference was that it represented feelings emerging from the therapist's own history. The conceptualization was that the patient simply told the story of his or her life and the analyst was to study it from an intellectual, blank slate perspective. The therapist's own feelings were to be detached from the therapeutic encounter. Transference was studied as a representation of the patient's unconscious memories, a projection, but not as an indicator of emotional communication between the patient and the therapist (Geltner, 2013). Winnicott introduced the idea that there was clinical data to be gleaned from the emotional communications triggering induced feelings in the clinician. He referred to this process as objective countertransference (Winnicott, 1949).

Winnicott's theory led to a renewed interest among psychoanalysts in emotional communication as a basis for understanding the patient's unconscious. Spotnitz further described the complexities of countertransference when he differentiated between objective and subjective countertransference. He referred to subjective countertransference as the analyst's contribution to the analytic relationship; feelings that are either in disproportion to the story being told or elicit responses from the listener that are reminiscent of personal history. Subjective countertransference usually arises from the clinician's unresolved emotional conflicts that resonate with what is being said (Ernsberger, 1979; Marshall & Marshall, 1988; Spotnitz, 1969, 1985). Or, they emanate from the dyadic interaction in the moment when empathic responses and unconscious memories combine with what is being listened to and with what the patient is experiencing, creating an analytic third. This analytic third is the newly formed emotional field co-created by the interaction of the therapist and the patient (Baranger, 2012; Bratt, 2012; Busch, 2001; Geltner, 2013; Grossmark, 2012; Katz, 2013; Kernberg, 2011; Ligiero & Gelso, 2002; Marshall, 2006).

Most clinical encounters will induce a blend of subjective and objective countertransference responses. It is important to recognize when these responses can lead to a countertransference resistance (Epstein, 2008; Gabbard, 1999; Liegner, 2003), triggered by the therapist's unresolved past. It can prompt him or her to avoid emotional openness in the therapeutic situation, and potentially have a negative impact on the treatment. While in earlier years the classical consensus about countertransference was that the feelings are to be avoided and processed out, today many schools of psychodynamic thought posit that these inductions, when studied, can reveal essential information about the case, as well as the clinician (Kernberg, 2011). They can be used to design interventions and therapeutic strategy (Epstein, 2008; Gabbard, 2001; Marshall & Marshall, 1988; Marshall, 2006).

In fact, some argue that the clinician's emotional receptivity that allows for subjective countertransference, may be the most important tool enabling a type of therapeutic mirroring, provided the therapist is aware of emotional triggers based on personal experiences (Geltner, 2013; Marshall, 2006; Spotnitz, 1979). The therapist remains in an actively receptive, empathic stance ready to welcome, hold, and process emotional communications from the patient. This willingness to hold and process through the filter of the therapist's feelings creates a safe emotional environment in which the patient may ultimately be able to tolerate a similar reintroduction of once toxic feelings now mediated by the therapist's willingness to hold and process them (Almond, 2003; Bratt, 2012; Bion, 1970; Brown, 2012). This co-creative therapeutic loop is what occurs in the process of developing Reciprocal Resilience.

Reciprocal Resilience

At present there is no controversy in the research about the possible positive effects of clinical work for the therapist, especially since so little is written about the phenomenon. What is discussed here are the few recent investigations of possible positive effects experienced within the process.

In considering the dynamics of the therapeutic dyad it has become clear that it represents an interactive model, with each side exerting some impact on the other.

> The degree to which this is possible depends obviously on the state of the patient and the trust in the relationship that has developed; it depends on the gradual creation of the intersubjective space for reflection, mutual regulation, recognition of vulnerability, humor, and so forth.
>
> (Benjamin, 2010, p. 115)

Grossmark, in *The Flow of Enactive Engagement*, states that:

> It [*the field*]—constituted by both participants' conscious and unconscious fantasies and fears, their worlds of internal object relations and the transferences that ensue—develops and takes on a transformative and generative quality of its own. Narratives and worlds are generated that are more than the sum of their parts — i.e., the internal and intersubjective worlds of the patient and analyst.
>
> (Grossmark, 2012, p. 292)

This growing attention to the psychical entity co-created in the therapeutic relationship is developing concurrently with interest in the impact of that interaction on the therapist, as well as the traditional focus on the patient's experience.

The idea of vicarious resilience is only recently mentioned in the literature (Brockhouse, Msetfi, Cohen, & Joseph, 2011; Cohen & Collens, 2012; Hernandez, Engstrom, & Gangsei, 2010). Hernandez, et al. noticed that there may also be effects other than vicarious trauma for those working with individuals exposed to dire or catastrophic life events. Hernandez, Gangsei, and Engstrom (2007), working in Colombia with an organization called Survivors of Torture, International, were part of a project studying vicarious trauma and its management in clinicians exposed to stories of torture experienced by their patients. They noticed a tendency among the therapists to refer to the positive impact they experienced in the course of listening to their patients' stories about the horror of the captivity and torture they survived. The investigators became curious about the unrecognized possible positive effect of the work and referred to the concept as "vicarious resilience" in contrast to vicarious trauma. Hernandez et al. (2010) describe the phenomenon as "[t]he positive meaning-making, growth, and transformations in the therapists' experience resulting from exposure to client's resilience in the course of therapeutic processes addressing trauma recovery" (p. 72). I will be referring to Hernandez's "vicarious resilience" as Reciprocal Resilience from herein. I believe the Hernandez description and explanations of the phenomenon include the reciprocity this study explores and that the term Reciprocal Resilience affirms the mutual interaction and influence in the therapeutic relationship that is being investigated.

According to Hernandez et al. (2007), Reciprocal Resilience can occur among specialists working on the front lines and in private offices or organizations, listening to stories told by individuals exposed to painful or horrifying life experiences. Their research results list several types of positive feedback responses that they consistently received from interviewees about the experience of the work. They state that those who facilitate and listen to the stories of survivors can experience an increase in their perception of personal resilience when doing this work. Despite their horror at what individuals may have been subjected to, and their dismay and empathy for the clients, there can be a concurrent surge and consolidation of the clinician's sense of resilience.

Several themes were noted in the Hernandez et al. 2007 study and the authors propose that there is a unique process of relational interaction that occurs in the course of trauma work and encourages resilience building in the clinician. They describe the impact as a transformation "in the therapist's inner experience resulting from empathic engagement with the client's trauma material" (Hernandez et al., 2007, p. 230).

Self-reflection is considered an important component of Reciprocal Resilience. Clinicians tend not to focus on personal benefits of their work and lose the opportunity for recognition of the positive impact for themselves in the course of their work. An important finding for resilience research emerging from the Hernandez studies (2007, 2010, 2014) was the implication that the act of helping clinicians become consciously aware of possible benefits could strengthen their experience of resilience. These researchers proposed this was an indicator for development of therapist awareness of potential positive reactions as a tool for building resilience.

In a subsequent study (Engstrom, Hernandez, & Gangsei, 2008) the same researchers further investigated the effects of trauma related work on clinicians. The 2008 findings corroborated the earlier study indicating themes of increased sense of meaning-making in their work, a sense of privilege in working with the challenged population, a more optimistic perspective on personal life issues, and an affirmation of the value of their work. Statements by the clinician interviewees demonstrated a sense of co-creation of meaning. That is, the therapists viewed themselves as interactive in the client's therapeutic journey in a way that transformed their own witnessing experience into one of mutual growth and meaning-making through the therapeutic dyad.

In their third study of vicarious or Reciprocal Resilience, Hernandez et al. (2010) found that the therapists' experiences working with Colombian victims of trauma and torture correlated with increased sense of satisfaction with the work, and a perceptible positive relationship with personal and interpersonal growth. The identified correlates of reciprocal resilience included:

> (1) reflecting on human beings' capacity to heal; (2) reaffirming the value of therapy; (3) regaining hope; (4) reassessing the dimensions of one's own problems; (5) understanding and valuing spiritual dimensions of healing; (6) discovering the power of community healing; and (7) making the professional and lay public aware of the impact and multiple dimensions of violence by writing and participating in public speaking forums.
>
> (Hernandez, et al., 2010, p. 72)

The concepts of vicarious trauma and vicarious or Reciprocal Resilience highlight the reciprocal relationship that can occur between clients and clinicians. The clinician participates in an empathic listening process that can lead to both positive and negative impacts on the clinician. Unlike posttraumatic growth (Bonanno, 2004), which relates specifically to a victim's transformation post trauma, vicarious trauma and Reciprocal Resilience are indicators of the therapist's responses within the therapeutic engagement, as well as after.

Hunter (2012), reporting on a study of clinicians' experience of agency work with difficult, distressing domestic situations that included violence and abuse, echoed the findings of the Hernandez studies. Hunter explored therapists' experience of the therapeutic bond in terms of three components: empathic connection between client and clinician, the client's role investment, and the mutual affirmation both client and therapist experienced in the course of the relationship. Therapists stated that they felt empathic resonance was essential to successful treatment. They recognized the dangers associated with allowing themselves to be open to the harrowing emotions expressed by their clients, but thought it crucial that clients knew someone was there, willing to listen to the stories and feel the emotions that others could not bear to experience. Therapists reported that it was easier to engage empathically with certain clients and not others, and attributed this to the more sympathetic position of some individuals. For example, it was said to be easier to empathize with someone who was exclusively a victim than with someone who was seen as both victim and perpetrator. Most therapists stated that they consider mutual affirmation an indicator of therapeutic success. They felt that the validation they provided in empathetic listening was reciprocated through a sense of respect and acceptance of trust in the relationship. Clients who were invested in the therapeutic process, who demonstrated a desire to recover and grow, instilled a greater sense of commitment on the part of their therapists. All three components of the therapeutic relationship examined indicated reciprocity within the dyad that could influence both the course of treatment and the experience of the sense of self of the clinician, as well as the client (Hunter, 2012).

In Hunter's study most therapists claimed a great satisfaction from their work. One described it as a feeling of "walking in the sacred places" of their clients' lives (Hunter, 2012, p. 185). All the clinicians reported both negative and positive responses to the work they did. More experienced clinicians said that they had become immunized over time listening to horrible stories. They felt the absence of shock value in listening allowed them to be more present, listening and resonating in a way that helped the client feel safe and more confident in telling their story. As Rutter hypothesized, not only may there may be a steeling effect from exposure to adverse experiences that allows the clinician to tolerate the inevitable negative aspects of the experience of trauma work, but it may also provide a resilience building factor that can strengthen one when exposed (Rutter, 2012).

"Reciprocity opens up the possibility of appreciating, attending to, and making meaning out of the process whereby therapists themselves may heal, learn, and change with clients" (Hernandez, et al., 2010, p. 74). Reciprocity implies both willingness and understanding on the part of at least one partner to bridge the gaps between contextual realities of socioeconomic, cultural, community, familial, and relational factors that influence the other's experience of events. One needs a capacity for mindfulness of the other's context in order to achieve empathic resonance. Without contextual understanding the clinician is imposing an interpretation of life experience that may resonate with the therapist, but not the client. It is a capacity for contextual openness that enables reciprocity in the therapeutic relationship.

According to Hernandez et al. (2010) one of the most important, and ignored, aspects of clinical practice is the therapist's awareness of their own contextual experience. Therapists and supervisors need to be mindful of the clinician's personal history and exposure to traumatic events to monitor possible reactions to repeatedly listening to overwhelming experiences. Clinician self-care needs to include opportunities for shared self-reflection through supervision, personal therapy, and opportunities for collegial interactions.

Therapist gratification has been a virtual taboo in the literature (Maroda, 2005). Maroda acknowledges that a cautious oversight of therapists' indulgence in gratifying narcissistic needs must be balanced with the understanding that the therapeutic relationship is the vehicle for change, and that growth in one part likely spurs growth in the other. Recognition of the reciprocity of mirror neurons helps conceptualize the interactive process between client and clinician (Marshall, 2006; Bargh & Morsella, 2008). We have a default tendency to behave or respond as those around us do.

Negative reactions to repetitive listening to stories of distress, pain, and trauma

Increased interest has been expressed in the literature about the negative impact working listening to stories of patients' overwhelming, horrible experiences can have on the therapist. Saakvitne (2002) states that:

> Vicarious trauma affects the same general aspects of self that are affected by traumatic life events: self capacities (affect management, object constancy, self-worth), frames of reference (identity, world view, spirituality), basic beliefs and psychological needs (safety, trust, esteem, intimacy, and control), and realms of perception and memory (verbal, somatic, visual imagery, emotional, relational, and behavioral). The most devastating impact of vicarious traumatization is in the realms of hope and meaning, specifically in cynicism and pessimism.
>
> (Saakvitne, 2002, p. 115)

Vicarious trauma represents an alteration in the inner experience of the clinician resulting from empathic listening to their clients' traumatic stories. It occurs as a process of accumulated stress over time.

The first use of the term compassion fatigue was used in 1992 by Johnson when talking about nurses experiencing burnout. Compassion fatigue involves becoming overly involved with a victim's situation until it feels as though it is happening to you. The clinician or caregiver becomes so wrapped up in the case it is hard to focus on anything else. Figley describes it as "a state of tension and preoccupation with the traumatized patients by re-experiencing the traumatic events, avoidance/numbing of reminder; persistent arousal (e.g. anxiety) associated with the patient. It is a function of bearing witness to the suffering of others" (Figley, 2002, p. 1435).

Clinicians may demonstrate the same characteristics and symptoms as their clients, such as hopelessness, confusion, cognitive functioning, and emotional distress. This does not reflect an emotional disorder or psychopathology of the clinicians. It is a direct response to induction over time listening to tragic and disturbing life stories (Pearlman & MacIan, 1995).

About vicarious trauma, Ghislaine Boulanger (2013), in her study of the effects on mental health professionals working with survivors of Hurricane Katrina, comments that therapists working under the conditions of shared trauma, listening to horror stories that echo their own experience, can feel overwhelmed by them. They may doubt their clinical ability to hold the patient's feelings and memories. The memories so resonate with the therapist's own that they can become helpless under the exponential impact of the trauma.

Burnout, a concept initially identified by Herbert Freudenberger (1974) refers to the exhaustion, cynicism, and inefficacy clinicians can develop from long-term exposure to intense workplace stress. In contrast to vicarious trauma, burnout conceptually may impact anyone experiencing persistent, overpowering stress, while vicarious trauma generally refers to responses of therapists specifically working with individuals who have experienced severe traumatic events or prolonged exposure to overwhelming and disastrous experiences of everyday life. Burnout is defined as "a psychological syndrome that involves a prolonged response to chronic interpersonal stressors on the job" (Leiter & Maslach, 2004, p. 93). Burnout consists of three components: emotional exhaustion, cynicism, and lowered personal efficacy. However, emotional exhaustion is considered the central element of burnout, resulting in cynicism about one's work and low efficacy (Leiter, Harvie, & Frizzell, 1998; Leiter & Maslach, 2004; Maslach & Leiter, 1997; Ray, Wong, White, & Heaslip, 2013).

In addition to vicarious trauma and burnout there are other concepts that describe possible negative effects of exposure to overwhelming or traumatic events, such as compassion fatigue and secondary trauma. Although not a robust area of study, alongside the dearth of attention paid to possible positive effects from clinical work, it can be noted that the pull to focus on the negatives remains consistently compelling over a positive, proactive approach.

Positive reactions to repetitive listening to stories of distress, pain, and trauma

The term compassion satisfaction, introduced by Phelps, Lloyd, Creamer, & Forbes (2009), "[is] commonly gauged by the Compassion Fatigue and Satisfaction Test" (Lloyd, et al. 2009, p. 321). Simply put, compassion satisfaction involves "the ability to receive gratification from caregiving" (Simon, Pryce, Roff, & Klemmack, 2006, p. 6). In their 2013 study, Ray et al. investigated the relationship between compassion fatigue and compassion satisfaction. They determined that the lower the compassion fatigue the higher the compassion satisfaction and vice versa. They outlined five Areas of Work Life (AWLs) whose input helps determine compassion fatigue and compassion satisfaction (Ray et al., 2013). This correlates with results from several other studies that claim that certain workplace elements need to be addressed to achieve compassion satisfaction.

Posttraumatic growth is a phenomenon that occurs after an individual has faced challenging, emotionally overwhelming, or traumatic life events. The individual, in facing the altered situation, finds ways to turn the event into a creative growth process. Personality traits that predispose one to a capacity for posttraumatic growth are extroversion, openness to new experiences, and optimism (Peterson, Park, Pole, D'Andrea, & Seligman, 2008). People and researchers report that some individuals experience positive change even after the most painful traumas. They describe a positive change in their sense of self, and indicate having a greater confidence about handling things in the future, and feel stronger and more self-assured (Calhoun & Tedeschi, 2012). Posttraumatic growth refers to the after-experience of an individual who has gone through a traumatic incident him/herself. Another term for growth after trauma is "benefit finding", in which one takes an active role in discerning positive outcomes occurring as a result of the trauma. Helgeson, Reynolds, & Tomich (2006) found that with benefit finding there was reduced depression and greater positive affect after the traumatic event.

References

Akhtar, S. (2013). *Psychoanalytic listening: Methods, limits, and innovations.* New York, NY: Karnac.

Almond, R. (2003). The holding function of theory. *Journal of the American Psychoanalytic Association*, 51, 131–153.

Anthony, E.J. (1974). The syndrome of the psychologically invulnerable. In: E.J. Anthony & C. Koupernik (Eds.), *The child in his family: Children at psychiatric risk* (pp. 3–10). Oxford: John Wiley & Sons.

Anthony, E.J., & Cohler, B.J. (1987). *The invulnerable child.* New York, NY: The Guilford Press.

Baranger, M. (2012). The intrapsychic and the intersubjective in contemporary psychoanalysis. *International Forum for Psychoanalysis*, 21, 130–135.

Bargh, J.A., & Morsella, E. (2008). The unconscious mind. *Perspectives in Psychological Science*, 3(1), 73–79.

Bartlett, D.W. (1994). On resilience: Questions of validity. In: M.C. Wang & E.W. Gordon (Eds.), *Educational resilience in inner-city America: Challenges and prospects* (pp. 97– 108). Hillsdale, NJ: Erlbaum.

Benjamin, J. (2010). Where's the gap and what's the difference? *Contemporary Psychoanalysis*, 46(1): 112–119.

Bion, W. (1970). *Attention and interpretation.* London: Tavistock.

Bonanno, G. (2004). Loss, trauma, and human resilience: Have we underestimated the human capacity to thrive after extremely aversive events? *American Psychologist*, 59, 20–28.

Bota, R., Munro, S., Nugyen, C., & Preda, A. (2011). Course of schizophrenia: What has been learned from longitudinal studies? In: M.S. Ritsner (Ed.), *Handbook of schizophrenia spectrum disorders: Volume II* (pp. 281–300). New York, NY: Springer.

Boulanger, G. (2013). Fearful symmetry: Shared trauma in New Orleans after Hurricane Katrina. *Psychoanalytic Dialogues*, 23, 31–44.

Bratt, P. (2012). Consulting the patient: The art of being together: Perspectives on technique and therapeutic field. *Modern Psychoanalysis*, 37, 193–202.

Brockhouse, R., Msetfi, R., Cohen, K., & Joseph, S. (2011). Vicarious exposure to trauma and growth in therapists: The moderating effects of sense of coherence, organizational support, and empathy. *Journal of Traumatic Stress*, 24(6), 735–742.

Brown, L.J. (2012). Bion's discovery of alpha function: Thinking under fire on the battlefield and in the consulting room. *International Journal of Psychoanalysis*, 93(5), 1191–1214.

Busch, F. (2001). Are we losing our mind? *Journal of the American Psychoanalytic Association*, 49 (3), 739–751.

Calhoun, L.G., & Tedeschi, R.G. (2012). *Posttraumatic growth in clinical practice.* New York, NY: Routledge.

Cicchetti, D. (2007). The construct of resilience: A critical evaluation and guidelines for future research. *Child Development*, 71 (3), 543–562.

Cicchetti, D., & Curtis, W.J. (2006). The developing brain and neural plasticity: Implications for normality, psychopathology, and resilience. In: D. Cicchetti, & D. Cohen (Eds.), *Developmental psychopathology: Vol 2: Developmental neurosciences* (pp. 1–64). New York, NY: Wiley.

Cicchetti, D., & Garmezy, N. (1993). Prospects and promises in the study of resilience. *Developmental Psychopathology*, 5, 497–502.

Cohen, K., & Collens, P. (2012). The impact of trauma work on trauma workers: A metasynthesis on vicarious trauma and vicarious posttraumatic growth. *Psychological Trauma: Theory, Research, Practice and Policy*, 5(6), 570–580.

Cowen, E.L., Wyman, P.A., Work, W.C., Kim, J., Fagen, D.B., & Magnus, K.B. (1997). Followup study of young stress affected and stress resilient urban children. *Development and Psychopathology*, 9, 565–577.

Docherty, N.M., St-Hilaire, A., Aakre, M.A., & Seghers, J.P. (2009). Life events and high-trait reactivity together predict psychotic symptom increases in schizophrenia. *Schizophrenia Bulletin*, 35(3), 638–645.

Egeland, B., Carlson, E., & Sroufe, L.A (1993). Resilience as process. *Development and Psychopathology*, 5(4), 517–528.

Engstrom, D., Hernandez, P., & Gangsei, D. (2008). Vicarious resilience: A qualitative investigation into its description. *Traumatology*, 3, 13–21.

Epstein, L. (2008). Some implications of conducting psychoanalysis as a talking cure. *Contemporary Psychoanalysis*, 44, 377–399.

Ernsberger, C. (1979). The concept of countertransference as therapeutic instrument: Its early history. *Modern Psychoanalysis*, 4, 141–164.

Figley, C.R. (2002). Compassion fatigue: Psychotherapists' chronic lack of self care. *JCLP/In Session Psychotherapy*, 58(11), 1433–1441.

Fletcher, D., & Sarkar, M. (2013). Psychological resilience. *European Psychologist*, 18(1), 12–23.

Freudenberger, H.J. (1974). Staff burnout. *Journal of Social Issues*, 30(1), 159–165.

Gabbard, G.O. (1999). *Countertransference issues in psychiatric treatment.* Washington, DC: American Psychiatric Press.

Gabbard, G.O. (2001). A contemporary psychoanalytic model of countertransference. *Journal of Clinical Psychology*, 57, 983–991.

Garmezy, N. (1970). Process and reactive schizophrenia: Some conceptions and issues. *Schizophrenia Bulletin*, 2, 30–74.

Garmezy, N. (1971). Vulnerability research and the issue of primary prevention. *American Journal of Orthopsychiatry*, 41, 101–116.

Garmezy, N. (1974). The study of competence in children at risk for severe psychopathology. In: E.J. Anthony & C. Koupernik (Eds.), *The child in his family: Children at psychiatric risk* (Vol. 3, pp. 77–97). New York: Wiley.

Garmezy, N. (1985). Stress-resistant children: The search for protective factors. In
J. E. Stevenson (Ed.), *Recent research in developmental psychopathology: Journal
of Child Psychology and Psychiatry Book Supplement 4* (pp. 213–233). Oxford,
UK: Pergamon Press.

Garmezy, N. (1987). Stress, competence, and development: Continuities in the study
of schizophrenic adults, children vulnerable to psychopathology, and the search
for stress-resistant children. *American Journal of Orthopsychiatry*, 159–174.

Garmezy, N. (1991). Resiliency and vulnerability to adverse developmental outcomes associated with poverty. *American Behavioral Scientist*, 34(4), 416–430.

Garmezy, N. (1993). Children in poverty: Resilience despite risk. *Psychiatry*, 56,
127–136.

Garmezy, N., Masten, A.S., & Tellegen, A. (1984). The study of stress and competence in children: A building block for developmental psychopathology. *Child
Development*, 55, 97–111.

Geltner, P. (2013). *Emotional communication: Countertransference analysis and the
use of feeling in psychoanalytic technique.* New York, NY: Routledge.

Gordon, E.W., & Song, L.D. (1994). Variations in the experience of resilience.
In: M.C. Wang & E.W. Gordon (Eds.), *Educational resilience in inner-city
America: Challenges and prospects* (pp. 27–43). Hillsdale, NJ: Lawrence Erlbaum
Associates.

Gottlieb, G. (2007). Probabilistic epigenetics. *Developmental Science*, 10, 1–11.

Grossmark, R. (2012). The flow of enactive engagement. *Contemporary Psychoanalysis*, 48, 287–300.

Helgeson, V.S., Reynolds, K.A., & Tomich, P.L. (2006). A meta-analytic review of benefit finding and growth. *Journal of Consulting and Clinical Psychology*, 74(5), 797–816.

Hernandez, P., Engstrom, D., & Gangsei, D. (2010). Exploring the impact of trauma
on therapists: Vicarious resilience and related concepts in training. *Journal of
Systemic Therapies*, 29(1), 67–83.

Hernandez, P., Gangsei, D., & Engstrom, D. (2007). Vicarious resilience: A new
concept in work with those who survive trauma. *Family Process*, 46(2), 229–241.

Hernandez-Wolfe, P., Killian, K., Engstrom, D., & Gangsei, D. (2014). Vicarious
resilience, vicarious trauma, and awareness of equity in trauma work. *Journal of
Humanistic Psychology*, 56(2), 153–172.

Herrman, H., Stewart, D.E., Diaz-Granados, N., Berger, E.L., Jackson, B., &
Yuen, T. (2011). What is resilience? *Canadian Journal of Psychiatry*, 56, 258–265.

Hunter, S.V. (2012). Walking in sacred spaces in the therapeutic bond: Therapists'
experiences of compassion satisfaction coupled with the potential for vicarious
traumatization. *Journal of Advanced Nursing*, 60(1), 1–9.

Kahneman, D. (2012). *Thinking, fast and slow.* New York, NY: Macmillan.

Katz, S.M. (2013). General psychoanalytic field theory: Its structure and applications to psychoanalytic perspectives. *Psychoanalytic Inquiry*, 33, 277–292.

Kernberg, O.F. (2011). Divergent contemporary trends in psychoanalytic theory.
Psychoanalytic Review, 98, 633–664.

Leipold, B., & Greve, W. (2009). Resilience: A conceptual bridge between coping
and development. *European Psychologist*, 14, 40–50.

Leiter, M.P., Harvie, P., & Frizzell, C. (1998). The correspondence of patient satisfaction and nurse burnout. *Social Science and Medicine*, 47, 1611–1617.

Leiter, M.P., & Maslach, C. (2004). Areas of worklife: A structured approach to organizational predictors of job burnout. In: P. Perrewé & D.C. Ganster, (Eds.), *Research in occupational stress and well being* (Vol. 3, pp. 91–134). Oxford, UK: Elsevier.

Liegner, E. (2003). Countertransference: Resistance and therapeutic leverage. *Modern Psychoanalysis*, 28, 7–13.

Ligiero, D.P., & Gelso, C.J. (2002). Countertransference, attachment, and the working alliance: The therapist's contribution. *Psychotherapy: Theory, Research, Practice, Training*, 39, 3–11.

Luthar, S., & Cicchetti, D. (2000). The construct of resilience: Implications for interventions and social policies. *Developmental Psychopathology*, 12(4), 857–885.

Maroda, K.J. (2005). Legitimate gratification of the analyst's needs. *Contemporary Psychoanalysis*, 41, 371–388.

Marshall, R.J. (2006). Suppose there were no mirrors: Converging concepts of mirroring. *Modern Psychoanalysis*, 31, 289–312.

Marshall, R.J., & Marshall, S. (1988). *The transference-countertransference matrix: The emotional-cognitive dialogue in psychotherapy, psychoanalysis and supervision.* New York, NY: Columbia University Press.

Martin-Breen, P., & Anderies, J.M. (2011). *Resilience: A literature review.* New York, NY: The Rockefeller Foundation.

Maslach, C., & Leiter, M.P. (1997). *The truth about burnout: How organizations cause personal stress and what to do about it.* San Francisco, CA: Jossey-Bass.

Masten, A.S. (1994). Resilience in individual development: Successful adaptation despite risk and adversity. In: M.C. Wang & E.W. Gordon (Eds.), *Educational resilience in inner-city America: Challenges and prospects* (pp. 3–25). Hillsdale, NJ: Lawrence Erlbaum.

Masten, A.S. (2001). Ordinary magic: Resilience processes in development. *American Psychologist*, 56(3), 227–238.

Masten, A.S. (2007). Resilience in developing systems: Progress and promise as the fourth wave rises. *Development and Psychopathology*, 19, 921–930.

Masten, A.S., Garmezy N., Tellegen, A., Pellegrini, D.S., Larkin, K., & Larsen, A. (1988). Competence and stress in school children: The moderating effects of individual and family qualities. *Journal for Child Psychiatry and Psychology*, 28, 745–764.

Pearlman, L.A., & MacIan, P.S. (1995). Vicarious traumatization: An empirical study of the effects of trauma work on trauma therapists. *Professional Psychology: Research and Practice*, 26(6), 558–565.

Peterson, C., Park, N., Pole, N., D'Andrea, W., & Seligman, M.E.P. (2008). Strengths of character and posttraumatic growth. *Journal of Traumatic Stress*, 21(2), 214–217.

Phelps, A., Lloyd, D., Creamer, M,. & Forbes, D. (2009). Caring for carers in the aftermath of trauma. *Journal of Aggression, Maltreatment & Trauma*, 18, 313–330.

Ray, S.L., Wong, C., White, D., & Heaslip, K. (2013). Compassion satisfaction, compassion fatigue, work life conditions, and burnout among frontline mental health care professionals. *Traumatology*, 19(4), 255–267.

Richardson, G.E. (2002). The metatheory of resilience and resiliency. *Journal of Clinical Psychology*, 58, 307–321.

Richardson, G.E., Neiger, B., Jensen, S., & Kumfer, K. (1990). The resiliency model. *Health Education*, 21, 33–39.

Rolf, J.E. (1999). An interview with Norman Garmezy. In: M. Glantz & J. Johnson (Eds.), *Resilience and development: Positive life adaptations* (pp. 5–14). New York, NY: Kluwer Academic/Plenum Publishers.

Rutter, M. (1987). Psychosocial resilience and protective mechanisms. *American Journal of Orthopsychiatry*, 57, 316–331.

Rutter, M. (2012). Resilience as a dynamic concept. *Development and Psychopathology*, 24, 335–344.

Saakvitne, K.W. (2002). Shared trauma: The therapist's increased vulnerability. *Psychoanalytic Dialogues*, 12, 443–449.

Simon, C.E., Pryce, J.G., Roff, L.L., & Klemmack, D. (2006). Secondary traumatic stress and oncology social work: Protecting compassion from fatigue and compromising the worker's worldview. *Journal of Psychosocial Oncology*, 23(4), 1–14.

Spotnitz, H. (1969). *Modern psychoanalysis of the schizophrenic patient*. New York, NY: Grune & Stratton.

Spotnitz, H. (1979). Narcissistic Countertransference. *Contemporary Psychoanalysis*, 15, 545–559.

Spotnitz, H. (1985). *Modern psychoanalysis of the schizophrenic patient* (Second Edition). New York, NY: Human Sciences Press.

Spotnitz, H. (1995). The need for insulation. In: *The Psychotherapy of Preoedipal Conditions* (pp. 117–136). New York, NY: Jason Aronson.

Stamm, B.H. (2005). The ProQOL manual. The professional quality of life scale: Compassion satisfaction, burnout & compassion fatigue/secondary trauma scales. Retrieved from: http://www.compassionfatigue.org/pages/ProQOLManualOct05.pdf.

Stamm, B.H. (2012). Helping the helpers: Compassion satisfaction and compassion fatigue in self-care, management, and policy. *Resources for Community Suicide Prevention*, 1–4.

Tusaie, K., & Dyer, J. (2004). Resilience: A historical review. *Holistic Nursing Practice*, 18, 3–10.

van Breda, A. (2001). Resilience theory: A literature review. Retrieved from: *http://www.vanbreda.org/adrian/resilience/resilience_theory_review.pdf*.

Werner, E. E. (1993). Risk, resilience, and recovery: Perspectives from the Kauai longitudinal study. *Development and Psychopathology*, 5, 503–515.

Werner, E.E, & Smith, R.S. (1992). *Overcoming the odds: High risk children from birth to adulthood*. Ithaca, NY: Cornell University Press.

Windle, G. (2011). What is resilience? A review and concept analysis. *Reviews in Clinical Gerontology*, 21(2), 152–169.

Winnicott, D.W. (1949). Hate in the counter-transference. *International Journal of Psychoanalysis*, 30, 69–74.

Wright, M.O.D., Masten, A.S., & Narayan, A.J. (2013). Resilience processes in development: Four waves of research on positive adaptation in the context of adversity. In S. Goldstein & R.B. Brooks (Eds.), *Handbook of resilience in children* (pp. 15–38). New York, NY: Springer.

Chapter 4

Mature Adaptive Defenses

Introduction

This chapter describes the theoretical foundation, George Vaillant's hierarchy of defenses, from which research volunteers' responses in the study reported are examined. It provides an historic perspective on the construct of defenses. The five Mature Adaptive Defenses are defined in this chapter, accompanied by excerpts, in table format, from research participants' interviews exemplifying use of that type of adaptive mechanism.

Mature Adaptive Defenses

Defense mechanisms are automatic, protective methods the psyche, or ego, develops to avoid experiencing anxiety and the intolerable tension produced by competing internal and external demands on it (Freud, 1894; Perry et al., 1998; APA, 1994; Vaillant, 2011). The concept of defenses originally described by Freud, in1894, depended intrinsically on a belief that an unconscious exists and operates on the basis of motivation, not simply by random reflex. According to Freud, defenses are unconscious, distinct from each other, dynamic, and can be either pathological or adaptive (Freud 1894; Vaillant, 1992). They are a form of self-deception devised to protect the self from internal or external assaults on the ego. This process of not-knowing is the ego's creative expression of an overarching quest for homeostasis. Defenses can be viewed from two perspectives: as coping or adaptive mechanisms to avoid overwhelming anxiety, and as protective processes that "transcend their role as defenses by contributing to the creation of new 'products' of value, such as new meanings, perspectives, modes of relating, and works of art or science" (Metzger, 2014, p. 478).

Defense mechanisms develop spontaneously, outside of the individual's awareness. If effective in warding off the painful feelings associated with anxiety, even if the immediate outcome itself is undesirable, the strategy may be mentally imprinted and called upon again when the person is next confronted with an anxiety-inducing situation (Valliant, 2011). In this way defenses may be situationally engaged and/or become fixed elements of the individual's response system through repetition reinforcement.

Because of the elusive quality of identifying and proving the existence of defense mechanisms, even Freud failed to pay much attention to their complex power in both adaptive and psychopathological influence. It was not until Anna Freud became more curious about the influence of defense mechanisms in everyday life that serious inquiry was begun about their existence and nature (Freud, 1979). She was interested in understanding how the parts of the psyche, id, ego, and superego, interacted and functioned, independently or interdependently, to protect against pain and encourage maturation. She agreed with Freud that the defense system existed to ward off the anxiety-guilt-producing pain the ego experienced mediating the demands of the primitive id impulses, the rigidly punitive superego, and external reality.

Research on the defenses has undergone periods of criticism based on issues such as flaws in empirical designs, disagreements about definitions, problems with identifying quantitative variables, reliance on self-reporting, and difficulty identifying reliably discrete defenses (Cramer, 2000; Vaillant, 1998). Early investigators raised questions about a defense as a stable functional style, whether certain defenses are age appropriate responses, and the reliability of attribution to an unconscious process (Cramer, 2000; Vaillant, 1998). Perry states that a 2011 review of the concept in literature produced seventy-two different approaches to defining and operationalizing defenses (Perry, 2014). While there was general agreement that defensive behavior influenced development of psychopathology, it was the growing interest in adaptive capacity that fostered the growth of empirical studies of the phenomena (Cramer, 2000). In addition to exploring how a defense mechanism approach to understanding and treating psychopathology can be useful (Perry & Cooper, 1986; Roth & Fonagy, 1999; Perry & Bond, 2000), investigators have taken a longitudinal approach to understanding the mechanisms and processes of the defenses as they may influence positive life adaptation (Vaillant, 1993; Perry & Bond, 2012).

The Harvard Grant Study was originally designed by Arlen Bock as a longitudinal study of 268 men, sophomores from the Harvard class of 1939–1944, to investigate factors contributing to healthy well-being across the lifespan. George Vaillant took leadership in the investigation in 1966. Bock's initiative marked the first major exploration of positive adaptation as opposed to studying psychopathology. It followed the lives of the men, through self-reporting questionnaires every two years, physical exams every five years, and personal interviews every fifteen years, over more than seven decades. Participants were selected on the bases of good health, academic achievement, IQ, and perception of future success by the school administration (Vaillant, 2000, 2012). The group represented a cohort of somewhat socio-economically diverse, Caucasian, educated men. A major conclusion of the study was that the most important factor contributing to general well-being over the life course is close relationships, particularly early warm relationships. This was found regardless of socio-economic status, intelligence, or career success. Interpersonal connections in life and work were the strongest predictors of life satisfaction. This finding echoes the research of Masten (2007), Garmezy (1970), and Luthar and Cicchetti (2000) about critical protective factors in the development of resilience.

Another important finding in the Harvard Study was that the men's adaptive abilities were not static. They changed and grew. Men whose early life was characterized by difficult development or life situations were able to learn to make different choices to positively impact their lives. Through observations and data collected in this massive study, Vaillant developed a theory of adaptive defense mechanisms that help one navigate life's challenges. The adaptive mechanisms flow on a continuum from low to high, reflecting the level of emotional maturation employed.

In a naturalistic style of research, Bond and Perry, both students of Vaillant, studied fifty-three women diagnosed with personality disorders over a period of three years. Their goal was to assess impact of long-term psychodynamic therapy on adaptive patterns. They found that participant defensive functioning and symptom formation improved over the three-year period. Because of the naturalistic nature of the study inferences about causation of improvements could not be made. Too many life events and changing environments may also have impacted defense use maturation. The results did provide a base and impetus for further investigation of the relationship between long-term psychodynamic therapy and increased use of higher level defenses among individuals diagnosed with personality disorders (Bond & Perry, 2004).

It has also been demonstrated that children's defense selection occurs in a developmentally predictable pattern (Cramer, 2000). Cramer and Blatt's fifteen-month study of psychiatric patients in therapy showed a significant increase in use of higher adaptive defenses and a lessening of psychiatric symptoms (Cramer & Blatt, 1993). Defenses used by psychiatric patients are often those formed in early developmental stages, where once they may have been appropriate or serviceable in a conflict situation, but now are part of an inadequate protective system.

Perry talks of the anomalies in the patient's communication that are indicators of the underlying meaning or defense that the experienced clinician readily notices through the analytic listening process and pattern recognition (Perry, 2014). He posits that the second step to understanding the nature of the defense is a deeper study of the meaning of the defensive behavior through the study of how it is expressed, hypothesizing that the observable behavior is a symbolic communication about the individual's internal protective processes. The external expressions are clues to the motives behind the behavior. Perry delineated four "defensive states of mind" (Perry, 2014, p. 407) that mirror the categories of defenses. They indicate that each defense state has an aim that is a response to where the threat was initiated. Defense anomalies appear in expression of affect, behavior, formal aspects of speech, and content of speech. The function of these expressions of defenses reflects:

- Working through to cope adequately with stressors and to promote growth (high level).
- Warding off to avoid uncomfortable conflicts or feelings, but giving the appearance of continuity of functioning (neurotic level).
- Externalizing and counterattacking to minimize perceived internal or external threats and stressors (immature level).
- Disregulation to avoid overwhelming anxiety regardless of the effectiveness of the strategy (psychotic defense).

(Perry, 2014, p. 408)

Case analyses presented by Perry demonstrate his method of studying anomalous expressions as clues to defensive action to inhibit or control or adapt to an internal or external stressor. Using transcripts from two interviews, he shows how the anomaly indicates the origin of the threat and its relationship to the defense unconsciously chosen. For example, a young man talks about his failure to get a driver's license. He acknowledges that this is unusual for someone his age, but effectively denies its significance by laughing as he reports the failure. He promises to rectify the dilemma while internally understanding that he will not take action. This is described as an example of a passive-aggressive defense. Another anomalous communication occurs when the interviewee says that he knows other people drive and it is irrational for him to be so fearful of getting his license. The interviewee then minimizes this allusion to his role in the conflict by stating that it is not really an important issue, not having a license. Perry identifies this as an instance of using the defense of undoing.

In presenting a systematic approach to studying defensive expression in vivo, Perry is attempting to provide a platform from which the clinician can be attuned to anomalous expressions in the moment. With this awareness one can readily explore the origin of the threat, recognize the aim of the defensive functioning, and address it before a cumulative, negative defense pattern becomes embedded (Perry, 2014).

The study of self-deception, as Vaillant refers to it, can only be evaluated in terms of its predictive ability as to whether identification of defenses in the moment can enable predictions about future behavior, defenses, and adaptation. He outlines five reasons why the study of defenses has met with much resistance and roller coaster attention over the past century. Firstly, the concept of defense was intrinsically identified with psychoanalysis and this created an aversion bias. Secondly, Vaillant mentions the difficulty in reliability of definition of the defenses, followed by a third drawback in many studies, in that they relied on self-reporting that is problematic. Another issue raised to inhibit defense research is the controversy over whether a defense is a situationally employed construct or a fixed personality trait. The final roadblock Vaillant raises is the question of the existence of the unconscious and its role in the defense activation and formation (Vaillant, 2002).

According to Modern Psychoanalytic theory, the defenses represent the fragile ego's attempt to protect itself from internal or external threat. The clinician studies the nature and intensity of the defenses through an exploratory process that enables the individual to feel safe to speak and engage. In this method the defenses are supported by not challenging perceptions, and by minimizing interactions unless requested. The therapeutic process is one of gradual building of ego strength within the safety of the analytic relationship until new, more mature coping defenses can be developed and the need for the less adaptive defenses spontaneously recedes (Spotnitz, 1985, Margolis, 1986; Bratt, 2002, 2012).

Defense, like resilience, is an active process. Vaillant maintains its greatest asset is the validity of the existence of observable defensive behaviors and communications. Again the similarity with the pros and cons of resilience research is notable. Vaillant offers remedies to the impediments to research and clinical use of the defense construct such as validation of defense activity through neuroscience, systematic interviewing techniques, longitudinal studies that are able to observe narrative distortions, exploration of genetic influences on defense choice, and dedicated professional efforts to reach consensus on definitions (Vaillant, 2002).

Defenses are a dynamic part of human response to an internal or external environment that presents a danger or a conflict. Resilience is a process of managing responses to threat, and consciously or unconsciously creating strategies for using the process to promote growth in the face, or aftermath, of adversity. Both constructs are metaphors for the meaning of the resultant behavior or process we can observe following a threat to emotional stability. Yet we can only assess observable and subsequent processes and do not yet have access to the process of their origination. It is the job of neuroscience to use their tools and technology to understand and describe the internal components of resilience and defense mechanisms so that clinicians and researchers may advance studies of adaptive defense, or involuntary coping mechanisms, and resilience building, as well as pathological responses to adversity (Vaillant, 2011).

Hierarchy of adaptive defenses

The hierarchy of adaptive defenses put forth by Vaillant continues to be used as the springboard for defense research and clinical theory (APA, 1994; Perry, 2014; Cramer, 2008; Bond & Perry, 2004). He described four levels of defense functioning: psychotic, immature, neurotic, and high mature. Adaptive defense mechanisms not only indicate the type, developmental level, and intensity of the individual's response to perceived threat, they are also correlates of emotional resilience (van Breda, 2001; Richardson, 2002; Yates & Masten, 2004; Vaillant, 2011; Metzger, 2014).

High-adaptive defenses are an individual's most productive way to cope with life stressors and challenges. With these high-adaptive defenses the internal or external stressors are fully perceived, the individual is aware of his/her role in both the stressor and possible solutions. While the individual is mindful of attempting to satisfy personal needs, personal limitations are also acknowledged, and there is a willingness to recruit others to help in implementing a solution (Perry, 2014). Adaptive mechanisms are often meaning-making strategies through which something new is devised or new understanding is built in the face of a conflict. They might address the response of "How could this happen to me?" or "Is there no end to this problem?" by developing a research project or creating a strategic plan to end the conflict. Vaillant's category of Mature Adaptive Defenses includes: altruism, sublimation, suppression, humor, and anticipation (Vaillant, 2011). Each of these will be discussed in depth, in terms of theory and through application, in vignettes in participants' own words, in the following chapters. In Chapter five, the cumulative and comparative use of higher level adaptive skills, and relationship to resilience, will be demonstrated through excerpts from research participants' own words, and vignettes from other sources. Chapters six through ten will provide in depth stories from the lives and work of several participants, in their own words and through a study of the meaning of the stories.

Spontaneous use of Mature Adaptive Defenses

The following excerpts are ordered, in each category, in terms of the research I.D. numbers assigned, and not in any system of importance. The objective is to provide a perspective on the frequency and manner in which volunteers spontaneously indicated resilient use of Mature Adaptive Defenses when problem solving in work or life. Some statements are longer in order to give the full flavor of the person's story. Quotes from research participants' transcripts, in table format, demonstrate use of specific coping skills culled from transcripts.

Altruism

"When used to transform conflict, altruism involves getting pleasure from giving to others what people would themselves like to receive" (Vaillant, 2000, p. 92). Corresponding resilience traits would be: concern about the welfare of others; a sense of mindful spirituality; moral reasoning capacity; insight capability and reflective skills; the ability to access interpersonal resources; and self-awareness. An example of altruism would be a person who experienced being homeless organizing a soup kitchen to take care of the homeless.

Expressions of altruism correlating with resilience are: caring about the welfare of others and relationships; a sense of the spiritual aspects of life; moral reasoning capacity; insight and interpersonal reflective skills; an ability to access interpersonal resources in times of need; and a capacity for self-awareness.

Healthy altruism allows the individual to cope with conflict and anxiety by providing an outlet to give to another what one may have needed at another time, or to be treated in the way one would like. It is an interesting form of adaptation in the clinical setting in that it benefits the patient and provides both an emotional buttress for the therapist as well as reciprocal refueling of emotional resources. The therapist is strengthened by the experience of competence and giving, and also experiences the interactive, emotional communication of the patient, reinforcing the empathic connection.

Table 4.1 Altrusim

014: (*Told by someone who had previously experienced the same kind of neglect and mistreatment.*) One intern, her supervisor's been gone all summer. So she's lost and nobody is open and friendly to her. She's come to me, needs someone to sign off on her hours. I said I know what it's like as a student here. It's terrible. You can't ask a question without getting picked on. You're a student, so you don't know anything. I've been helping her get situated and acclimate. Cause if not, she would be floundering in water.

015: And she was going through a time where she was struggling with her drinking. She was also schizoaffective so she was hearing voices. She couldn't sleep at night because the shadows were scaring her. Just the act of seeing, every session how she would come in, and watching the process of her painting and her be able to gather her thoughts, had a really emotional impact on me. It helped me connect with her more, so I could understand what's going on. I empathized with her and I understood where she was coming from because of my own past.

017: (*Told by someone who experienced early maternal loss and abuse.*) And they've survived well enough to be at the site. I mean they're not in a cardboard box on the corner. They're taking care of themselves in some way or fashion. They're a productive member of society, so that's remarkable. The human spirit is very resilient, I think. Also [I have] the hope that I can help them in the ways that they want to be helped, that the therapy can make a difference and I can be part of that.

021: I didn't have a problem with it, because I thought it was the right thing to do. It was worth standing up for people, and I got through it. We used to have a saying for what we did, that we were protecting people that couldn't protect themselves. So we thought that was a noble thing, to protect the unprotected.

023: And he was brutally run down, purposely. And I was debriefing all these kids, meanwhile I'm I in shock inside. And then it was just, it was awful. That I lost him. That's how I felt. And his poor mother and everything. At the wake, other students of ours showed up bawling their eyes out, but I have to comfort them and myself. Somehow I was OK at that point. I had made peace at that moment, and could be there for them. Even though no one was for me.

029: So I'm trying to get them, medical residents, to think more humanely about their patients as opposed to the gallbladder in room six. Think as though they might be the patients, and what would they want. OK, its medical ethics, I've been doing this as a volunteer for, I'd say six years.

As related in interviews for the project described in this book, by someone who had experienced loss, abandonment and the struggle to take care of herself and her family alone, Volunteer 029 said the following (*going forward I will refer to volunteers by their assigned number to protect anonymity. In the stories in Part II of this book participants names, and other characteristics have been changed or condensed for further privacy*):

> When someone needs to be in residential treatment, they're in pretty bad shape. You know, they're not just going to an AA meeting ... some of them are doing it instead of going to jail... So to see them actually look good, you know ... you know, their complexions change ... movements change. The way they carry themselves ... their, their makeup changes ... they just start getting better and so it's, yeah, that's rewarding to see.

She mentioned on several occasions allusions to treating people as she would like to be treated, thought this had helped her be successful in several arenas, and coupled this with the feeling of the interaction with the patients having positive meaning for her.

Sublimation

Sublimation "allows an indirect resolution of conflict with neither adverse consequences nor marked loss of pleasure ... Sublimation does more than make the affect acceptable; it also makes ideas exciting" (Vaillant, 2000, p. 94). Corresponding resilience traits are: viewing problems as opportunities; seeking out new, challenging experiences; not experiencing shame or depression when facing a failure; an ability to transform helplessness into power; capacity to move from being a victim to a survivor; a belief in the uniqueness of oneself; flexibility and an ability to tolerate adversity, silence, or solitude; and an ability to tolerate frustration.

An example of sublimation would be a child experiencing chronic anger at a parent and then taking up wrestling. Another example would be a woman taken advantage of by an auto salesperson writing a negative review to the manufacturer. In each situation a destructive impulse is allowed discharge in a way that allows the affect without self-damage.

The creativity involved in the use of sublimation offers a way to diplomatically balance the sides of the conflict or stressor by devising an alternative action or solution that will ameliorate the stress while providing some satisfaction.

Volunteer 016 described a poignant example of resolving intense, near paralyzing anxiety around starting and being competent at a new job. He devised several strategies to cope with this, one being that he and his wife would exchange notes or texts during the day where she would tell him how lucky the organization is to have him, and they will soon know he is a

top-level find. He read and re-read these notes through the day to center
and remind himself of his competence and his connectedness with his wife.
This is a resilient individual, someone who expects to find a way to manage
adversity and then designs a way to handle it and grow.

Table 4.2 Sublimation

014:	I've been spending less [time in the office] now. I've been trying to be with patients, I've asked for more groups, the only person probably ever that's asked for more work to do. I'm trying to get involved with more committees. Because the less I'm in there, the less stressed I am, and the less toxic I feel in both my being toxic and them being toxic. So I've been listening to the music, a book, I doodle. Anything to keep myself levelheaded.
016:	I just was starting this job. It was a very stressful thing for me, not knowing if I'm up to the job. The mornings are ... I feel a little bit sick to my stomach. But if I'm able to tell myself to just keep moving forward, take the next step, I'm able to gradually overcome that anxiety. If I start to get nervous again, sometimes in the car I just start telling myself, keep moving forward, and take the next step. And I think about the reassurances people in my life have given me. I express that I'm nervous or anxious to my wife; she sends me notes or texts, lucky to have you, that sort of thing. So the words are a tool. I can use the texts to walk me through the anxiety.
017:	There were these student evaluations of the faculty. Number 5 was "displays a sense of humor." The other faculty [said] that shouldn't be there because they'll be making jokes or they're going to get a raise higher than the other faculty. And this other person and I said, are you kidding me? If you don't have a sense of humor teaching ten students in the clinical area you couldn't survive all the trauma. So we decided to find out what this could be related to academically. We looked up humor, and we wrote this little paper that documented that having a sense of humor's related to critical thinking. So we presented our little paper and the item stayed in the questionnaire ... a triumph.
020:	I have found myself, in my initial encounter with you I was a little shielded, not knowing what to expect. This time I was a little shielded because of this situation [at home], not wanting that to intrude and yet wanting to be honest by the end of the time that something is happening in my life right now. So I've considered the question of resiliency. I find myself hoping that my humor didn't derail, wasn't just derailing me from facing something that I didn't want to talk about. I'm half suspicious of humor but know I used humor and detachment to avoid thinking about it [crisis at home] while we've been talking.
021:	Yes, I'll hold off, you know, and then I'll eventually act. I think it's that fear that makes me humble. That's something that I didn't realize until just recently. I think the fear comes from when I was a kid and has a lot to do with my father and the relationship that I had, being afraid of him. The funny thing is that, even though I'm not a confrontational person the ones I had [on that job], I realized later that was me standing up to my dad. That was me standing up and saying "No," to him.

Suppression

> Suppression always sacrifices beauty for truth. It involves the semiconscious decision to postpone paying attention to a conscious impulse and/or conflict ... A critical difference between suppression and repression, between suppression and isolation, and between stoical suppression and Spartan reaction formation is the degree to which suppression allows all the components of conflict to exist at least partially in consciousness.
>
> (Vaillant, 2000, p. 94)

Examples of expressions of suppression correlating with resilience are: a capacity to succeed despite their hardships; willingness to learn from mistakes/failures; refusal to allow anxiety and doubts to overwhelm; not feeling shame or depression in the face of failure; demonstrating determination and perseverance; independence; healthy optimism despite the odds; and self-esteem and ability to restore it when challenged.

A downhill skier experiencing an anxiety attack, waiting at the top of the hill in a race, feels the tension and does pressure breathing, whooshing sounds expelling oxygen from the system. This is a strategy to deal with lowered oxygen in high altitudes when you need it for powering your actions. By taking deep inhalations you force oxygen into your body and blood stream in preparation to meet an increased demand. You acclimate lungs to expanding to full potential. You can also use it to momentarily take the focus off the fearsome task in front of you, focus inward, and push off from the gate. This is suppression. Another example would be someone angry at being passed over at work deciding to stay and do a superior job on an assignment, while at the same time job-hunting, rather than walk out in a huff. Suppression requires a balancing act of awareness of the conflict and a response that pushes impulsive action aside, allowing functioning to continue.

Unlike dissociation or repression, suppression allows a person to be at least partially aware of the aspects of the conflict. It is a conscious or semiconscious decision to opt for one course over another, despite possible negative consequences, based on the belief that a solution will be found. This is a strategy for problem-solving that requires some mental tightrope walking, in that you are aware of the ground dangerously below, and of the reward at the other end of the rope, so need to keep your gaze straight ahead and keep moving. Volunteer 017, a medical professional, stated that after receiving a frightening diagnosis and meeting with a "deadly" physician whom she believed was using the wrong protocol, she bolstered herself, walked out the door, and found a better physician. Despite her fears and anxiety about the condition, she pushed them aside in order to advocate for herself:

I learned early on from that experience that ... patients need to stand up for themselves ... It's doing it when you're so vulnerable. You don't let the fears and anxiety overpower you. You push through because you know you need to.

Table 4.3 Suppression

014:	They discharged her and then she tried to commit suicide. So twenty-four hours later she was back. Quite traumatic [after being assaulted by that patient]. I was like; I'm fine, there are no marks. The doctor checked me out. If anything, my heart just feels like it's pounding out of my chest. My supervisor's very understanding. She said to take a full week off to get yourself back together. I said no. I'll be in on Monday. This is the nature of the work. If I get scared away by that, I'm never going to survive in mental health. So, yes. That's ... that's one of the traumatic events.
014:	Goes again, back to that whole I don't care thing. I think it's my way of justifying, cause I know truly I do care. But in my head it's easier for me to keep saying I don't care cause it helps process things a little bit better, and not take things too personally. It makes me feel better and it truly has helped me remarkably. I can keep on going, or just walk away.
016:	I think that's what I do to deal with challenging and difficult situations. I take time for myself, and look at the difficult situation that's in front of me, or look at this sort of pain that I feel and let it out. I have to put the anxiety aside, let the feelings be. Sit with the pain and then pick myself up, and I can go take care of other things. I've had a lot of pain and a lot of loss and I've dealt with it in all different ways before I came to this realization. This is the way that I need to deal with it and the way that is healthy for me to deal with it. It was hard, because I had to go through all that other stuff in my past to get where I am now.
021:	I just couldn't stand that. I couldn't stand that [bullying]. But I still didn't like the confrontation. There was a manager that was trying to get heavy with me once. He just bumped up against me and glared up at me. I was really annoyed at him but I got really composed and said, "This doesn't work with me, does it? You're not my boss." I said, "I know you're trying to intimidate me. You can't do anything to me; you're just a bully." But I wasn't afraid when I did that. I wasn't afraid. And I think that was like part of the thing that, you know, that whole thing about fighting my father, pushing the fear down.
027:	And because I learned to just do so much on my own, and I just kept working through so much adversity, that's what I did for so many years in my work, and as a kid. I just, kept pushing, pushing, pushing. And, knowing it will work for me.
029:	I care about my son and his state of mind, and I think you can always get sucked into these kinds of conflicts that if you just stop for a minute and say why am I feeling this, why am I so angry and what control do they have over me, or me over them, and what's the worst that could happen? I mean that was one of my favorite phrases, forever. What's the worst thing that could happen here, assess it right and just, OK, well that's not so bad. I'll be able to just calm myself down. It's a crazy situation but it will be resolved.

Anticipation

> Anticipation is the capacity to keep affective response to an unbeara-
> ble future in mind ... The defense of anticipation reflects the capacity
> to perceive future danger affectively as well as cognitively and by this
> means to master conflict in small steps. Anticipation involves more than
> just the ideational work of cognitive planning. Anticipation involves
> both thinking and feeling about the future.
>
> (Vaillant, 2000, p. 94)

Healthy anticipation is not easy to achieve. It is predicated on the notion that
a potentially undesirable situation is going to occur and that you may need to
prepare despite anxiety or dread. The use of anticipation may be voluntary.
When you know a hurricane is predicted to hit landfall before you can leave,
using anticipation you would make as many arrangements as possible to
secure yourself and your property safely during and after the storm. Knowing there is an assignment deadline at the same time as a major family event,
using anticipation one would arrange to complete the assignment to the
degree possible before the family event. Corresponding resilience traits are:
realistic goals and expectations; being able to ask for help; problem-solving
skills; dreams/goals and purpose in life; internal locus of control, hopefulness, and optimism; believe in ability to influence current environment and
future destiny; flexibility; and seeking novelty and new challenges.

Table 4.4 Anticipation

017:	On the night shift, a patient was admitted and the chart was blank. Her symptoms and signs were odd and there was something wrong. I just knew there was something wrong. So I called the intern. You have to examine this patient. Well, I'm not coming, it's like two or three o'clock in the morning. He said. I said you have to come, it's very important. He refused. So I called the resident who was over them. He came, examined her. She was going into heart failure and so she was whisked off to the ICU. The next morning as I was leaving, the resident had the intern in the hallway, dressing him down about this, and said when a nurse calls you and says there's something wrong, you're supposed to respond. That was something important. I shared that with students. I said when you think something's wrong, stand your ground, say something.
019:	I've been told I'm very compassionate and caring, and sometimes I can be very stubborn and determined. I can be hard on myself but I have changed from that a bit. I didn't realize it till somebody close to me said you know that you're very, very stubborn. I said well yes I'm stubborn with the things I'm determined to do, like if I'm going to open a new business. I don't think anybody would stop me from doing that because it's what I believe in. I plan for what's difficult. That's my passion, and they're like how can you do this business, you're not a business person? I said whatever you say, I love you. I said I love you but I'm doing this.

(Continued)

025: I always go to the worst case scenario. I am a worst-case scenario thinker, that's how I manage myself. Right, that's how you manage that kind of thinking, by going straight to it. So what's the worst-case scenario? Agonize about these trivial things, and then someone can be dying in front of you, OK. You just know exactly where to go. And that's anxiety provoking all right. But then it's in your control; you've walked it through. You're not dependent on others. I know the difference. Then it's dependent on me. I'm delivering the message. I'm not going leave them till I get it right.

029: I think I'll figure that out [an impending, conflicted, major life change], but it's less clear than it's ever been to me with these things. I'm trying to just let that be, and not just anxiously fill it with what's familiar because that's a little too easy, and I think would miss an opportunity for me if I just planted myself with what's familiar and kept tap-dancing. Something tells me that's not the thing to do. I have to grow in a different path ... let yourself turn a page, not try to reinvent the last one. Take it step by step.

029: I think being this kind of person allowed me to be successful. In order to do whatever job I'm given I have to have some level of determination, and be able to use whatever skills I have to figure it out. Whether it's curiosity, or intelligence, or strength, or other mental or physical strength. I have to just get done what I need to get done. I think it's how I learned to lead people and maybe by being the way I'd like to be treated and treating others that way. I've always been that way. I see a problem and say, "there's a gap here". There's some disorganization, something. Somebody needs to control the situation, just move ahead and get out of the confusion ... and it was always easy for me to do that.

Humor

> Humor permits the expression of emotion without individual discomfort and without unpleasant effects on others. Humor, like anticipation and suppression, is such a sensible coping device that it ought to be conscious, but almost by definition, humor always surprises people ... Humor keeps both idea and affect in mind. Mature humor allows people to look directly at what is painful.
>
> (Vaillant, 2000, p. 95)

Humor takes a known reality and presents it from a different, startling, yet true way that feels syntonic. It promotes an appreciation of life's absurdities. Corresponding resilience traits are: an ability to laugh at oneself and life's absurdities; a sense of humor and realistic optimism under stress; and a concern about the welfare of others and about relationships. An example of humor as an adaptive defense would be responding to the hospitalized patient who says, "I feel so guilty about causing everyone bother," with, "You can't imagine what kind of punishment we'll think up once you get out of here!" Humor allows us to take the difficult moments, as well as ourselves, less seriously. It also creates a bond between people who are able to share a humorous moment.

Table 4.5 Humor

Question: *Do you find that humor is important?*

014: It has to be in multiple ways for your own personal sanity and to work with the patients because it definitely cuts some of the tension and some of the aggression. For example today I had a patient, and he was fake smoking weed, sitting there disrupting the group. I try to compose myself, and I say, can you please stop smoking in here? Everyone starts laughing. So I use that to break the silence, and plus it makes me more human. I'm not just a therapist, and not an authoritative figure. I have that playful side. Cause you don't want to walk in and lay down the law. Especially with psychotic patients.

015: We would have this guided imagery and I was very serious faced while we were doing it. I was like, "It's okay to laugh," cause they would look around, be worried. I said, "It's okay to laugh, you can laugh, it's fine, and it's funny." Or if they would make a joke, I would always laugh with them and even sometimes in different situations they could feel free to joke back. I always joked with them and laughed with them if they brought that in with them. So that was important. That's what they needed right there.

016: I think that I've always enjoyed laughing and making people laugh and I like listening to things that will make me laugh. I've got about four stations on the presets and when one goes into a commercial I'll switch to the other. Some of them are sports related, some of them are humor related, and some of them are a combination. So I find that it just, it helps, laughter. If I can find something that will make me laugh, it dissipates the anxiety.

017: You know the patient I've seen the longest, we laugh together. She'll say something and I'll join her and I'll respond, she'll agree and she'll laugh. I mean it's not necessarily about some serious things, but other things that are happening in her life and relationships with people, and that kind of thing. So I do think it's important. I think a sense of humor is what makes us human.

020: As long as it humor doesn't become an excuse for not facing our own tears. That would be my self-caution. I think it can be helpful, for me it helps me keep things in perspective. Frequently when my anxiety is beyond reasonable proportions, I find humor can help to bring things back into, into proper ratios. But sometimes underneath that humor there are tears, and maybe I'm not wanting to see them.

025: If I had to choose a single quality that I would say what makes people, what's the difference between those who are emotionally resilient and those who aren't ... I think it would be a sense of humor ... I think in a broader sense it would ... perhaps go to a more optimistic explanatory style, perhaps ... but I know a sense of humor is critical ... And I think without that it is very hard to be resilient.

According to Vaillant:

> Adaptive defenses are more than simply "healthy wound healing": They allow us to create—to put ideas, actions, objects into the world that were not there before. In other words, they often transcend their function as defenses: They can "turn lead to gold."
>
> (Vaillant, 2000, p. 89)

References

Bond, M. & Perry, J.C. (2004). Long-term changes in defense styles with psychodynamic psychotherapy for depressive, anxiety, and personality disorders. *American Journal of Psychiatry*, 161(9), 1665–1671.

Bratt, P. (2002). The impact of strategic emotional communication on memory and identity development. Communication in the 3rd International Neuropsychoanalysis Congress, Stockholm, September 1–3.

Bratt, P. (2012). Consulting the patient: The art of being together: Perspectives on technique and therapeutic field. *Modern Psychoanalysis*, 37, 193–202. Cramer, P. (2000). Defense mechanisms in psychology today: Further processes for adaptation. *The American Psychologist*, 55(6), 637–646.

Cramer, P. (2008). Seven pillars of defense mechanism theory. *Social and Personality Psychology Compass*, 2, 1–19.

Cramer, P., & Blatt, S.J. (1993). Change in defense mechanisms follow intensive treatment, as related to personality organization and gender. In: U. Hentschel, G.J.W. Smith, W. Ehlers, & J.G. Draguus (Eds.), *The concept of defense mechanisms in contemporary psychology* (pp. 310–320). New York: Springer-Verlag. Freud, A. (1979). *The ego and the mechanisms of defense.* New York, NY: International University Press.

Freud, S. (1894). The neuro-psychoses of defence. *The complete psychological works of Sigmund Freud* (Vol. 3, Standard Ed.) (pp. 43–61). London: Hogarth Press.

Garmezy, N. (1970). Process and reactive schizophrenia: Some conceptions and issues. *Schizophrenia Bulletin*, 2, 30–74.

Luthar, S., & Cicchetti, D. (2000). The construct of resilience: Implications for interventions and social policies. *Developmental Psychopathology*, 12(4), 857–885.

Margolis, B. (1986). Joining, mirroring, psychological reflection: Terminology, definitions, theoretical considerations. *Modern Psychoanalysis*, 11, 19–35.

Masten, A.S. (2007). Resilience in developing systems: Progress and promise as the fourth wave rises. *Development and Psychopathology*, 19, 921–930.

Metzger, J.A. (2014). Adaptive defense mechanisms: Function and transcendence. *Journal of Clinical Psychology*, 70(5), 478–488.

Perry, J.C. (2014). Anomalies and specific functions in the clinical identification of defense mechanisms. *Journal of Clinical Psychology*, 70(5), 405–488.

Perry J.C., & Bond, M. (2000). Empirical studies of psychotherapy for personality disorders. In: J.G. Gunderson & G.O. Gabbard (Eds.), *Psychotherapy for personality disorders* (pp. 1–31). Washington, DC: American Psychiatric Press.

Perry J.C., & Bond, M. (2012). Change in defense mechanisms during long-term dynamic five-year outcome. *American Journal of Psychiatry*, 169(9), 916–925.

Perry, J.C., & Cooper, S. H. (1986). A preliminary report on defenses and conflicts associated with borderline personality disorder. *Journal of American Psychoanalytic Association*, 34(4), 863–893.

Perry J.C., Hoglend, P., Shear, K., Vaillant, G.E., Horowitz, M.J., Kardos, M.E., & Bille, H. (1998). Field trial of a diagnostic axis for defense mechanisms for DSM-IV. *Journal of Personality Disorders*, 12, 56–68. Richardson, G.E. (2002). The metatheory of resilience and resiliency. *Journal of Clinical Psychology*, 58, 307–321.

Roth, A., & Fonagy, P. (1999). *What works for whom? A critical review of psychotherapy research*. NY: Guilford Press.

Spotnitz, H. (1985). *Modern psychoanalysis of the schizophrenic patient* (Second Edition). New York, NY: Human Sciences Press.

Vaillant, G.E. (1992). *Ego mechanisms of defense: A guide for clinicians and researchers*. Washington, DC: American Psychiatric Association Press.

Vaillant, G.E. (1993). *The wisdom of ego*. Cambridge, MA: Harvard University Press.

Vaillant, G.E. (1998). Where do we go from here? *Journal of Personality*, 66, 1147–1157.

Vaillant, G.E. (2000). Adaptive mental mechanisms: Their role in a positive psychology. *American Psychology*, 55(1), 89–98.

Vaillant, G. (2002). *Aging well*. Boston: Little, Brown and Company.

Vallaint, G.E. (2011). Involuntary coping mechanisms: A psychodynamic perspective. *Dialogues in Clinical Neuroscience*, 13(3), 366–370.

Vaillant, G. E. (2012). *Triumph of experience*. Boston: Harvard University Press.

van Breda, A. (2001). Resilience theory : A literature review. Retrieved from: http://www.vanbreda.org/adrian/resilience/resilience_theory_review.pdf.

Yates, T.M., & Masten, A.S. (2004). Fostering the future: Resilience theory and the practice of positive psychology. In: P.A. Linley & S. Joseph (Eds.), *Positive psychology in practice* (pp. 521–539). Hoboken, NJ: John Wiley and Sons.

Chapter 5

Reciprocal Resilience in the therapeutic relationship

Chapter Five outlines what was learned from the investigation of possible benefits to clinicians of repetitive listening to stressful, overwhelming, or tragic stories. It focuses on three areas of exploration:

1. Emerging themes representing how therapists interviewed view themselves or would like to be perceived, in the world, and what they believe is essential for them to continue working with confidence, competence, and a sense of personal accomplishment and satisfaction are examined. It describes patterns of conscious and unconscious inferences of the therapists' desires for themselves/identity/self-concept, as related in the research interviews. These provide valuable insight into their perception of what is needed to enhance well-being.

2. A graphic representation of frequency of types of Mature Adaptive Defenses demonstrated in interviews, with a comparative analysis of usage, and its rise between sessions is presented. It supports the proposal that the experience of personal resilience may increase with brief, resilience-oriented interventions.

3. Reports of therapists' perceived experiences of benefits from listening repetitively to overwhelming stories are included in table and narrative format. This gives an overview of responses, to direct questions and revelations made in spontaneous statements, about benefits experienced in their work and the therapeutic relationship. Examples of therapists' comments demonstrate how their words conveyed the stories of their conscious and unconscious expressions of self, resilience, and meaning.

Therapists' narratives were examined in terms of their use of adaptive defenses and associated resilience correlates, giving access to both conscious and unconscious self-descriptors. Studying interview responses from the perspective of defenses used, to either remain responsive to patients' overwhelming stories, or to navigate in trying personal situations, permits development of a framework for understanding the clinicians' personal, psychic resources. Defenses employed repeatedly can help create a portrait of the individual's sense of, and wishes for, their place in the world. Higher

Adaptive Defenses are most closely aligned with resilience traits. Tracking resilience references through adaptive defense use provides an enriched conceptual base from which to explore the topic.

Repeated reviews of the interview transcripts revealed that responses to questions or stories told could represent multiple defenses, as well as references to wishes and beliefs about self and identity. Wishes became an important sub-category of inferences from therapists' reports in building a profile of the needs, assets, and values of clinicians. A person's conscious and unconscious statements about the experience of their place in the world and sense of self, offer a window to understanding their emotional resilience.

Wishes: *Patterns of conscious and unconscious inferences of interviewees' desires for themselves/identity/ self-concept*

Whether in answer to specific questions, or as part of a general pattern of communicating attitudes, preferences, ideals, and wishes, certain themes appeared in the interviews that marked a generic predisposition of the therapists and their experience of their place in the world. For example, it could be hypothesized that people who enter fields where they must listen to terrible, heart-wrenching stories may be looking for a job that gives meaning by offering hope or help to the helpless. This notion of "wanting to give back", of "being grateful" or "privileged" to be the person the client chooses to share their story with was in the fabric of every clinician's transcript. One could also look further for a more complex meaningfulness in that surface statement of wanting to help.

When I first tried to recruit participants, offering an opportunity to be a part of research on resilience, I got minimal responses. It was not until I sent a recruitment letter headed "A few minutes of your help needed" that more people began to volunteer. As time progressed I recognized that as an early unconscious communication about the respondents view of themselves and how they would like to be perceived. A negative perspective on the choice of such a demanding career might hypothesize sadistic gratification from listening to stories of pain and anguish, but there are easier and more lucrative ways to accomplish that. Other than the indirect reference to feeling grateful not to be in the predicament of the client/victim, there was no indication of sadistic gratification as a motive for doing clinical work.

We walk with an organic, integrated and unverbalized belief system about our identity that encompasses all aspects of our self. How one sees oneself, and perceives that others see them, informs structure of the self. It is the foundation for wishes and dreams in the present and the future. It both limits and inspires choices made, actions taken, and possibilities for tomorrow. All of these are, in turn, reflections of the individual's actual resilience, and of their experience of personal resilience that may differ from the former.

Four themes emerged in relation to patterns of conscious and unconscious inferences of interviewees' desires for themselves/identity/self-concept.

First, therapists demonstrated a strong desire to have their own stories heard. There was a clear resonance throughout the interviews saying that these are people who value the opportunity to be heard and known.

Allied, but not identical, two other emergent themes were the desire to be part of a community of like-minded people who appreciate what it is like to listen to painful stories, and the ability to emotionally connect in the clinical setting and in their personal lives. Connecting emotionally can be a part of being a member of a like-minded group, but it also implies a connection on a one-to-one basis. Participants repeatedly commented that the most important thing they can bring to their clients is the ability to be emotionally connected. They stated that this was fuel for themselves as well the patients. It is a goal, a burden, and a benefit of the work they do. There was group consensus that the most significant aspect of the work is the therapeutic relationship. That relies on the therapist's capacity for emotional connectedness, regardless of the patient's current capacity to relate and connect. They expressed a sense that the clinician's willingness to connect and stay with it, even in the face of patient withdrawal or abject narcissism, is the tool to eventually, successfully bring the client into the relationship as a participating partner.

The fourth theme was the wish to make a difference, to have a positive impact on the world. This can be viewed as a combination of wanting to view oneself as an effective, productive individual, and as healing oneself at the same time. These clinicians, representatives of diverse socio-economic backgrounds, education, age, life-long health status, and personal histories, all chose a career where they could make a difference through the tools of a relationship and emotional connectedness. They view this role as a valued part of their identity, and it is syntonic with their unconscious experience of themselves.

Wish I – To be heard, to be known

An interesting phenomenon that emerged from the data was the fact that several of the interviewees commented during the second interview that they could not remember what they talked about in the first interview. They either apologized or said something like the following the remarks in Table 5.1.

In each second interview there was an initial period where the respondent told me about what had been happening in their lives since we last met. It was an ice-breaking moment, a sense of catching up. Then I would move toward the research questions and begin with a version of, "Have you had any thoughts or feelings about what we discussed since we last spoke?" The question was designed to help get the interviewee into the mode of thinking about stories they listen to, or their lives, reflecting about themselves in light of this process. It was surprising to learn so many claimed not to remember our previous meeting. The process of the first interview had seemed a distinctly emotional experience where they spoke, often in an open and interpersonally connected manner, of events profoundly impacting them. As the interviews proceeded I noticed that not only did people apologize for not remembering the content of the previous meeting, but also some repeated stories from that interview with no apparent recollection of it being a repetition.

What started as an ice-breaker question may have accomplished that, but it also transformed into another window on participants' unconscious processing. It seems that the emotional environment of telling *their* stories to an attentive listener provided a safe, holding experience in which the feelings connected to both the stories and the interview blended. The thoughts or ideas discussed receded and the emotional memory was more easily retrievable. At the same time, since the stories described in the earlier interview resurfaced spontaneously in the second, even though the questions were different, it is likely that the conflicts those memories represented were unconsciously processing, memories being reintegrated from a present-day perspective, between interviews. The wish to be heard, known as oneself, and possibly process unresolved conflicts was understood as a strong motivator for open participation in the research once the nature of the interviews was understood. It was the experience of revealing themselves in a comfortable, attentive, nonthreatening encounter that became the dominant, conscious memory.

Table 5.1 WISH I – To be heard, to be known

Question: Have you thought about anything we talked about since we last met?
015: Not really too much. Only this morning when I knew I was coming. I was like what exactly did I tell them. Then I was like whatever, I don't remember.
016: I don't remember exactly what we talked about. Uh, the conference was a, I enjoyed it. It was very interesting for a number of reasons, very interesting. I really enjoyed the, the different ... seminars that I sat in.
019: I, just refresh my memory if you don't mind. Sorry ... Maybe it'll come to me as we speak about it.
020: I, honestly I'm having trouble remembering what we discussed.
021: Uh, yeah. I have. Do you have any examples of what I said?
025: What we spoke about? Oh, I just remember thinking that it was, uh, painless and didn't feel like an interview.
027: No. I was thinking, oh shit. No. Now it's time to get me back into the swing. *(She'd been away from work for some time.)*
028: Um, [pause] I hate to say this but not really.

Wish 2 – To be part of a community of like-minded people

Another theme that emerged in the initial interview, and followed up in the second, was the idea that respondents are looking for a place where they can meet with like-minded people who appreciate what it's like to listen to painful stories. They want a place to talk about what they are doing without feeling judged, a community of people who "get" what it means to be a therapist. The excerpts in Table 5.2 are examples of clinicians' comments about community.

Table 5.2 WISH 2 – To be part of a community of like-minded people

014:	I think that it's important ... a decent community support system ... this field is really lonely at times ... it is nice to have ... some sort of connection and people who understand what you do ... it's, it's validating.
015:	I miss it a lot... But I definitely miss that community, I miss it, cause for me that was like a really, a nice, a good motivator ... to keep going, keep moving forward, and now I don't have that ... and I miss it ... Not around, like-minded people.
016:	Uh, I think community is a very important concept ... the whole idea of community and people coming together to help each other, to be there for each other ... to provide a sense of identity to, to the group.
017:	Yes. I think that the other therapists at the clinic, I think we're community for each other. You can see that, they always talk to each other ... before and after we see patients ... I think there is... that the sense of community is strong.
021:	It means a lot. It means an awful lot. You know, that's the first conference that I've gone to ... I just loved it ... It was great ... when you do this kind of work you have to have a community ... if you don't have a community to support you ... in this job, it's too much. It'll stress you out.
027:	I think if you try to do this work without a support system, whether it's a consult group or a community of therapists that you see, or a strong personal life, I think it's kind of deadly ... really drains you of resources, that you're already so depleted.
028:	Yeah. I need a group of like-minded people doing the same kind of work ... when I was teaching as an adjunct it was very isolating ... I wasn't part of any group, I had no colleagues really ... so that's one of the reasons that I left. It was very isolating.
029:	Oh sure... I find this to be a great community of people ... who are like-minded ... I'm having intelligent conversations ... with people who, who I can relate to ... we don't have to be huggy, huggy, kissy, kissy in order to feel like we have ... a bond, or support, or community that you feel a part of and I think that's truly important ... definitely.
030:	That's really what it's all about. What's wonderful about having a community is we don't have to hide it. We all understand what we're doing and we look to support one another ... we can go in that lounge area, and sort of let the armor down and share with each other ... I cherish it actually. I think that's the good, that's what keeps me going. That's what gets me through all the hard stuff.

Several participants described the sense of community they seek as essential for personal and professional survival when working with cases where they are continually listening to overwhelming stories. They commented that the things they hear and witness daily are not fit for light conversation at dinner. There was a sense of protecting those close to them from hearing the grueling stories, as well as concern about others simply not wanting to listen. They spoke of feeling validated when able to talk freely about some of the difficult emotions experienced and stories heard. There is a sense of needing to believe that someone else grasps the enormity of what the therapist holds, the secrets, and appreciates its value. Also, there is relief in being able to share the type of gallows humor necessary to put things in perspective, as with many professions where horror and conflict are part of the daily routine.

Wish 3 – To emotionally connect

In addition to expressing the desire for a community, the therapists indicated a strong wish to feel emotionally connected to others in the clinical setting and in personal life. This was manifested both in terms of discussing client contact and interpersonal relationships. Connecting represented more of a wish to be known, or emotionally touched/touching, than the concept of a community of people. The excerpts in Table 5.3 from transcripts relate to the notion of emotional connectedness.

Table 5.3 WISH 3 – To emotionally connect

014:	I do enjoy having that connection with the patients and knowing that me providing them forty-five minutes to do whatever they want in the art room and not something specific ... feels like I'm giving them the world.
016:	I learned things and made connections and that was probably the most important thing ... became more a part of this, the community ... every seminar that I sat in, you got this feeling that, you know, people want to connect.
020:	The moment when I listen to someone else's story and I become aware of the way I'm connecting with what they're saying. It's sort of a process ... of [emotional] navigating. Essential.
021:	I thought, "Why are you feeling good? He just told you this terrible thing last night." What I realized that I made a connection with somebody ... That I could make a connection with somebody. It's important.
025:	I think listening to the stories of others in some ways is an opportunity to connect.
026:	I think the caring component ... makes me stay in the work I do. Cause I like ... being with people in that way, having a career, being able to listen to people and find out about people.
028:	Yeah, where everyone is connecting ... connected ... There's just energy in the hallways ... energy in the room ... auditorium and during the presentations ... I feel very connected to the participants in the room. And I think they feel connected to one another by sharing their stories.
030:	I don't necessarily have all the answers, but if I can connect emotionally with them ... they end up performing way beyond what seems to be expected in other parts of life ... You know then there was an attachment made. And that's what counts.
030:	I think it's a relief for people. When they finally start talking you feel like they've never talked about this or, or wow, somebody else has that feeling also ... it's useful for people who are not in this field [to feel connected and free to talk]. I think I see relief ... Sharing feelings, it's palpable. It's our humanness keeping us alive.

Connecting might happen within the community but it is through an emotional exchange with specific individuals. This could be colleagues, family, or clients. What was notable in the interviews was that all participants indicated, either directly or indirectly, that the experience of emotional connection carries significant importance for them.

Interviewees rarely reported feeling lonely when working with patients. If lonely feelings were reported they were about times when they felt isolated with the residual of being witness to their patients' stories. They described feeling alive and connected when engaged in the therapeutic process, but in a sense with nothing to talk about when with friends or family. How does one answer the question, "So what's happening at work?" or even, "How was your day?" One might interpret the quest for a combination of need for a community of like-minded people who get it, coupled with the capacity to stay connected when in the process of listening to disturbing material, and a sense of limits on avenues for discharge of work related tension, as a form of healthy sublimation. The impulse to disclose, reveal when in the presence of family or friends, is satisfied in a self-protective yet interpersonally generative way through connecting in the therapeutic relationship, as well as in the personal sphere, and in community building.

Wish 4 – To make a difference

A combination of a sense of wanting to make a difference and being grateful for what is described as the privilege of being with the patient, sharing the journey, was an emergent theme in the interviews. Interviewees wanted to view themselves as impacting the world and healing others. It could be expected that those drawn to professions where the task is the processing of overwhelming life stories would have a natural inclination to be helpful. This might grow out of a need to repair aspects of their own lives or those they had witnessed in developmental stages. It might grow from a sense that interpersonal problem-solving is something at which they could excel. Table 5.4 shows interview excerpts demonstrating the desire to make a difference, help someone grow by providing a safe emotional "container", and the reciprocal growth it can signal in the clinician.

Therapists discussed the impulse to problem solve for patients and the commitment to training or supervision to minimize acting on those impulses. Several demonstrated a high level of self-awareness in this regard. Along with the wish to make a difference, a trend toward describing how that happens, besides the talking, is a sense of holding, of being a container. In the realm of connecting in the professional world, it was recognized that a significant factor in the therapeutic relationship is the clinician's willingness to hold the patient's horrors, not back off. The act of empathic listening and being a holding container, along with following the patient's agenda, rather than the therapist's, was described as the way the therapeutic relationship can make a difference in life and society.

Table 5.4 WISH 4 – To make a difference

017:	Also the hope that I can help them in the ways that they want to be helped ... that the therapy can make a difference and I can be part of that.
019:	What can I do? I don't believe in talking about it. Be and make a positive change. So I said what can I do to make a difference?
019:	I'm very grateful [to be able to connect]. I feel honored about it ... it'll happen in time, and I feel privileged to be part of the change.
021:	She said something and it really stuck with me. She said what we forget is that as a therapist, we provide an important function for the patient: we are holding that patient's secrets for them. The listening and holding make a difference.
025:	That's the animal that defines us [making a difference]. Your phone is always on. They can call you at any time, and it satisfies that whole Florence Nightingale fantasy that helpers are motivated by. Then it becomes something you need to manage, keep things going in the right way. But, you're always connected to it. Wanting to make a difference. It's satisfying something.
026:	I feel like I'm doing something for their future. I'm creating movement with them in their life and their progression. In the maturation. And with me too. It feels like I'm moving along.
027:	I do truly believe it's a privilege to be sitting with people, when they're sharing, you know, from those places, trying to get back to their lives, themself. And so, I do feel privileged and appreciate people who chose me to do that with them. I see them growing, and myself too.
030:	Just holding all that. [That's the hardest.] Maintaining all of it, trying to do it successfully. I just sort of become a container in a sense, just deal with whatever is going on, and hold the feelings. If they're having a hard time, something they're going through that's really horrible and I empathize with them, I feel that pain. But that doesn't feel too stressful to me. We're in it together and it means something.

Use of Mature Adaptive Defenses

This section addresses the clinicians' cumulative use in the interviews of Mature Adaptive Defenses as related to emotional resilience. In several instances accounts of their experiences, and assessment of how they demonstrated use of adaptive defenses, could be viewed from two perspectives: exemplification or description. For example, while most people described their ideas about the value or hazards of using humor, few actually demonstrated the use of it in their stories. Table 5.5 and its analysis, along with the Chapter four excerpts from interviews in Tables 4.1– 4.5, provide examples of use of Higher Adaptive Defenses drawn from statements about both personal and professional experience of the clinicians.

Interview transcripts were analyzed for evidence in the respondents' stories of the use of Mature Adaptive Defenses. These were signified by the use of resilience characteristics that correspond to Higher Adaptive Defenses. Table 5.5 indicates the types of defenses used by each Volunteer, their frequency in the first and second interviews, and degrees of change between them. The results noted provide support for the notion that the use of higher-level defenses may be positively influenced by an individual's guided self-reflection about personal assessment and use of their own emotional resources. An increase in use of higher-level defenses is a marker of enhanced resilience, flexibility, and strength of a sense of self.

Table 5.5 Tabulations of participants' use of Mature Adaptive Defenses listed anonymously by number assigned

Name	Altruism	Sublimation	Suppression	Anticipation	Humor	Total	D	% Ch
014	7	4	3	1	0	15		
	9	8	6	5	3	31	16	107
015	6	5	4	2	0	17		
	5	3	3	1	1	13	-4	-24
016	9	2	3	3	0	17		
	9	3	2	3	3	20	3	18
017	8	5	4	5	1	23		
	10	5	3	2	3	23	0	0
019	9	2	0	2	0	13		
	10	4	2	3	3	22	9	69
020	6	4	4	4	3	21		
	12	6	4	8	3	33	12	57
021	10	4	4	4	2	24		
	12	14	6	8	3	43	19	79
023	4	1	2	2	0	9		
	1	1	0	0	0	2	-7	-77
025	12	6	5	4	0	27		
	14	5	2	4	4	29	2	7
026	4	1	5	2	0	12		
	12	5	2	2	0	21	9	75
027	5	0	1	5	0	11		
	4	5	2	0	0	11	0	0
028	7	1	3	0	0	11		
	2	4	5	3	0	14	3	27
029	6	5	1	2	1	15		
	9	6	4	6	1	26	11	73
030	7	2	2	4	0	15		
	13	8	0	6	3	29	14	93
Int 1 total	91	42	41	40	7	230		
Int 2 total	122	87	41	51	27	317		
% Ch	34	107	0	22	286	38		

Numbers indicate times responses reflected the use of each defense.
D = the difference in total use of Mature Adaptive Defenses between interviews for each respondent.
% Ch = Percent of change between Interviews I & II for each respondent.

As seen in the graph, altruism was the most frequently used Higher Adaptive Defense. It was used 120% more often than the next most frequently used, sublimation. Anticipation, sublimation and suppression were nearly equal in use in the first interview. However, there was wide variability in the increase of their use in the second interview. Humor, by far the least called upon defense in either interview, increased dramatically between interviews, 286%, although that was a large increase in an extremely small total. Use of Mature Adaptive Defenses as a whole increased between interviews by 38%.

Respondents with the lowest use of Mature Adaptive Defenses also happened to be those with the least experience, if any, of personal psychotherapy. In contrast, interviewees with the highest adaptive defense use were mainly those with the most exposure to personal therapy and/or ongoing clinical supervision. This could be an indication that either the therapy helped with resilience formation or that people with higher levels of resilience tend to seek therapy as a solution to internal and external conflicts. Those who expressed the least connectedness with, or need for, "community" demonstrated the lowest incidence of Mature Adaptive Defenses. From this it might be hypothesized that a lack of motivation, or capacity to utilize interpersonal resources for emotional nurturing or problem-solving, correspond with lower general resiliency, regardless of the cause.

What can be understood from this profile? First, it appears that a substantial increase in use of Mature Adaptive Defenses is noted from Interview I to Interview II. Among these respondents the clear, near default adaptive defense utilized was altruism. It is not surprising that altruism might be a primary, higher adaptive defense and motivator employed by mental health professionals. The use of altruism in this research increased 34% between Interview I and II.

Differentiating between sublimation and suppression can be a fine line. However, it can be seen from the table that while these defenses were relatively equal in usage in the first interview, sublimation's use increased by 107%, as compared with suppression's 0%, between interviews. One could take from this that, regardless of potential overlap in inference, the scope of the difference in change may indicate a meaningful shift in respondents' assessment of their ability to be assertive in resolving conflict and meeting needs. Sublimation allows the discharge of affect without endangering the individual or foregoing pleasure. Suppression requires a healthy compartmentalization where satisfaction may be sacrificed for the capacity to function within the conflict situation.

Looking at interview responses of individual respondents it is seen that seven out of the fourteen listed showed an increase in Mature Adaptive Defense responses ranging from 57–93%. Two participants showed a decrease in adaptive defenses. Two had no change in use, and three range in increase from 7–27%. So while the overall increase in deployment of Higher Adaptive Defenses was 38%, there was substantial variability among individual participants. This is a small and select sample, but if the number of respondents were increased and even a smaller percent demonstrated the type of increase in mature defenses demonstrated here, that would be an indication that promoting increased resilience among clinicians through brief intervention is possible.

The individuals represented by numbers 015 and 023 in the table above show low use of adaptive defenses compared to the other participants. Interviewee 015 fell at the 63rd and 18th percentiles in Interview I and II, respectively. Interviewee 023 was at the 4th percentile in both interviews. Looking at the overall score, 015 was at the 35th percentile and 023 continued at the 4th. This means that if there were one hundred respondents, sixty-five would score higher than 015, and ninety-six higher than 023 in use of Mature Adaptive Defenses.

What might this difference represent? It could be an indicator that 015, whose adaptive responses decreased between interviews, in contrast to 72% of the respondents whose higher defense use increased, experienced personal or professional stressors between interviews that weakened their resilience response. In fact, 015 is part of an ongoing family situation that escalated to a crisis between interviews. This required her to be the caregiver for the family members when she was already in an emotionally stressed state. Ten of the other respondents used a higher number of adaptive defenses in the second interview than in the first. This could imply an ability on their part to be more responsive to a short-term resilience intervention than 015 and 023. Also, only one person's results were lower in Interview II than both 015 and 023. Despite 015's overall responses falling within the normal range for the group interviewed, her resilience responses decreased 24% between interviews. This strong trend in the negative direction, compared with other respondents, supports the hypothesis that increased between-interview stressors interfered with resilience capacity.

From the perspective of the table of interview responses it can be seen that there was a strong trend toward increased resilience responses in Interview II over Interview I. Altruism and then sublimation were the most commonly employed defenses. Humor was the least used, but its usage increased considerably from Interview I to II.

Descriptions of experiences of benefits from listening repetitively to overwhelming stories

This section gives examples, in therapists' own words, of how they consciously or unconsciously indicated awareness of benefits from their work, and employ specific, higher-level defenses in personal and professional life. These are brief excerpts from the interviews that, when presented as a group, communicate the flavor of commonality among the respondents. In Chapters six through eleven, cases representing these patterns, as freely described by volunteers, will be discussed in detail. My aim, with the two types of presentation of material, is:

1. To demonstrate the multiple ways the therapists spontaneously, and unconsciously, described themselves as relying on higher level coping mechanisms to navigate conflict.
2. To understand the socio-emotional and psychological environments that triggered and encouraged development of adaptive defenses, and how this may impact the clinician, and therefore the patients.
3. To provide an in-depth, three dimensional view, in their own words, of how these therapists understand and experience the work they do, the resilience it requires of them, and the embedded benefits that often go unnoticed.

Throughout the interviews statements were made acknowledging the difficult nature of working with people who have experienced disaster, trauma, and overwhelming life events. There was a keen awareness of the perils of this type of work in terms of therapeutic relationship stability, the clinician's well-being, and the impact on one's personal life. As seen in the Wishes section of this chapter, many people expressed a desire for resources that would support or bolster their sense of identity, self, and place in the world. These resources, they believe, would help balance the negative and draining aspects of clinical work with a camaraderie and group identity that recognizes the difficulties and appreciates the satisfaction and joy in the work.

There was an initial tendency among interviewees to ignore or deny any benefit from their work. They might mention it in an offhand way, sometimes followed by an undoing, mentioning a negative impact. Still, the spontaneous statements about pleasure from their work subtly laced the interviews. When they felt as though permission to consider benefits was given, they were expressive and enthusiastic.

Table 5.6 presents examples of statements by the therapists describing their experience of the benefits they were able to recognize. This awareness in no way denies the intrinsic difficulties in the work. It reflects the participants' assessment of their experience from a different perspective than they typically maintain. Transcript excerpts chosen were on the basis of the way the experience was described, as well as an effort to provide a sampling of the wide range of benefits mentioned. There were many other, similar statements in the interviews, but here is a sampling.

It is interesting to note that in addition to being able to list the benefits described by volunteers, their responses could be broken down into two types of benefits: one of enhanced personal well-being, and the other of increased clinical skills. An example of ideas about increased clinical skills is volunteer 016's statement:

Every patient I've ever had ... when I hear stories of trauma, I ... can always glean from that something about ... how that person ... learned from that, how they coped ... There is always something ... registers in my pre-conscious ... just storing in my memory banks ... that you think of the next time you see somebody with this same situation.

Table 5.6 Interviewees' descriptions of benefits from listening repetitively to overwhelming stories

014:	Repeatedly listening to stories of trauma and overwhelming experiences puts things into perspective. I realize how lucky I really am. To have my health, and to have physical things: a home, a bed, a supportive family, a normal brain, to be completely put together.
014:	I love what I do. That's the one thing that keeps me going to work every day. I do enjoy having that connection with the patients in the hospital, and knowing that providing forty-five minutes to do whatever they want in my space and not something specific, it feels like I'm giving them the world.
014:	Working with illnesses and listening to their stories, and reading their stories, can be very emotional at times. I remember one time when I was complaining that I didn't get something, or I wanted something, and then I saw a patient being discharged with three Shop-rite bags, and that's all he had to his name. I was like, OK, well now you don't complain about anything. You have your health, don't have to worry about going outside at night and getting shot at, where some of these patients go [if released]. You have a support system, an education, so now stop complaining, and put things into perspective. So for that I'm grateful for what they've indirectly given me.
015:	I was always very aware, in the back of my head, I would think to say something to like push the clients along, and be like, no, they have to figure it out on their own. It's not your sister or your mother. This is a client, so I think that actually impacted me positively. It's nice to feel that self-awareness. I never really had it when I was younger. It's a really good feeling to have it because when you don't have it, you behave on impulse. I always behaved on impulse. To not always have to be behaving on impulse, it's a good feeling.
015:	Hearing difficult stories about others and what they've experienced, it helps you grow as a person. You learn, gain this knowledge of terrible things that happen, but you're able to help them manage it. I think that that's a really positive experience.
015:	It's not just like a one-time thing. Like hearing these traumatic experiences and being able to help them, facilitate their working through that, is what would be positive. I can see the negative aspects, but I don't think that it has to be negative. I think that you hear this traumatic story and, yes, you empathize, but you don't internalize. I think it helps you to be more resilient, to hear that.
017:	Sometimes listening, it's traumatic, and it brings up my own experiences, similar experiences. Many times I have thought how remarkable it was that the person survived, thrived, managed to come in and say I think I need therapy.

(Continued)

017:    You hear some appalling stories of how people were tortured. It is
        a form of resilience, because as tortured as some people might be
        coming into therapy, they have survived, they have survived. The human
        spirit is very resilient. I have admiration for their strength to fight. And
        also the hope that I can help them in the ways that they want to be
        helped, that the therapy can make a difference and I can be part of that.

019:    So I'm very grateful. I really am. I feel honored about it. I tell myself
        whenever that happens [concern about the patient moving forward],
        it'll happen in time. I feel privileged to be able to help people, to just
        be on the journey with them. So we can never, ever forget that.

026:    It might have changed the way I see things [listening to traumatic stories], in
        my own work, my life, being able to listen to what's needed in a situation.
        I think the caring component makes me stay in the work. I like being with
        people in that way, having a career, being able to listen, to find out about
        people, though I have all these difficult emotions and feelings. It can it feel like
        it's the end of the world, but I've learned I can come out of it, we can together.

026:    I love the work I do, it's an extremely fulfilling job, it's a fulfillment. When
        I first started in analysis I got this feeling of being heard, that I've never had
        before. So it was such a new experience, and I guess I'd like to, I always
        wanted to, give back to other people, being really listened to. I hadn't been
        listened [to] all my life. The feeling of knowing that I am available to hear
        these people and nobody else might've done that, knowing that's a relief to
        them because of what I've experienced being a patient. It's big.

027:    Well, sometimes I come home; I go, oh, I'm so grateful for my life.

027:    I can tell you, you can compare them [the terrible stories you listen to]
        and your life looks pretty darn good. And sometimes too, working with
        some of these people, it has helped me understand myself more, too.

027:    I do truly believe it's a privilege to be sitting with people, when
        they're sharing ... from those places [of terrible pain] ... I do feel
        privileged and appreciate people who chose me to do that.

028:    I think it's made me overall just appreciate what I have in my life. I don't
        have financial difficulties. I have a stable marriage, my kids are doing fine,
        not that I don't have my own issues, I do. It's made me look at my life in a
        different way, or at least understand the emotional resources that I have,
        or whatever resources I have. I think it's made me more grateful for that.

029:    It's rewarding in many ways, being able to help another human being, relating
        to another person in a way you know that you can help them, and their life
        to improve, and try to have a better life and strive just to live wholly.

Further, the personal growth concept can be broken into two subtypes.
First, a comparative assessment, 027, "I can tell you, you can compare
them [the terrible stories you listen to] and your life looks pretty darn good.
And sometimes too, working with some of these people, it has helped me
understand myself more, too." Second, a recognition of personal growth,
029, "I'm getting something out of every interaction ... I'm getting personal
growth and knowledge. Out of every interaction, I learn something about
myself." Many statements were made about the feeling of honor or privilege
to be accompanying someone on their journey from a disastrous situation to
one of greater well-being. This is emblematic of the meaningfulness imbued
in the work and the reciprocal nature of the healing relationship.

Part II

Clinical applications

Introduction

Part I, Chapters one through five, introduced the concept of Reciprocal Resilience in the therapeutic relationship, and a research project exploring it. It described the relationship between mature adaptive defense mechanisms and emotional resilience, outlining their correlates. Part II, Clinical applications, provides a deeper look at how these coping skills can manifest in a therapists' functioning and self-reporting, as recounted in their own words. Shifts in resilience self-indicators after minor resilience-building interventions are described through case vignettes and interviews, as well as examples of personal benefits therapists experienced in the process of listening to stories of trauma and hardship. Each chapter in Part II includes at least one, and often several, in-depth stories and analyses of Mature Adaptive Defense usage and its relation to resilience expression and enhancement.

Many of the stories presented in this section are based on transcripts of actual interviews, with modifications to protect the storytellers' privacy. Although all agreed to the use of their material, I am always leery of the possibility someone may later regret giving their approval. It is an odd phenomenon to see words one has spoken now in black and white on paper. I know from my own experiences being interviewed. You are certain what you mean when speaking, but somehow it can get lost in transition to the written word. Or, you may realize it is more revealing than you intended.

One of the things I have found in giving talks and writing about my work is that people can come up to me later and say one of two remarkable things. First, they know I was talking about them. Second scenario, they insist they know who it was and then tell me. It has never happened that they were correct. Not once. Perhaps the stories here, because drawn from extensive interviews, will be more recognizable to the speaker than the smaller pieces found in articles or presentations. If you think you recognize your words, please also enjoy the tales woven around them as disguises to your identity.

We see ourselves in stories or recognize our acquaintances because all stories about the human dilemma are resonant. When I tell people I often forget whom I was writing about after all the anonymity changes, they shake their heads in disbelief. But it is true. I regularly have to look at a legend of characters to remember who's who when I go back after a period to review what I have written. In first writing they are exact, in disguising they become the familiar characters in my mind, in reviewing they meld. In Chapters Six through Ten you will read passages from actual meetings with research participants and vignettes from sessions with patients or supervisees. All are disguised, but at the same time genuine.

Chapter 6

Altruism
The runaway

Altruism, the most highly used adaptive defense among those interviewed, enables one to cope with conflict and anxiety by offering a channel for giving to another what might have sustained oneself at another time, or to treat another in the way one would wish to have been. It provides an emotional structure for the therapist as well as reciprocal replenishing of psychic resources. The therapist's ego is strengthened by the experience of generosity and usefulness, and the interactive, emotional communication reinforcing the empathic connection. Corresponding resilience traits are: concern about the welfare of others; a sense of mindful spirituality; moral reasoning capacity; insight capability and reflective skills; the ability to access interpersonal resources; and self-awareness. An example of altruism as a coping mechanism would be a former refugee from a war zone becoming involved in helping resettle new immigrants.

People reveal their motives in both direct and subtle ways. One of the wonderful aspects of the research interview process is that you can learn about an individual's sense of self and personal history indirectly while gathering information and data about another area of interest. This approach provides an opening into conscious and unconscious motives propelling current behavior and beliefs.

In their own words...

Dina: The runaway

An example of a more direct allusion to a desire to treat others as she would like to be treated was made by a therapist – let's call her Dina – who has worked in a VA hospital for many years. Her father was in the military and the family moved frequently from base to base during her childhood. This disruption of stability and relationships had a harsh impact on Dina's capacity for intimacy and her sense of centeredness. Worse, her father was a self-absorbed, demanding man, relentless in his criticism of everything about her from the way she walked, talked, and played sports, to how she worked or socialized. It is ironic that after years of running away from family oppression, Dina often finds herself locked down in a military hospital, the exponential reflection of her perceived childhood environment. The mind is ingenious at organizing situations that compel us to re-experience old conflicts without our conscious awareness that we are echoing the past with a need to master it, or simply be it.

Dina was initially hesitant to participate in the study, stating, "I'm not sure I have anything to contribute." She assumed the interviews involved being asked questions about clinical practice and technique. I reassured her, saying that I was mainly interested in simply hearing stories from practitioners about their experience of listening to patients recounting of grim life situations.

Dina entered the office smiling, with a shy giggle. "Hello." She said, eyes averted. She is a tall, slender, and attractive young woman who seems to flutter to life with energy, and then subtly withdraws inward. She dresses in lavender hues and flowing scarves. A soft, short blonde cut frames her face like an angelic halo, belying the defiance that surfaces quickly on getting to know her. When meeting with Dina, engaging in conversation or listening to her stories, one has the feeling that there is much more core strength behind the surface delicacy she conveys. There is a wistful quality to her presence, as though she is secretly longing for something or someone. It creates a melancholy undertone even when she is joking or engaged in story-telling about other people.

Dina: I retreated to my own world a lot … when I was really young, into my own fantasy world. A lot of playing … very quiet. Hardly ever saying anything. I mean, if I talked, I might be criticized, or … a lot of it I don't remember. Probably there's a lot of reasons for that. I don't remember them … I tried to do well. One of the big things in our family was golf, it was a big sport. My father played. Everyone played, my mother, and my brothers, and I. And I got really … I was naturally gifted at it. That was one thing that I could do well. He was pleased. But then sometimes, some days I did terribly, and some days I'd do really well. So it was very, it was interesting … I think it was very emotionally driven, I mean you can't just do terribly one day in a sport and really good on another day … so I was probably communicating something … How terrible I was. I don't know.

… Oh, it was awful … I'd feel awful about not winning … playing so terribly; I'd feel terrible about myself. I was useless. So yeah, why didn't I make myself feel good all the time by winning? I could've, I was capable … There was lots of silent treatment, and my mother, too. She had the same experience with her father. They both had issues with their fathers. My dad didn't have a father of his own. He died when my father was six … and his mother had died in childbirth when he was three, with his younger sister who also didn't survive. So he was alone. Then he was part of a family, his godfather and his wife, where he was always judged, and perfection was demanded. I knew them, my grandparents. They didn't really want children, didn't know how to raise a young boy, and they were pretty religious. My father isn't. And my mother's family was extremely competitive … when she didn't do well … it was worse even than my father's. Her father would go for months without talking with her if she did badly.

Despite the battering her self-esteem took during childhood, Dina decided she needed to leave home and found a way to get to college without any help from her parents. She describes it as running away to herself. She thinks her parents might have helped if asked, but the fear of rejection was so pervasive she avoided the possibility by taking charge on her own. Dina worked throughout college and graduate school, paying for everything with multiple jobs, scholarships, and loans. She lived in boarding houses, laughed when telling me about being homeless for a while, and how she finally got her own apartment.

It was after that success, and several years of therapy, that she was able to re-establish a relationship with the parents who did not want her to talk, did not listen when she did, and do not even now. It is Dina's ability to step back from the situation and view her parents for who they are that enables her to sustain the connection. Still, the dynamic continues to influence her feelings about worth, competence, and identity. It impacts her choices and aspirations, fostering a hesitance and ambivalence about committing to having a need or desire. It is reflected in Dina's ambivalence about every decision, each aspect of life.

In our first meeting Dina talked about her chronic fear of being a disappointment, of being too passive at work and in her personal life. As with the other volunteers, I listened to Dina's stories with an ear to hearing both strengths and fragilities. My intent was to gently reflect on the positives I anticipated would be downplayed, and reinforce their existence for Dina. I was aware of a sense I should be doing something else, something more. Although we had comfortable, engaged discussions, I had the notion that I was disappointing Dina. I noticed an impulse to say more, to be talkative, though I am usually at ease with silence. It was as though in the silence Dina was willing me to help, rescue her, say something.

For the most part I observed this pattern silently or asked a neutral, object-oriented question that would not be ego threatening. For example, after one stretch of sitting quietly, where Dina seemed to have drifted off mid-sentence, I inquired, "Should I ask another question now?" Another time I asked, "Is this a comfortable silence?" In more direct reference to what was her last comment, "I was the mother … it totally felt like…", I responded, "What's that feeling, of being the mother?" To which Dina was able to reply and continue describing her experience with a difficult patient.

In one story Dina described a repulsive, psychotic patient who had a revolving door relationship with the hospital, and constantly resurfaced in one of her groups. She loathed him, felt inadequate in his presence.

Dina: There's a patient who comes over, over, and over gets admitted. He gives you such a strong feeling of you're disappointing him always. I don't know, to me that's difficult. I can't get around, around that. It's hard to explain it. Sorry. It's not clear. I try to avoid him.

P: Ah. Why does he keep coming back?

Dina: On some level he probably wants to get the reaction that I have. I don't want him around.. It's kind of redoing something he's experienced, maybe from his military service. But probably much earlier than that, because nobody wants to have him around them. So he can be very sexual, he goes in your space whether you want him there or not. And, I don't even want to talk about him in supervision.

P: Don't want to talk about about him?

Dina: I don't want to talk about him, want to avoid everything about him at all cost. Not even in supervision. I'm disgusted by him.

P: What's disgusting besides that he's invasive?

Dina: Well, it's the feeling. He gets, he can come really close but it's more like, he's not touching you, he's, more like, it's like an induction. He's just kind of going into you like he, it's somewhat like a sexual assault, he's intruding on you psychically instead of physically.

P: There's a threat?

Dina: Yes.

P: And everybody experiences that?

Dina: Most women are disgusted, but men are too. He just gets in you. And he gets you to get rid of him but he stays, he sticks. You can't get rid of him.

P: Like a disease.

Dina: Yes. He's very much like a disease. So that's probably why he keeps on coming back and back.

P: You're faced with these pretty challenging, scary encounters a lot of the time. I'm wondering, how would you describe the way you handle them?

Dina: I guess the best thing for me is to talk about them. That's how I keep on, I'm able to continue going into those challenging situations. I don't want to get rid of all my patients, so I talk about my patients. Or with that guy, I try, but too often he slips my mind when I'd intended to talk about him. In supervision, therapy, wherever I can talk. I don't react instantly unless I need to. Very rarely do I need to really react. But sometimes you might. I kind of sit with the feeling, and wait for a contact.

P: How might other people describe you dealing with these disturbing situations?

Dina: They probably think she's not doing anything. She should be more aggressive. She's letting them run over the top of her. That's not the case at all.

P: So they don't see what's happening, what's really going on?

Dina: They just think that's the patient's inappropriate behavior and want it to stop, get rid of whatever the situation is. They don't want to work with the feeling at all. They put limits, and not that that's a bad thing, but they just, they cut them off very easily. I don't. I don't really cut them off as easy.

P: How about outside of work? How would people describe you handling tough situations?

Dina: Probably the same I imagine.

P: They'd say you're a softie?

Dina: A softie. Don't know what I'm doing.

P: So they don't know you either.

Dina: No, probably not.

P: What gets them to think like that?

Dina: Cause that's how the world thinks. You should be active. You shouldn't, you should, it's just very limited. You shouldn't see what's going on in the situation. You shouldn't see a person for more than what you actually see. If a man comes into a room and he's very smelly and disheveled and angry looking, most people would be scared of that person. And just react and assume things, assume this person's dangerous. So you have to look under that. But a lot of people don't. They just assume you should react and get out of that situation as opposed to start understanding what that person's about.

P: Instead of studying and being curious about what makes them that way?

Dina: Yeah.

P: Are there, are there any times that you can think of where people or you didn't think of yourself that way, thought of yourself as strong and assertive?

Dina: Yes, maybe sticking with things. Sticking with all the commitments on jobs and getting through graduate school. People say that they don't know how I did that.

P: Uh huh.

Dina: It's a hard situation, working and going to school. Sticking with any academic program. I did it by myself. I did everything in that respect. I'm answering your questions, which I knew would be hard for me. But keeping the commitment. So, that's one of, I guess, a strength. I'm able to stay with whatever I'm doing and not back out. Does that help?

P: Sure, very much so.

Dina: Yeah, I don't back down easy.

P: So people would also think of you as someone who has strength of perseverance? That when things get tough, you persevere. You like to know the details, have choices?
    Dina: Mm hm.

Dina talked about the way her attitude of defiance has helped and hurt her. She says she adopted a passive personality style, even while oppositional, and thinks it would be better if she could be direct. She should have been with her father. What would she have said, or say now, I asked.

> **Dina:** I would say, you have (*hesitates, laughs*) to pay attention to me and love me no matter what I do. No matter how I say it. I'm doing the golf thing cause you probably want me to do it, and you feel good about it. It makes you happy ... encourage me ... They didn't listen then, wouldn't now ... Very involved in himself, my mother too. So I'd tell them now how I felt about it anyway.

Throughout the first interview I worked to learn about Dina's experience of herself in relationships, self-assessment, and identity, and to make note of instances when she demonstrated resourceful resilience. During the second interview, I asked her to tell another story about how she handles things in difficult situations with patients at work. Dina recounted a recent incident when a patient ran away from the hospital. Usually she is calm, thinks things through, but feels the pattern is another example of passivity. She dislikes this passive aspect of her personality, describing it as a win on the part of her parents. It holds her like a prisoner. But she commented that she is determined now to stick with it, to tolerate the discomfort of breaking out of passivity. She wants to be free to make choices. This time with the runaway patient, Dina told me, she joined in helping find the patient and returned with her to the unit.

> **Dina:** This time I decided to assist ... a patient took off up the drive and then down into an alley. One of the other staff followed her ... another guy came by car, and we're communicating on cells. When they found her, she was crying ... it was just very scary and sad because she heard voices that said they were going to hurt her. She'd recently come back from Afghanistan, where it was awful. Hallucinations, hallucinations ... She was crying, and then I started talking, and tried to calm her down by saying it's all right ...
>   I'm used to just kind of being there. So that was a first, an interesting situation, being actively involved. And then she came up and wanted to hug me ... I have a no touching policy. But that went out the door during this period, and she just cried and wanted to be right next to me. I was like ... she needed it and we're outside, there's no protection. We needed

to do something to keep her there or else she would take off, or they would have to be aggressive or restrain her.

She was a baby basically. I was the mother suddenly ... I stayed with her on the unit a little bit. It totally felt like ... I was the mother ... like I'm going to do whatever I can to give this person, give her the feeling I'm there ... and I think about my patients and how they're coming to me because probably they're a baby and they want a mother. So I need to make that happen with words and listening.

We see Dina becoming more comfortable recognizing and confronting her default position of passivity from the first to second interviews. Perhaps by acknowledging some of her strengths, and by having them noted by me, she was able to challenge the compulsion to hold back. The goal, of course, would be to have choices to step back and study, or take action. Neither is always right, but being compelled to one or the other diminishes all psychic resources.

Often people who struggle with ambivalence, as Dina has, view the world through a black and white filter. They believe there is one correct answer to any question or problem. This can render even the simplest decision paralyzing. It can become better, safer, to see no choices than to recognize alternatives. Dina did not consciously recognize the parallel dilemma she and her runaway patient faced. But her unconscious was working on it. She was offering the patient what Dina, herself, craves.

A patient once complained to me that we probably could not work together because he recognized I see things in shades of possibilities, and he needs someone who is black and white, either or, like himself. No quibbling. After much time in therapy, this same patient complained that I am too stuck in my thinking. I need to be able to think out of the box, like him. He wondered how I could function as a therapist without exploring all shades of potential solutions. In finding a place where his criticisms and self-doubts could be safely spoken, through a narcissistic transference, he was eventually able to loose himself from the overpowering shadow of a tyrannical father and a submissive mother. Dina is on a similar quest.

At another point, I asked Dina if she could think of any benefit therapists might gain from listening repeatedly to their patients' traumatic stories. She said:

I think, well my experience when I first started in therapy was of being heard. I've never had that before. So it was such a new, it was such a new experience and I guess I'd like to, I always wanted to give it back to other people ... being really listened to. I guess I hadn't been heard all my life. Listening, that means knowing them, if that makes sense. Knowing that I'm doing ... the feeling of knowing I am a person available to hear these people and nobody else might've done that ... that's big ... that's a relief ...

to them. I know because of what I've experienced being a patient. And then they're calmed, or soothed, like I'm understanding them, and it does something for them more than just letting them talk.

Dina's experiences with intermittently critical and neglectful parents trained her to doubt her own capacities, while at the same time demanded she take care of herself if she were to survive. This dynamic can have a paralytic impact on a person's ability to make accurate assessments about life circumstances, relationships, and sense of self. The pummeling of her self-esteem triggered a trauma response enlisting all elements of the fight-flight-freeze triad. Dina fought to forge her own identity. She fled both into a world of her own fantasy making, and later from home to a life where she depended on herself alone for survival. She froze, refusing to insist on having emotional needs addressed, with a debilitating effect on her capacity to judge self-worth, personal aspirations, or contextual conditions.

Each new situation was judged from the perspective of Dina's life experience as a child, where the refusal to acknowledge needs first froze in place. The pattern protected her, back then, from having to face the horrifying fear that her parents could reject or abandon her completely, and she would not survive. Dina intuited that if she could be the child they envisioned, she would be safe. But her fundamental survival instinct drove her to look for other means to meet maturational needs – through defiance. This defense, in its alternating pattern of approach-avoidance as manifested in Dina's use, laid the groundwork for a lifetime of ambivalence in all quarters.

The pattern was strikingly visible in my encounters with Dina, from her ambivalence about participating in the interviews, to her hesitant entrance to the office, to her vacillation between confident descriptions of clinical issues to humorous, self-effacing comments. Dina's ability to see circumstances from multiple perspectives is inhibited, and further encourages reliance on the flight-fight-freeze triad.

When reliance on the trauma defense triad occurs, the individual tends to process situations in terms of the dangers and needs of that original frozen moment. A child cannot envision alternative solutions to a problem in the same way a person with many years of life experience can. Their viewpoint is stunted, and repetitive responses will become persistently more embedded unless some intervention can disrupt the pattern, introducing alternate possibilities. As we will see next in the case of Sam, an influential other, for Dina a therapist, bridged the gap to challenge her frozen position.

Dina's history reflects someone predisposed to fighting for survival. Like her runaway patient, she had been running from a threat and to an unknown relief and consolation all her life. She wanted to break out, but not break away. It is the human challenge to grapple with what we intuit our parents want so they will love us as they should, and the instinct that we need to separate to survive.

In cases like Dina's, where the parents provide an untenable road map to healthy maturity, the obstacles are formidable. It is fascinating that Dina chose to challenge her passivity with the runaway patient, and then to follow it through with being the holding container for all the sadness, loss, anger, and release outpouring from her patient. Also interesting is the fact that she chose to seize that moment and report it to me, out of the carousel of stories she could tell. It is a testimony to the power of reciprocity in the emotional field created by the therapist and patient, in this case by the researcher and volunteer, and of the potential impact of positive priming for resilience building.

Dina had enough positive experiences in her early years to reinforce understanding that with sharply honed instincts she could hopefully assure her existence. Her therapist touched a resonant chord. She demonstrated the power of listening to connect. This experience enabled Dina to begin expanding her worldview, sharing it with another. She learned the value of listening to hear the symbolic communications, and the reciprocity one can experience in that dyad. Armed with this understanding, she is now experimenting with embracing altruism as a coping mechanism that feeds her, as well as those who are its recipients.

In their own words...

Sam: A little shielded

Another therapist, Sam, related an example of an indirect, subtler reference to unspoken motives. He sent a quick, formal response to my email about the research project, stating that he would be happy to help. Sam mentioned his own current research, and anxiety about whether people would be willing to participate there, too. He would be pulling from a different population than this project involved, he said, but you never know about people's resistances. Sam's opening salvo offered a preview, as initial contacts often do, of what might be expected in our sessions: cooperation, reserve, and resistance. For our meeting, he arrived casually dressed and ready to get into the work. His measured, somewhat precise language hinted at a life wrapped in university academia.

Sam is a fit-looking, slim-framed man whose age would be difficult to guess. He speaks in a soft voice, often laced with self-deprecating humor, and seems to be intently concentrating. He gives the impression of someone who wants to be where they are, a great asset to anyone working in human services fields.

As we talked about the research and got to feel comfortable together, Sam told me about his personal and professional life. He spoke with the cadence of one accustomed to telling details of his life as though from a resume, yet he poignantly painted a picture of all aspects, internal and external. This mode of speaking can have a distancing quality. For me, it raised a sense of caution, a red flag to be careful of the potential fragility of the cooperative, who can be over-revealing too soon. I followed that instinct, mindful of containing boundaries, while working to foster an easy, relaxed, and interactive environment. At times I noticed that I got lost in Sam's stories, several of them about incredibly tragic situations. I wondered if this capacity to eloquently spin a riveting tale was also a cloak behind which he could hide.

Sam grew up in an extended family where everyone lived nearby. This was helpful because his father was an explosive type, and you never knew when the monster would appear. Occasional escapes were necessary. There would be a few months of "wonderful parenting", then an eruption lasting weeks. There was no predicting the emotional climate. What was predictable was the possibility things could change in a heartbeat, and mechanisms of escape were vital. It helped that extended family members were available for protection and retreat. Sam commented that many people in the healing professions need healing for themselves. He spoke affectionately about his mother, grandmother, and aunts, all of whom seemed to have had a hand at raising him.

He is in a long-term second marriage. His first wife died very young of breast cancer, leaving him with three young children. Eventually he married his current wife, an economist, and they have one child. Sam is close to his children, all adults now, with whom he is actively involved, and has grandchildren he adores. He surrounds himself with family just as he was in childhood. As suspected from his initial letter, Sam is both a mental health professional and an academic deeply immersed in university life and politics.

After introductory conversation and several opening questions from the interview protocol, I asked if Sam ever found that he suddenly feels he cannot do his job another day.

Sam: (*Laughs*) By the end of the semester I'm ready to retire... I would say that's it. Let me put it this way; I have to deal with such a variety of people's points of view, a variety of emotional conditions. There's a student in my class right now who's bipolar, went off his medication six months ago. It's become a horrible crisis for his family. So knowing there are these emotional issues in my classes, and I could go into long lists, I'm trying to give you kind of snapshots of things. I try to be aware of the emotional dynamics in class because this is about training young people to go into the world to help others. They need to be aware of their own issues, and so do I.

So I have to cope with students who are resistant, and I do mean resistance, to what I'm teaching. It's Philosophy of Psychology now, and they're philosophy and psych grad students. They derive security from sticking to what they believe, naturally. It's threatening to think of changing when there's a crisis confronting you. I have to be careful to remain true to what I'm teaching, and mindful of their vulnerabilities at the same time. I have to try not to trip their wire so to speak. At the same time, I'm continuing to do my own thinking through the issue presented because these aren't fixed ideas for me about ethics or handling tough situations either. I invite students to walk with me as I begin the topic that we're studying. So all this becomes very exhausting.

P: Yes.

Sam: I mean, yes, it's very rewarding and I get a thrill out of those moments when the students and I are really in sync. I know you know that feeling.

P: Yes, very much.

Sam: But then by the end of the semester I'm like, ah. I just can't go to another class or I can't grade another paper. So that's the kind of moment when that happens.

I'm on the training review committee. We always meet after the semester. I think, I just can't do another year of meeting with students and watching the agony they go through as we say things like we're going to have to say to one of them this year, "We feel you need to do more work in supervision before moving on." We really have to do that sometimes. Because at times they really need it or we wouldn't ask them. And if they don't want to do it and take it seriously, they can't go forward. We owe that to the people who they'll work with after graduation. Yeah. So I get a little tired.

At another point Sam told me a story about his own mentor.

P: Has there been anybody, anyone who's really impressed you? Who you've admired the way that they handle these kinds of difficult situations?

Sam: Hm. Well my mentor, Jack. He was very good at handling situations and just letting things kind of play out. We're still in touch. He's in his late 70s now. We've shared many family events and professional ups and downs over the years ... I'm crazy about him, just really love him. So he's someone I admire.

P: Can you give me an example of something he did that really impressed you?

Sam: We worked as volunteers at the university counseling center. It was open to the public and a young girl came in, an immature young girl. She was probably seventeen at the time. Got pregnant, didn't want to marry the young man and wasn't, just wasn't sure what to do with the pregnancy. At the time I felt I was too immature and not trained to handle an issue like that. I was not the person to help her through it. So I suggested Jack meet with her.

P: Good recommendation.

Sam: It was tough, but Jack just walked her through it so well. And, you know, he was so good at caring people through their circumstances. So he's one that comes to mind, someone I've greatly admired. A couple of men in the university were just out to get him, the politics of academia. And he handled them with such grace, most of the time. I mean, Jack does have a temper.

P: Mm hm.

Sam: And we, we did so well together. I would run interference for his temper (*laughing*).

P: How would you do that?

Sam: I'd see that he was starting to get agitated at meetings, and I would just speak up. I had a way of acknowledging a concern but saying, you know, this is another way of looking at it and give him time to defuse (*lots of laughing, happy*). And we would move on. So he was a good caretaker of people and a great mentor of mine. He's got a broad spectrum of gifts ... open about his life questions. More open than I was ... He would challenge me when I would get overconfident. So he shepherded me very well.

Sam responded positively, and was drawn as a young graduate student, to his mentor's consistent interactive and collaborative approach. It was the polar opposite of his early life experience with his father that had made him question his own stability and judgment. He developed tactics for traversing disturbing encounters, by lying low and being almost invisible, as he had needed to at home. Then, the objective was to not draw fire. Later, the same skills helped him persevere and succeed in school, but became more of a drawback for clinical work in their interference with his emotional availability for clients and students.

It was with Jack's modeling of a stable mentor with whom Sam could agree or disagree without fear of vengeful retaliation, that he noticed the handicap his default defenses presented in his work. He might glide through the conflict, but miss the important cues necessary for therapeutic efficacy. Jack encouraged him to welcome the reciprocity in the relationship by treating his input with respect, while maintaining his role as the supervising mentor. It is clear from Sam's story about his position at the university now that, as a teacher and mentor, he thrived with Jack's modeling.

Today Sam deals with the conflicts and struggles in his work with students by using the early mentoring experience as a rudder. He treats students as he would like to be in their situation, as he was treated. When the emotional climate in the classroom gets challenging, he can rely on a sense of altruism as a bolster enabling him to successfully navigate the difficulty. With access to this ego defense, Sam augments his ability to choose to be the container for his students' anxieties and their emotional issues in relation to clinical training. He can elect to be present, or retreat; whichever is more useful in the moment.

Sam was one of the volunteers who expressed apologies or dismay during the second interview when I asked whether he had any thoughts about what we had discussed in the first interview.

P: Since we last met, have you had any thoughts about what we discussed?

Sam: I, honestly, I'm having trouble remembering what we discussed.

P: You aren't the only one, believe me. It's so interesting.

Sam: I've been thinking more about, I've been thinking more about the conference than the interview.

P: Yes, mm hm.

Sam: But, well I, I've had kind of a daily reminder of the conference so that's where my mind has gravitated.

P: It's OK. I can remind you a bit, then we can talk about the conference. One of the things we talked about was how people, or you, would describe yourself dealing with challenging, difficult situations, listening to stories of trauma, impossible situations, heart-wrenching. Can you tell me a little more about that?

Sam: I remember sharing some of those horrible stories I had heard.

P: Mm hm.

Sam: I felt it was not only listening to other people's stories but part of the holding of people's terrible ordeals.

Unfortunately, I missed an opportunity there to follow up on what was actually important in Sam's mind at the moment. I was focused on the notion and surprise that several volunteers remarked that they could not remember things from the first interview. Had I been in more of a therapeutic mode, I might have noticed that Sam was telling me there was a specific issue on his mind daily that resonated with the theme of the conference. In fact, he ultimately circled back to it, an example of increasing resilience resources I will describe here.

Sam's participation in the first interview was thoughtful and collaborative. As mentioned earlier, despite his collegiality I had a feeling of reticence or masking on his part. I did not think much of it because the interview process, in itself, is an oddly personal encounter one does not expect in everyday life. Hesitation and anxiety are to be expected, and all part of the great mix of studying human relationships.

The following exchange occurred toward the end of Sam's second interview:

Sam: I've enjoyed getting to know you a little better though I know it's been kind of one-sided. You haven't been doing the sharing as much as I have done.

P: True.

Sam: I have found myself, in my initial encounter with you, I was a little shielded. You know, not knowing what to expect.

P: Of course.

Sam: This time I was a little shielded because of this situation, a personal crisis, not wanting that to intrude, and yet wanting to be honest by the end of the time that it's something in my own life right now. So I've really considered the question of resiliency, unlike what I said in the beginning.

P: Yes.

Sam: It's something that I have been sort of making a point of under-standing resiliency, my own. In the process here, I find myself hoping that my humor didn't derail, wasn't just derailing me from facing some-thing I didn't want to talk about, but really did. I'm half suspicious of humor but...

P: Mm hm.

Sam: One other thing. Yeah, the resilience, I think I'm more resilient.

P: How so?

Sam then chose to describe the consuming problem he was facing with a sister and her family. He had berated himself for not stepping up sooner, for not noticing what was going on with a nephew.

Sam: I realize I can't make decisions for them. But I can be there to support her and to help encourage the strengthening of her ego so she can deal with this with greater and greater strength. He's her son, her baby. She's like the mother bear. So she tries to take care of it by herself, and kind of shuts you out. Then I experienced some relief just in making that observation, not automatically laying on the guilt. I realize that part of my lack of resilience when things happen in my family is just the lost kid in me resurfacing from way back when. Same for her, we both struggle with that legacy.

So I think dealing with it in the moment, thinking in terms of re-silience, I became more resilient. It's an experience that created more resilience than I would have had dealing with this before, I think.

P: Yes.

Sam: And I never know in the study of the mind where, if some of these things get tucked away ... they're affecting me, helping me, but I'm not necessarily conscious of it.

P: It's organic?

Sam: Yeah, it becomes more organic. So to say well at this point in time there was this insight, that's really what is shaping it. That's not the way it works, for me at least.

P: Mm hm. It's cumulative?

Sam: Yeah, that's a good word for it. It's a cumulative thing.

P: Mm hm.

Sam: I like the idea of maturation. It's optimistic.

In his search to navigate the trauma of early abuse and familial instability, Sam turned to the resources he had known as a child: relationships and talking. Even in this brief interviewing process he was able to utilize them. His commitment to what he describes as maturation, and helping others heal when you have come from a background that demands healing, enabled him to join in a reciprocal process with me in the interviews. He was keenly aware of the skewed character of our conversations, was able to comment on it, but still chanced reaching across to someone ready to listen. Awareness of that capacity itself created a greater sense of efficacy, in addition to the collaborative, emotional reciprocity between us.

In their own words...

Jeff: Men don't talk to each other

Jeff described his early life as one of loss, abandonment, abuse, and the struggle to stay safe in a volatile family environment. Unlike Dina, Jeff seemed eager to participate in the research interviews. He said that it was an opportunity to share what he thinks are valuable clinical and professional experiences people might learn from. It is how he learns best, hearing about how others traverse similar challenges.

Jeff was one of the first volunteers to respond to my request for help with the research. We spoke briefly on the phone to schedule time to meet, and I had the impression of a jovial, enthusiastic person. I was not prepared for the gruff, but insecure, middle-aged man who appeared at the office. My first thought was really a memory. He immediately reminded me of a former supervisor who always joked he was a truck driver in an earlier life. I later discovered my supervisor had grown up in New York City among rival street gangs. His language was coarse, speckled with endless, near inappropriate jokes. He made outrageous recommendations that even then, I recognized, were clinical gems. At that time in my training, he was the antithesis of the polished and serious New York psychoanalysts I usually encountered.

It was not a big surprise to learn that Jeff, who resonated for me with the old supervisory memories, had spent many years as a labor organizer. What was surprising was his open discussion of early childhood trauma, and his awareness of the connection between some of his actions and the relationship with his father. Jeff was not in therapy when we first met, nor had he ever been. He described his journey from labor organizer to mental health professional as an evolution in his development that spurred him in his mid-forties to retire and pursue further graduate training. By the time of our interview, he had completed his degree, was working in an inner city, dual diagnosis unit of a major hospital, and attempting to build a private practice.

Finding himself unhappy and enmeshed in another smothering bureaucracy at the hospital, Jeff commented that perhaps it is his destiny to always land in the midst of conflict and chaos. His marriage is contentious and he is responsible for a special needs child now in her early thirties. Yet somehow he retained an air of quiet optimism and good humor. He spoke of the advantages of his difficult job, of his appreciation for the good supervision and support he got by post-grad networking through his university program.

Jeff related the following story when describing difficult moments in his work as a labor organizer, when he had to help young members during a financial downturn that triggered widespread anxiety:

Jeff: And, you know, what? I found that I was very sympathetic to young people and to how hard it is for them, you know. How hard it is with this economy. They've got kids. They want to buy houses. And you can't afford these houses. They're not making enough money.

And I would tell them, like this one young guy who came to me, I'd say, "This is going to be the hardest part of your life. You'll get through this. You got to hang in there and get through it."

P: Had that been your experience?

Jeff: It was my experience, that early on it's tough. Early on, it's tough. And, you know, and eventually things get better. That was my experience.

P: So it came naturally to tell him that.

Jeff: Yeah. You know what? I was worried about him. I was concerned about them all, you know.

P: What was the concern?

Jeff: The concern was that he was going to throw everything away because he was frustrated. That was what I was concerned about. And I think he'd needed somebody to tell him, "Look ... let's just take stock of things here. You're going to be OK."

Because, what I find is that, in my experience, a lot of people don't get that, you know? A lot of people don't have somebody to talk to.

P: That's true.

Jeff: And especially ... I think it's especially bad for men. Men don't talk to each other.

P: Absolutely true.

Jeff: Yeah. They just don't talk to each other. And, some men are lucky enough to have fathers or uncles who can put their arm around them and say. "Look, here's ... you know, things are going to be OK. You've just got to take stock of things here." But, I mean, for the most part, men don't talk to each other.

P: So they don't know what to expect? That young man was lucky to have you.

Jeff: They don't know what to expect. They don't know. They don't realize that if they talk about this stuff with somebody else, they realize that they're not alone, that they're not the only ones going through this stuff, that things can get better for them.

So, I think I had that in mind when I was talking to him, that I could have talked to this kid like he needed.

Jeff's empathic capacity, bolstered by the higher adaptive mechanism of altruism gave him the resources to tolerate listening to the painful anxieties of his young employees. At the same time, it was an opportunity for a mulligan, a do-over repairing long-carried trauma from his experiences as a youngster. He is another volunteer who initially said he could not remember from one interview to the next what was discussed, but later reported the same story he had in the first interview.

> **P:** Well, since we last met, have you had a chance to think about any of the things that we discussed?
>
> **Jeff:** Uh, yeah. I have. Do you have any examples?
>
> **P:** Sure. We talked about resilience. I asked how you would describe yourself responding in difficult situations, and then how other people might describe you.
>
> **Jeff:** You know, I'm wondering now if that's changed a little bit about how I would describe myself.
>
> **P:** Mm hm.
>
> **Jeff:** You know as far as resilience goes. I started my own therapy recently.
>
> **P:** Uh huh.
>
> **Jeff:** And it's been a really positive experience for me. I think I'm starting to realize that I'm more resilient than I thought I was.
>
> **P:** Uh huh.
>
> **Jeff:** I'm starting to realize that I have more ego strength than I thought I did. For some reason I never thought I did.
>
> **P:** Mm hm.
>
> **Jeff:** You know, I'm fifty-three years old and a lot of my friends, the people I know that are the same age, they kind of stopped. They're ... they look older. I saw a friend of mine over the weekend. He asked, "How do you do that, all that you do? I don't know how you do it." I said I enjoy it.

Jeff told me some horrifying stories about clients, young men, who had been multiply abused, incarcerated, addicted, and alone. There were tales about men and women living on the street, or bi-polar patients coming to him battered and off their medication. He told me about an experience at work in the weeks between our interviews, and of a new way of listening to clients he is developing.

> **Jeff:** It's funny, they had a new counselor come in. They introduced me and they said, "Jeff does intensive outpatient. That's the worst of the worst." You know, I was like well I'm glad they think that. Because, everybody's really just the same. Everybody's the same. But, because they think that, I have fewer clients, I only have fourteen, and I do three groups a week with them. It gives me the opportunity to spend time with them, and to develop a relationship with them. You know, to take the time to let them talk when they want to talk or, you know, to learn how to listen to them.

P: How does it feel? What's the difference in the feeling for you of listening in this new way?

Jeff: Well, what I'm feeling is that this person is trying to tell me something, you know? Even if they go off on a tangent, they're complaining about something, you know, this is why I couldn't make group and this is why I missed the clinic yesterday. You know, there's something going on there. And so I started to realize that in their own way, everybody's trying to tell me something. I'd learned it in classes, but suddenly it hit home.

P: Hm.

Jeff: Yeah, and I guess I never thought that before. I mean I feel a little more emotionally connected to, like to that bi-polar woman who's really abrasive. She's very difficult, and I've noticed the last few weeks that I haven't been thinking of her as difficult. I'm thinking of her as somebody who ... she almost seems desperate to me. Someone who's desperately trying to tell me what's going on. You know? I don't know, I picked up on what was behind the aggressiveness ... I think it's just that I've become more patient with people. You know, I'm becoming less judgmental. It really means something.

P: Mm hm. You're aware you enjoy it?

Jeff: I'm aware I enjoy it ... it's part of this thing that I'm realizing, that everybody, I mean even though it might not be the way you would react, but most people do things for a reason.

The story Jeff recounted in both interviews was about an exercise he had done in class where a classmate suddenly revealed to him, for the first time he had talked with anyone outside the family, that his son had died in a fatal car accident the month before. As a fledgling therapist Jeff was terrified that he would say the wrong thing. He described himself as just sitting and nodding. When they were finished with the exercise, his partner thanked him profusely. He claimed it was the most helpful thing, just having him listen, that had happened since the funeral. Jeff was astonished. "I didn't do anything," he thought. On the way home he was whistling cheerily, and questioned why he was so happy when his classmate had just revealed the tragic story. He said it was the first time he really recognized the importance of the way one listens to hear what is the real story.

As he began, in Interview II, telling me the story for the second time, Jeff prefaced it by saying, "I'm not sure if I mentioned this one before." Of course, since he had and was repeating it, I understood it was one of significance to him. I asked if that was a story with special meaning. He said that he had been thinking of what I might ask in the interview, and this encounter came to mind. I commented that it was a terrific story, but wondered what made it stand out so for him. He said he had questioned that himself. He thought it had to do with how terrified he was of his father most of his life. There had been encounters on the old job where he had been forced to stand up to bullies, and felt obligated to protect some of the junior staff. There were times when he had to use brute will to conquer fears. This was one of those, even though in the closed environment of the class exercise. He believes all such incidents are connected to facing down the father who had ruthlessly bullied him. This time, it was his own fear of incompetence at providing the emotional strength his classmate needed, the grit he had craved as a youngster that caused him to falter. That he was able to do it and get recognition by being there for his classmate, was transformative.

Chapter 7

Sublimation
My handy dandy smart phone

Sublimation "allows an indirect resolution of conflict with neither adverse consequences nor marked loss of pleasure ... Sublimation does more than make the affect acceptable; it also makes ideas exciting" (Vaillant, 2000, p. 94). With the use of sublimation, a socially unacceptable, or personally dangerous, impulse is transformed into a positive channel. The energy from the original wish is redirected toward another activity or expression of desire that reduces the potential for psychic conflict and creates a satisfying alternative. Those who use sublimation as a coping skill are able to find satisfaction, pleasure and/or meaning in what they do, regardless of whether it would have been their original choice or impulse.

Resilience traits corresponding with sublimation are: viewing problems as opportunities; seeking out new, challenging experiences; not experiencing shame or depression when facing a failure; an ability to transform helplessness into power; capacity to move from being a victim to a survivor; a belief in the uniqueness of oneself; flexibility; and an ability to tolerate adversity, silence, solitude, and frustration.

An example of sublimation employed as a higher-level coping skill would be a person who wants to spy on others, a voyeur, becoming a bill collector. A therapist whose landlord refuses to fix a heating problem and purchases a space heater, deciding that is a more useful approach than acting on the impulse to take the case to court, is sublimating. A woman who is tempted to cheat on her husband, but instead takes him for a romantic getaway has used this adaptive device.

Sublimation was the second most frequently used adaptive defense mechanism by volunteers in this research. Anyone who trains for years in an academic setting – graduate school, military, or professional training – learns to sublimate to survive. The same holds true for parents, law enforcement professionals, and many positions where aggressive impulses are tempted and challenged daily. Without the capacity for sublimation, you are left with a mounting psychic energy from urges and needs not met, which may trigger behaviors momentarily gratifying, but carrying harsh consequences.

Imagine a mother at home with three young children, one of them with special needs. She only wants her kids to cooperate in the simplest ways, like come to the table. The day has been harrowing with medical and insurance calls, school responsibilities, and with contractors who do not show. Two of her children tumble fighting into the kitchen knocking dinner off the table. The dog chomps it down. It takes all her restraint to stop from swatting them. Instead, she challenges them to a race to clean up the mess while she orders take out. Accidents happen.

A patient reports to his therapist that he discussed the therapy with his girlfriend. She thinks it is not helping and recommends he discontinue. The therapist is tempted to say something crushing about relying on the recommendation of someone who has been so abusive to him. She opts to explore what the girlfriend has in mind and what the dissatisfactions are. She recognizes that the patient is communicating a complaint of his own. She wants to continue working with him, so demonstrates seriousness about his statements, rather than indulge in being critical of the girlfriend.

Several of the higher level coping skills use a form of replacement, or standing back, as a means of psychic conflict resolution. With sublimation there is the special, added benefit that the replacement may be exciting as well as effective. Remember Dina, who chased a runaway in Chapter six, swinging her way through criticism and rejection by her family on the golf greens? How exciting it may have been to indulge in terrible performances, testing her father's reactions. She continually balanced the conflict, using golf to club herself and her father.

In their own words...

Jen: My handy dandy smart phone

Jen is a small, voluptuous Asian woman in her early thirties. When annoyed she can appear more tank-like than sensual, barreling into confrontations. But her appearance, at our interviews or on the conference days, was undeniably geared toward the seductive. Her clothes were stylish and well-coordinated, slightly too short, too revealing, or too tight for appropriate professional wear. Though she was simply coming to interviews with me, or to a weekend, casual conference, she had also come directly from work as director of a residential facility, where her attire might be experienced as provocative. Jen is gorgeous, with haunting, dark hazel eyes, a sign of her mixed racial heritage, that change color with the light. This was especially noticeable in my office where she faced an expanse of sunlit windows. She is one of the few people whose eyes I have observed shifting color with her affect as well as the light. There's a slight disconnect in the coordination of both eyes that can be disconcerting, too. It can create a feeling of edginess or startle, as though something unexpectedly came into view with one eye darting after the other. I later learned that this is a congenital condition for which Jen underwent surgeries and eye training throughout her younger years. She speaks with a faintly noticeable lisp that is somehow lovely to hear. It was hard to tell whether this pattern was an accent incorporated growing up at home with immigrant parents, or functional. The slight speech anomaly encourages a more intense attentiveness to what is being said.

For a small person, Jen has a big presence. She told me that she works as a clinical director at a residential facility for adolescent girls. She loves her job. Most patients there are diagnosed with schizophrenia or borderline conditions. Many are dual diagnosed. Often trouble with the law, acting out school behavior, or domestic violence is the trigger for referral to the facility. I asked if she would tell me some stories about difficult situations at work that had a strong emotional impact on her.

Once Jen started talking, it was clear the floodgates had opened. Stories cascaded one after the other in great detail. It made me think about her wardrobe choices and how she seemed to almost erupt from everywhere, physically, affectively, and verbally. I had a sense of unease, as she cooperatively continued telling the stories, that this was more of a download than sharing, and that I needed to help her stay contained.

Jen: Oh, OK. This was when I first started. I've been at the site for about five years now. So it was a holiday and we were down-staffed. We had a young patient, Donna, diagnosed with schizophrenia, but my idea was borderline. She suddenly flew across the room and physically attacked me. That took an extreme emotional toll on me at the time because I thought I had a pretty good rapport with her and I learned how naïve I could be. I'll set the stage up for you. Donna's a self-harmer, but she said she had stopped. For some reason she was afraid to tell me she had back slid, so she left me a note and asked me to meet her in the dayroom.

Once I heard that she was hurting herself again, my gut reaction was to get her back to the unit so the staff could examine her to see how bad it was, what she needed. But she refused to go. She showed me some of the spots. It was worse than I could imagine. She'd gotten matches and was burning holes all over her body where you couldn't see when she was dressed. I'm surprised I didn't pass out when I saw it. I needed her back on the unit. My idea was to slowly kind of walk her back without her knowing. I didn't want to escalate it. I kept a safe distance.

We were standing at opposite walls. She's much bigger than me, so it's not like I was very intimidating. Donna was in continuous motion, kept rolling against the wall, back and forth. She began telling me her story in a sing-song voice in rhythm with her movements. She needed to be punished. That's how she kept the bad guys away. Her father sexually abused her. Her uncle attempted suicide in front of her. Everyone lived in a small space, and there was constant violence. Someone was always getting hurt or thrown out. While she talked she started itching then digging at herself. I asked if she could stop it. She wouldn't. Suddenly she was all over me scratching and choking. We weren't trained to deal with violent outbursts, which we should have been, but I've made changes about that since. It was awful. Luckily I was in an area where staff could hear. Otherwise it would have been me, on my own. So, they escorted her back to the unit and she was seething.

My heart was pounding out of my chest. My supervisor said I should take a few days off to recover. I said no, this is the nature of the work. If I get scared away by that, I'm never going to survive in mental health. So, yes, that's one of the traumatic events. It was brutal, and my family wanted me to press charges, but that made me feel even more powerfully. I am not always the strongest person in a group. I can get overwhelmed or intimidated. I decided this was one place where I would hold my ground. I would not be kept from my job, but I would insist on proper protections and training. So it worked well.

I asked if there were many more stories like that. Tons, she responded, and from the other hospital she had worked at before, too. How does she manage keeping so many balls in the air with unpredictable, potentially violent patients and not enough staff support?

Jen: Oh, boy. I handle things very well under pressure. I was a unit director for a few years. So under pressure and split-second decisions, I'm very good at. Things that linger, like going back on the unit with that girl who choked me, I don't like. I don't like at all. I don't like the feelings. I probably don't usually react in the best way. I mean, I'm not a physical threat to anybody. My language can get pretty vulgar. I get pretty heated. Overall, though, I handle crisis situations well in the moment. But that was one time when it felt really good to be able to say I am going to make this work, stick it out, and use it to get the other staff to learn to respect me more.

P: Are there things that you do or use sometimes that help you to get through these difficult situations?

Jen: I read a lot, I guess that would be somewhat of a coping skill. I read a lot. Anything I get on my Kindle, and whatever's free. I subscribe to different things and download. So I just stock up my Kindle. That's what I actually do at work, when I have a few moments, if I don't have anything to do, which has been very rare now. I read because I'm able to block everything out around me and focus on something I like. I do art. You know, I started as an artist. I'm making more art lately, new things. I've been making these masks, carvings, from amalgams of materials. I'm starting to get some attention at craft shows. All those things I do, they help me let go for a few. I like reading and it makes me forget I want to run out of there at times, not hear any more. Obviously I go out with friends, socialize, being connected with professional peers is a big thing for me too. I recently got connected with someone who works at another facility. We've been in situations where we're managing staff who are not cooperative, we're dealing with patients. So it's great to have that bond and have that professional and personal relationship because it is a tough population and you don't realize it until you're in it.

P: Working with this population, does it ever impact your personal life?

Jen: I think that's natural. I think it does. Sometimes a stressful day, I just want to go home and shut the door and leave the world on the outside, you know? And sometimes I want to talk about it with others and I might project my anger onto somebody who doesn't deserve to have it towards them. So I think any population that I would work with, it would affect my personal life one way or another because you're … yes, you have to learn how to balance and separate. But at the same time, we're in a helping profession, so it's, it's kind of a fine line. It's not like I'm going into a bank and dealing with money, and dealing with people's finances, and then going home. It's kind of like work is home and home is work.

Like others I interviewed, in fact most of the people I have met over the course of doing resilience-building seminars and research, Jen is courageously dedicated. She is creative in using sublimation to make what others might consider intolerable working conditions, and a thankless job, meaningful. She recognizes the value in it, and strives to understand her own clinical weaknesses. Jen continues training and supervision to improve her skills, and finds delight in activities that give her solace or pleasure in the midst of chaos and potential danger.

In our second interview, Jen revealed that she had been bullied throughout childhood. This was surprising to learn. The grit and self-assessments she disclosed during the first meeting would not have suggested someone chronically mistreated, either at home or in social settings. She became tearful, turning away embarrassed as she spoke. It was apparent she had been thinking about this history of her trauma, and was torn deciding whether to share or hold back. It was as though having told me the story of standing up for herself after the assault was giving her courage, or license, to take a stand with me, to share the story of her past shames and watch for my reaction.

Jen: Up until high school I was picked on and teased. All throughout my childhood actually, up until about my senior year … Oh, I was teased for my speech, I had really bad speech problems, and you can't believe the things kids said. Between my speech, and I'm obviously mixed race, and there was this problem with my eyes. (*She wiggled and rolled her eyes, and accentuated her lisp playfully*). So we had to move a couple of times, Dad's job transfers. I guess they were critical ages: six and nine. I don't remember, I don't remember much of my childhood aside from being miserable, teased, and left out. Each time we moved I prayed this would be to a better place, the kids would like me. It just didn't work. I'm in therapy now. We're working this out ... It was, it's a trauma. The moves, the kids were a trauma. And there's a lot of it that I don't remember and I'm sorting it out now and trying to integrate it all. Each place was a different set up to get used to. You know, my Dad would get promoted, we'd move to a better neighborhood, and then have to adjust to how they did things. But my father wasn't around so much so everything he heard was like hearsay. He didn't witness me coming home in tears. He didn't witness the comments, you know, the phone calls and things like that. He didn't really understand all the anxiety that I started to get, which led me into therapy then.

They did as best as they could, whatever is considered good for a child. My mom was very supportive. She did what she could do. She got involved with the school, I mean there's only so much parents can do. It wasn't easy for her either. I was the target of everybody's ... I don't know... how do I say ... I was the target of being picked on, being teased about everything. So it stuck with me up until I finished high school. But by that point, I learned how to blow it off more. Yeah, but it was all the time.

P: All the time?

Jen: Yes. I went through a lot. I had a few friends and then everyone else was, you know, picking on my speech, even after I had years of speech therapy and you could barely notice anything, I was still picked on. So your conference, the talk on social media and bullying, I keep going back to that and thinking, like, with the technology that there is today how much that would have made things even more terrible for me. I could just imagine the disaster it would be for me to get through school.

I was thinking about, like, the instant gratification from cell phones and what you can access now with the blink of an eye. And how much, how much torture and torment I went through as a child, would probably have been a hundred times worse knowing that someone could just go on Facebook and write something. Someone could go on Twitter and say whatever they wanted, send a picture on Instagram, and all those other apps.

Regardless of Jen's possible role in perpetuating the childhood torture, it was heart wrenching to listen to her stories. The feelings were palpable in the room, in the present. She talked about how the teasing has shaped most of her relationships and mentioned an upcoming high school reunion. I was

shocked to hear she was considering going. Whatever would induce someone to risk exposing herself to a possible repetition of the high school nightmare? She laughed when I asked, tilted her chin in defiance, straightened her
linen jacket as though primping.

> **Jen:** Because I feel like I've grown into my skin now. I left high school,
> I went away to college, I went away to grad school, and I've never gone
> back. It's really kind of interesting for me to want to even go back to
> the reunion because of all the torment I went through. And the reason
> why I'm going back is I look at who I am now, and yes, I know that the
> teasing has taken a toll on my self-image, even as an adult I still have
> residual side effects from it. But I look at where I got, where I got myself;
> at thirty-four I've got multiple graduate degrees, I've purchased my own
> home, and I've got a hefty amount in savings. I have a career where I'm
> doing something important and am appreciated. You know, I'm doing
> productive things with my life and I'm succeeding. With Facebook, you
> can see what other people are doing with their lives, so then you say
> wow, the popular kids are working as Uber drivers. I have bright goals
> for the future. I'm career-driven. I've come a long way. In a sense I want
> to say look at me now! That's kind of where I am. It's going to be inter-
> esting to see all those people that made my life hell and see how unpro-
> ductive some are right now.
>
> **P:** Sweet revenge.
>
> **Jen:** Yes. And that's exactly what it will be.

I listened in fascination to Jen's story unwind, witnessed the transformation
in the description of her experience as a chronically helpless, hopeless child
to a woman so pleased with how she had defeated her torturers. Not that I
think the issues are truly history. I am curious about how Jen is currently,
deviously organizing parts of her world to replay and re-vanquish, continually prove that she can beat her oppressor. But, as in her own words, it is
remarkable to see how far she has come.

Jen never mentioned the parallels between herself and the patients at the
residence. They, too, were moved from place to place, constantly required
to adapt. Like Jen, they had challenges that put them at the social fringes,
interrupting a linear process of maturation and personality development.
Jen brings a wonderful gift of empathic resonance to her work, which is her
greatest asset and challenge at the same time. Whether because of family
dynamics, environmental input or constitution, she managed to navigate
to adulthood building the stronger coping mechanisms that enabled her to
flourish rather than withdraw.

Being able to use Higher Adaptive Defenses like sublimation does not automatically mean that an individual is free from psychic conflict, neuroses,
or the compulsion to repeat and repair old wounds. It does indicate that the

person is capable of using healthful, self-protective tools, rather than being locked into patterns of persistent self-sabotage. Jen told me she had started her own therapy since we first talked. With a happy grin she announced, "I'm ready to move up to the next level!" Many weeks after our last meeting I received a note from her. The reunion was a great success. It was all she had hoped it would be.

During our last meeting, I heard more stories from Jen about patients at the residence. I had come to think of the young women as the extension, or psychic externalization of the parts of Jen's self she both loathed and wanted to salvage. At one point she recounted the following about her experience:

Jen: So, running the residence, I think I'm more proactive than reactive now, and I'm more observant to catch things before they escalate or happen. I also learned I have to set limits with a lot of patients or they'll drain you by the end of the day. And it's about time. No pun intended.

P: How do you set limits?

Jen: I give them a set time each week. Seems ridiculously simple, right? In the outside world it would have been automatic. That's their time and then they don't bother me, or interrupt me, or break up my group, or follow me down the hall all the time. By giving them that guaranteed time, they know I'll be there. It's helped with my stress level of dealing with some very needy patients, not to mention staff, too.

P: And they're able to organize the time? They'll know when it's time?

Jen: Well, we're still working on that (*laughs*). They ask, do I meet with you today? No, we meet on Tuesday at three o'clock. Well can we meet today? No, it's Tuesday at three o'clock. I have to be very firm. That's not who I am with them, feel with them, because I have a lot of compassion, and a lot of them don't have support systems when they're released. So we're their support system in addition to their therapists. I have a very difficult time putting limits on some of them, knowing where they come from. I want to give them everything. But then I'm sucked dry and that's not fair to myself or everybody else.

P: What happens when you're sucked dry?

Jen: Oh, I get very irritated and agitated and frustrated. I just, you know, I'm at my wits end. And then the slightest thing can make me go to the anger zone. Or I'll just start crying.

P: Oh...

Jen: Those are my options. I've gotten better though.

P: Uh huh.

Jen: I worked it out, this month I downloaded a whole bunch of music on my handy dandy smart phone device. I listen to the music as a way of coping. It's a way of de-escalating before I hit the wall, which I haven't hit in some time ... I just put my headphones in, tune out, and do my thing. I learned to put these in (*brandishes earbuds*), and I'm good to go.

P: Head down, music on.

Jen: That's me now: setting limits, keeping boundaries, and every now and then good sounds in my head.

Jen did not remember she had told me about reading and using different devices to transport her when things started pressing in on her, challenging her to act on impulsive urges, as she had at school, lashing out at the kids who tormented her. This version, though, had a more vital and connected tenor. It sounded optimistic, uplifting, rather than submerging into the Kindle stories. Each is a positive tack, a sublimation of conflicted energies, but the music allows Jen to roam the halls herself, to choose to smile, simply nod, or be occupied. Taking the risk of holding herself to boundary setting, as much as her patients, was a challenge to a comforting self-image: someone spontaneous and all giving. She was right; it is on to a new level for her, being able to recognize that being firm about being there is a different kind of giving.

Her new approach is actually a compounding higher-level defense, combining both sublimation and altruism. Jen has gotten much gratification in the past from giving to patients unconditionally, without assessing therapeutic strategies. She acted on the unverbalized belief that what they need is her total, spontaneous acceptance. In stepping back to examine her own motives she realizes that the boundaries she resisted imposing are protective resources that help patients tolerate stimulation. Once able to recognize that, Jen was chagrined to admit that the gratitude from patients when she disregarded boundaries for them was something she desired. With the growing awareness of the important meaningfulness of boundary protection, Jen was able to forego the instant gratification and found the increasing responsiveness and stability of her patients rewarding. She is able to look back now and identify moments when things could have been different had she put the brakes on her own impulses to be gratifying.

I mentioned this is a compounding defense because of the overlap between sublimation and altruism. To quiet the conflict about being all-giving or a responsible boundary setter, Jen has introduced a new perspective on the meaning of giving within the treatment relationship. She is giving to the patients by being willing to reign in her own impulses, observe boundaries, and do it with an empathetic, not punitive mindset. Being able to consciously choose to sublimate her impulses and replace with another clinically driven approach is not only exciting for her, but there is increased positive feedback in patient progress. In addition, this is an altruistic gesture, a coping devise that resonates with Jen's own life experiences. She yearned for someone to really see her, to understand what she was going through, rather than tease and reject her for what they saw on the surface. Remember her unanswered wish, "Each time we moved I prayed this would be to a better place, the kids would like me. It just didn't work." She gets it now, that her patients need a similar generosity of spirit, to be seen for themselves, and it frees her and rebounds to her child within at the same time.

Nuances of sublimation

One supervisee told me that each time he meets with a patient in the hospital, this paranoid individual reaches out to shake his hand. The therapist feels most uncomfortable, suggesting that everything in the room get put into words. It is common courtesy that if someone moves to shake your hand, you reciprocate. But he followed supervisory recommendations and spent many sessions where the patient suggested instead of a handshake, a fist bump. Or how about just finger tips touching, like in ET? Or a quick head or butt bump? The patient became creative in his suggestions, laughing and teasing with the therapist about how long it would take to figure this out. The therapist stood firm and the patient, who had previously refused to attend sessions with other interns, continued. Recently my supervisee told me he realized the importance of this simple boundary setting and exploration. Despite the discomfort, it tells his patient he is someone who can be trusted not to cave in, not to break protective boundaries. He is someone who will continue with the patient despite uncomfortable feelings. His interest is more about protecting the patient's ego boundaries than in taking an expedient route. The therapist believes this mutual exploration of a seemingly minor interaction is a large factor in the patient's ability to tolerate the intimacy of the sessions in which he is revealing more about his internal life. The words and mutual, joking exploration provide a sublimation tool with which each can accept the discomfort of holding back impulses, and connect at the same time.

Some demonstrations of sublimation are easily observable. They result from concrete substitute of an impulse with another recognizable replacement. A child longs to smash in his crabby neighbor's window with a snowball. At the last minute he changes direction, artfully hitting a tree branch that sends snow cascading from limb to limb to a mound on the ground. Grinning, he thrusts a victory pump in the air and saunters off. He successfully saved himself from certain disaster and punishment if there had been a direct hit on the window, and pleasurably enjoyed the discharge and reward of his well-aimed pitch at the tree. The capacity to assess risks and consequences, and to choose alternate satisfaction routes gets reinforced each time it is exercised. With every successful choice, the neuro-psychic imprint is deeper embedded, and the coping strategy carried forward for use in other situations.

Other examples of sublimation are more organically woven into our way of navigating life. They become the fabric of a personality pattern that centers the individual, becoming a core, defining characteristic on which other coping skills are based. They can be positive, adaptive, and supportive patterns or divert into pathology when ego strength is not sufficient to support the power of primitive impulses. While a person may use specific defense mechanisms as their primary coping tool, personality and functioning style are not always static. People generally have several mechanisms in their arsenal, and respond to situations based on life experiences. Successful adaptation relies on both the ability to develop coping tools and the maturation of a stable personality that can employ them.

Someone with a powerful aggressive drive might become a surgeon. Redirection and release of overpowering impulses can play out as a path of action and satisfaction over the course of life. In a strange blend of sublimation and rationalization, or self-serving bias, Dr. Hannibal Lecter, of the Thomas Harris novels, became a surgeon and a cannibal. He pursued surgery to sublimate homicidal cravings, and then used surgical skills to dismember those he deemed unfit to live. He was ridding society of useless or damaging people. Lecter was an outstanding chef, serving lavish meals to his guests. He later revealed that his savory dishes were actually organs and body parts of his victims. In that process he repeatedly vanquished the trauma and tortures of his childhood as a captive during WWII, and his sister's cannibalization by looters while they were in captivity. Hannibal's psychopathic behavior can be seen as the use of psychological defenses gone haywire. It demonstrates that even though coping mechanisms are adaptive, in extreme they can be perverted into disguised mechanisms of destruction.

A man I worked with some time ago was a chemist and a firefighter. He told me with absolute sincerity and lack of guilt that, when his wife was at work, he tied his children naked to chairs in his workshop to teach them the basics of chemistry and to reinforce the need to be cautious around equipment. His parents had died in a chemical fire and an aunt and uncle who were childless raised him. The uncle was sexually abusive. My patient believed his aunt denied this so that her husband would leave her alone, and choose him, their adoptive son, as a sexual substitute. Becoming a firefighter was his way of repairing and undoing the fire that killed his parents. It was also a sublimation of his overwhelming rage at having been orphaned, abused, and never rescued. Unfortunately, these defenses, shifting from the higher level of sublimation to the more primitive of reaction formation and denial, were not sufficient to keep his fragile ego cohesive. Impulses broke through, got translated through rationalizations, and his children became a second generation of substitute victims. It was only because one of them confided in a school counselor that the terrible situation came to light.

In their own words...

Carol: It doesn't scare me

There will be more about Carol in a later chapter, but she told me some wonderful stories that rang so true with the use of sublimation that I want to share here as well. Carol is a delightful, energetic woman who communicates an eagerness to engage in everything around her. She is articulate and open to connecting. She impresses as a strong presence in the room, but holding back a bit to size up the situation before jumping into it. Carol has had several professional incarnations, among them owning an art gallery. She described a life history involving many moves and separations that were challenges, though always exciting. She does not view herself as someone suffering serious separation anxiety, but experienced it when her daughter went off on a job taking her to many remote areas in third world countries. The depth of her own anxiety about the job shocked Carol. She panicked and wanted to insist her daughter change the plans. She also felt guilty about not being as supportive as she thought she should.

Carol: Besides my day job, I've been running a gallery since about 2010, and I don't know if I ever told you the story. The way I got into it is my daughter is a graphic designer, an artist. Not as her job. She actually works for NGOs setting up programs for women's literacy in disadvantaged areas. But she's great with graphic design and communicating through her art what she experiences in her travels. She wanted to do a showing of her work, and she was going off on some trip to Africa, or whatever. I said, "So keep the project in mind, and when you get back you can try to put it all together, and I'll arrange a venue. Just keep sending me material."

So she did pull it all together, and then we found out she had only six months between coming back from that trip and going to Brazil. I just said, "OK, how are we going to get it done? Where's the gallery?" She wanted it, and I'm like, you produce the art and I'll go figure it out.

That was the first step. I found a small space in the center of town, researched how to publicize and market a showing, and voila! It was quite successful. Since then we do a few showings a year and have someone running the gallery for us. I don't do a ton of the work, but I do select the art. It takes a lot of time because it's just us, and she's still traveling. Thank goodness for a wired world. It's not a huge organization by any stretch. So, let's see, I just finished one exhibit, and we're starting to review for the next. It keeps us connected and I feel like she's part of my everyday life no matter where in the world she's off to now.

Carol's resolve, in the face of powerful urges to override her daughter's commitment to work in faraway and frightening areas, is impressive. Instead of becoming demanding or crumbling, she found a way to redirect her energies into a pursuit that would tap her own and her daughter's passions, and keep them connected. It was a way to maintain a sense of control and knowledge of ongoing events that helped lower her anxiety, allowing her to support her daughter.

In another instance, Carol told the following story about experiences as an intern at a psychiatric hospital:

> **Carol:** It doesn't scare me, the voices and crazy talk. No it doesn't scare me. I just look at these people and thank God. It brings to mind the question, like what happened? What happened to these people? And I have a guy who tells me I was this kind of child and I was this kind of person, and then I was twenty-three and I went crazy. So he can tell his story. But he can't control how it unfolds. He's schizophrenic, schizo-affective.
>
> He even asked me the other day, so what would you do if you had a choice of being homeless, being in jail, or being in an asylum, which would you choose? I started to say something and then he barely gave me a chance to answer. He started rambling on. He talks a mile a minute. But then he sat back and said you never answered my question.
>
> **P:** He's testing you?
>
> **Carol:** Yeah, yeah, and I was waiting, you know. So I said, well, I've, I've done some work at a prison so I don't think I'd like to be there. And being homeless, you could do it for a while, but you couldn't do it for a long time. I wouldn't want to do it for a long time. So, I said if I don't have an option to have a job and earn money, I guess I'm left with the choice of being in an asylum.
>
> **P:** Was there a reason he mentioned prison?
>
> **Carol:** Because he did some stuff and someone called the police on him. He said he really wanted to fight them off or run. But he also didn't want to go to jail, so he said crazy shit to them basically. So they'll either leave him alone or send him to psych for an evaluation. Then he gets to a safe place where someone else controls his impulses for him.

With the little information she had about this patient, Carol managed to mirror him by sorting through options and choosing being sent to the hospital over prison. He was besieged by paranoid impulses to assault people for not treating him right. In a moment of clarity he chose to "act crazy" instead of belligerent, and this got him at least some of the treatment he wanted. Carol's own default mechanism, to find a substitute solution that will meet a thwarted need, kicked in and helped her be in sync with her patient. She modeled the appropriateness of his choices regarding detainment, and reinforced his fragile connection to an awareness of his condition, and to her. Carol reported her confidence is boosted in situations like this, where she feels backed into a corner clinically, but can find an intervention that balances acceptance of the patient's perceptions, however distorted, with a genuine understanding of the validity of their choices.

Sublimation is such a useful tool. But it takes a cohesive sense of self-organization and internal centeredness to sustain it. The competing pulls of powerful impulses create psychic conflict that can drive someone to an irresistible need to act. Caught in a traumatic, threatening situation the ego tends to regress toward disintegration if not already bolstered with existing coping mechanisms. This is not an indication that something is wrong with, or inadequate about, the individual whose defenses begin failing when facing a serious challenge. It implies that their defense structure has simply not matured enough to meet the present test. This event might present an opportunity to rally and initiate a new pattern of response, or the opposite: regression. It's a measure of resilience, and a chance to increase it.

In their own words...

Melanie: Skating through a dream

Melanie, a nine-year-old figure skater, suffered from intermittent, but serious performance anxiety. She came in one day with a video of her latest performance, and told me she found a new way to face the ice and the crowds. She started up the video and we saw her skate into the scene, looking minute and alone in the massive rink. She was so tiny it seemed to take forever to get to the far end where she was to begin. She warmed up, doing turns and flips rounding the rink. With a slight nod she acknowledged the audience and judges, before gliding to a stop. Everything was silent, as she stood immobile, arms stretched to the side. She stared straight ahead, the music started and she seemed transported, moving through her routine beautifully, smiling, but with a faraway look in her eyes. It was breath taking, beautiful. When it was over I automatically began clapping and cheering.

What a performance! I asked what was the new, secret strategy that let her feel so free? Grinning that knock out all-over smile, she said, "I imagined myself at my home rink. I looked around and in my head, saw all the bleachers and the kids, my team, waving." Melanie allowed herself to feel the comfort of the home ice, the boards as she skated the warm up, the familiar breezes through her hair, the sounds of blades glazing the ice, and to hear the music in her muscles. "When I could do that, it was like dancing through a dream."

Was this dissociation or sublimation? I, too, was lost in the imagery of this sliver of child alone on enormous rink; arms aloft ready to fly, waiting for the music, letting all eyes in the stands disappear. The fantasy and mind-body collaboration were a message to her troubled psyche. It was the sublimation tool that allowed her to manage the warring drives: fight, flight, freeze, and use it as the momentary transport for conflict resolution. The tool gave her muscles and psyche a chance to perform, rather than retreat or stumble. It will not always be enough to carry the moment, but is another nuance of sublimation in her repertoire.

In their own words...

Lisa: Alarm bells and life jackets

Another research volunteer you will hear more about in a later chapter, told me a wonderful story about an experience in an Emergency Room when she was a young intern.

> **Lisa:** And there was another case, again on the night shift. I was really a newbie. A patient was admitted, they admitted her, they don't do this anymore either. They're supposed to do some kind of admission assessment, physical exam, before they admit somebody to the hospital. The chart was blank. The patient's doctor was a cardiologist. I think they had some kind of vague diagnosis on it. And she's, she was behaving ... I mean, her symptoms and signs were odd and there was something wrong. I just knew there was something wrong. Her vital signs weren't what they should have been. She had a fever. She seemed to be disoriented. It didn't quite make sense. And I called the resident. "You have to examine this patient. She's just been admitted and I don't have any history. She's not had an exam and I think there's something really wrong with this patient." "Well, I'm not coming," he said, "it's the middle of the night, it's like two or three o'clock in the morning." I said, "You have to come, it's very important." He refused, said there's got to be someone else on the floor, just wait till they come back, and hung up. I was furious. I tried calling him back. No answer. He made me feel like a fool, and I began to doubt my instincts. Even thought I might get into trouble. Then I looked in on the woman and said, "No, something's not right."
>
> So I called the chief resident who was over the guy I'd called. And I told him my concern. He came down and examined her. She was going into heart failure and so she was whisked off to the ICU. They gave IV antibiotics, everything. She was not even responsive by the time she was whisked off. The next morning as I was leaving, the chief had the resident in the hallway, dressing him down about this, and said when an intern calls you and says there's something wrong, you're supposed to respond. And I just cherish that memory. That was an important moment. That was something key for me. I shared that years later with

my students, too. I said, when you think something's wrong, stand your ground, say something. It's better to risk getting called out by your boss than to let something awful happen to a patient.

P: Wonderfully supportive for your students: reinforcing that you should recognize when you have a gut feeling and respect it, pay attention to it.

Lisa: Yeah. Intuition ... something about your brain putting the pieces together before you have the words to say it. It had happened with me before and I just had to go with it. It's like all the alarm bells were ringing. I could have ignored it. The ER was jammed with patients. But knowing how on target it had been in the past gave me the strength to override my anxiety, and call the chief. I was shaking, I'll tell you. There's been some research done on that, on intuition and ER work. It was too soon in my career for me to really recognize it, but I just couldn't ignore the feeling either. You have this intuitive feeling. And you are usually accurate about what's going on.

P: And you learn to trust it.

Lisa: Yes. Exactly.

Lisa's example demonstrates how she was able to step back from the fear of being wrong and use belief in her intuition as a tool to resolve the conflict. Like wearing a life jacket on a white water raft, she was able to withstand the anxiety triggered by the resident's response, and take a problem-solving attitude despite potential risk to herself. She did not deny or ignore her fears, she used faith in her intuition to bolster her courage. She had the satisfaction of getting the chief to pay attention, and of knowing she surely saved a woman's life. She also got the special fringe benefit of knowing that the resident publically had a taste of the same treatment he had given her.

In their own words...

Chris: A private eye

A patient, Chris, was diagnosed with a paranoid disorder. He had a brain tumor removed when he was an adolescent and the surgery left him with residual brain damage. It was not clear whether his intermittent lapses into thought disordered speech were connected to the traumatic brain injury, or to living at home alone with a mother who was diagnosed with schizophrenia. She had been hospitalized several times, and attempted suicide in front of my patient. He was an intrusive, unlikable young man. He spoke in the most denigrating way about women, sex, and me. He was wildly self-pitying, always bemoaning that if his father had cared anything about him he would not have abandoned him and his mother. The father supposedly disappeared when Chris was an infant. There were no other family members, so he was alone all his life with a suicidally depressed mother. His mother's parents supported the two, but were never much involved in his life. Chris became obsessed with finding his father, and seeing him punished for what he believed was a betrayal. It was never clear if there really was a husband, if Chris was the product of a relationship, a one-night stand, or an assault. At times he suggested all of these possibilities. He got a job working in a debt collection office. With this he had access to files and financial records of anyone he chose to investigate, including me and others he discovered were connected to me.

It was difficult to tolerate working with this young man. Just the idea that he had an appointment that day triggered feelings of disgust. I would be relieved whenever he called to cancel, and always made sure there was a patient scheduled right after him so he could not linger in the office. I spent endless hours in supervision discussing the case, trying to brace myself for the next vicious torrent of narcissistic rage he would direct toward me. I was everything evil or withholding that had ruined his life. Very gradually, as the negative narcissistic transfer rolled out, the drive to barrage and discharge at me subtly decreased. There was more talk of wanting to meet people, of moving into his own place, always of wanting a girlfriend. That was something unimaginable to me. Yet, Chris persisted, we both did, and there was a calming of his rage. He did manage to date a few women, and established a relationship with one. Through her he became involved with her circle of friends, and a different life.

But Chris's obsession with finding the dirt on his father, and all the people he labeled as crooks, continued in the background. He became adept at tracking people down and at getting them to pay their debts. He got a private investigator's license and opened his own business. Regardless of the verbal learning disability, whether from birth or the brain surgery, he was quite skilled with technology. His business did well, and he needed more staff. This presented a problem because his ability to manage people was poor, at best. His girlfriend agreed to manage the office and staff, and this brought the business to an even higher level. One day in my office, Chris regressed to his old, despicable way of lambasting me. He screamed that I had never helped him find his father. I was a failure as a therapist. He was building the premier private investigation service, and could track down anyone. He lived to uncover and expose the things people had done. He thrived on getting them to repay debts. He loved that doing this made money for him, and he could do or buy anything he wanted. Except, he could not find his father.

I thought the debt collecting and the investigative service were brilliant sublimations of Chris's compulsive need to find the father who had abandoned him. But I began to wonder more about why none of his successes seemed to mitigate the longing for his father. I understood he desperately did not want to believe he was like his mother. Their relationship had been pathologically symbiotic for so long that he frequently lost track of who was who. Who had been in the hospital? Who was allergic to nuts? Even though furious at his father, it seemed Chris wanted to believe the man was actually a decent, well-functioning person who had been tricked by his mother into marriage, and may never have even known there was a child. We began to explore more his fantasies about his father. These were not the dreams of mutilating and humiliating him, but became ones where Chris pulled in characters from films or books, describing the man he wished was his father.

This went on for a long time until one day Chris sat down, looked directly at me, and said, "I'm never going to find him, am I? He only exists in my head." He was enormously sad. A rush of tears streamed down his face, and he buried his head in his hands sobbing with grief. Finally he quieted, and looked up. "I guess the only way that guy is going to exist is if I become the one I wish he were." This started a new path for Chris where he worked to find in himself the good qualities he wished for in the father he lost. It was a fantastic journey from the young boy bent on insuring everyone loathed him, to the man determined to become the role model he constructed in his mind.

With all of the pathology and environmental hardships, Chris was able to intuitively develop at least two higher-level coping sublimation strategies that helped reshape his life. He became an investigator to cope with his obsessional drive to track down his father and make him pay. This business allowed him to become independent and develop new interpersonal resources. The other sublimation tool he used was the fantasy, the puzzle pieces he put together to define the man the father should be. This enabled Chris to eventually let the panic and dread about not knowing his father recede, and for him to decide it was he who needed to be that man in his own life.

Reference

Vaillant, G.E. (2000). Adaptive mental mechanisms: Their role in a positive psychology. *American Psychology, 55*(1), 89–98.

Chapter 8

Suppression
I just kept going

Suppression as a coping defense requires a semiconscious choice, a balancing act of awareness of a conflict and a response pushing impulsive action aside, allowing functioning to continue. One is aware of impending danger, but opts to minimize or ignore it in order to cope with powerful, competing impulses. Corresponding resilience traits are: a capacity to succeed despite hardships; willingness to learn from mistakes/failures; refusal to allow anxiety and doubts to overwhelm; not feeling shame or depression in the face of failure; demonstrating determination and perseverance; comfort with independence; and an ability to restore self-esteem when challenged.

Nick works with a domestic violence support agency where flashbacks of his own childhood with alcoholic parents, who he later cared for while in graduate school, can be overwhelming. He does not know how he continued working between the depression and rage client situations triggered. Nick claims he just powered through, kept his eye on the end goal: building a private practice. During our talks he acknowledged his ability to compartmentalize is a positive tool he uses, and one he helps clients develop to manage impulses. Professionally, he has combined two disciplines, physical therapy and mental health counseling, where suppression is useful for success. In PT, both the patient and the therapist must suspend fears of potential pain or re-injury and trust in the method, and clinical skill, to repair not harm. A counselor faced with a repulsive patient, or a situation that resonates with painful personal history, must develop tools that enable staying in the moment with the difficult case. Many times therapists need to mentally distance themselves, compartmentalize, in order to be the container for all the stories and feelings they must hold.

Suppression may not have some of the added benefits of sublimation or altruism. There is no replacement element for the unwanted feelings or condition that triggers a need for conflict relief. One does not experience the pleasure of a new option with suppression. Nor does one have the satisfaction found in altruism as a defense, where there can be reciprocal gratification that the other person is being treated as you would like to be under the same circumstances. Still, suppression is a mighty and useful tool that can keep one safe while reinforcing feelings of strength, competency, and value. It connects directly with one's sense of self and identity. When suppression is healthfully successful, the capacity to persist under adverse conditions bolsters resilience and a willingness to take risks with confidence they can be managed.

In their own words...

Sam: Have to crush feelings or can't function

Sam, the academic who was discussed in Chapter Six, reported the following story:

> **Sam:** Sadly one of our students died a couple of years ago under what seemed suspicious circumstances. I had to say something at a memorial at school. There were his parents, sitting up front, grieving and not fully knowing what had happened. They were in shock. And ... the fraternity brothers were all there around them. It was emotional, and difficult, and frightening for me. I was terrified I'd say something that would reveal my suspicions. At the same time I was so sad and wanted to say something meaningful, comforting for the parents and the community. Situations like that raised the question, what do I do with my own feelings? Obviously I have to keep them in check, and stay in touch with them at the same time. Otherwise I can't function ... I had to de-connect, disconnect, or let my feelings overwhelm me, and maybe everyone there. I didn't know what the rest of them were thinking. Did they wonder about foul play or were they simply mourning a tragic accident? Being there with my feelings ... very difficult ... That's when I understood I had to push my feelings down somewhere deep inside to go on. I discovered, too, that if I did not talk about them at some point they would accumulate as a kind of reservoir that would burn me out. Luckily I had a good therapist who could tolerate my ambivalences, my anxieties.

Sam's retreat from his feelings, the "de-connecting" he describes, allowed him to be emotionally available for the mourners, while it protected him from psychic disintegration or making a mistake that could disrupt the whole service. He felt strongly that fraternity events played a role in the young man's untimely death. He also knew it would be inappropriate to contaminate the present service with his suspicions. Discussing them with the authorities would be for another venue.

The difficulty with suppression is that in someone with a poorly integrated ego, a person less self-aware, or resilient than Sam, the impulses can break through the compartmentalizing barrier. They can overwhelm feelings and functionality. For example, if suppression was not working for Sam, he might have regressed to another method of coping and freeze. His feelings could have overwhelmed and overtaken him, rendering him unable to speak at the service at all. Sam has a more highly developed coping capacity so he was able to continue on, confident he would deal with his suspicions and questions later.

Denial vs. suppression

A more primitive cousin of suppression is denial, and sometimes confused with suppression or repression. Denial involves active refusal to believe that something is true or exists, regardless of objective facts. It is considered one of the most infantile defenses because of its fragile relationship with reality and the dangers it ultimately presents for the person. When denial is shattered, the ego and the individual's relationship with the world can be broken too. The intrusion of reality on the mind trying to cope with overwhelming experiences or knowledge can be disastrous. But denial may temporarily assist tolerating a specific event, even if it leads to an observably unwanted outcome.

You see an elderly man caught in a burning, overturned car. As you rush to snatch him from the flames your friend grabs you, imploring you to stop. "It's going to explode. You'll be burned." You shuck off her hand and yell back, "My jacket's flame proof." Of course, that is a ridiculous answer or rationalization for heading into the fire. Even if your jacket is fireproof, your body and the rest of your clothing are not. Denial can help propel powerful actions. In the burning car situation, without more developed coping resources, you simply must believe that you are immune to the flames. Your desire to save the victim outweighs your assessment of reality.

In the more developed personality facing the same conflict, use of suppression, rather than denial, would involve understanding that you are putting yourself at risk, and deciding that saving the trapped man supersedes it. The danger is acknowledged. This puts one in a stronger position to problem solve. You throw a coat over your head, tamp down the fear, and run to the car as your friend douses you with water from bottles in your own car.

You were able to intervene in the feeling-impulse-action thread by stepping back, if momentarily, to take stock of the situation regardless of powerful urges. You could scan the environment for protective resources while judging what is required to save the man. Thus armed, you could make a conscious decision about choice of action, but would still have to compartmentalize, suppress one of the competing impulses, stop or go, in order to persist.

In their own words...

Andrea: I just kept powering on

Whenever Andrea came into the office she brought an aura of anxious anticipation with her. She is a cordial woman, who appears engaged in the moment. Yet she radiates a tension hinting at fear that she might say or do the wrong thing. Andrea described an early history of feeling lonely and sometimes lost in her family environment, shadowed by gloomy feelings juxtaposed with intermittent critical or angry outbursts by both parents. Regardless of several siblings at home, Andrea described herself as on her own and aware of a longing for approval and attachment to her parents. Stories of childhood ranged from hanging around the kitchen wanting to help out, or just be noticed, to self-prescribed isolation behind a closed bedroom door. Her world was a mystery she often dealt with by escape into reading. She was a voracious reader, and a good student. She drew solace from knowing that by studying she could get approval.

It was not surprising to learn that Andrea's parents, her grandparents, and her extended remaining family, were Holocaust survivors. Feelings of secrecy, posttraumatic stress, depression, an undercurrent of belief that the world cannot be trusted, and guilt at surviving are shared among many survivors. While some adapt and lead satisfying, productive lives, certain factors have been found to more negatively influence adaptation. Child survivors were often subjected to starvation, abuse, and separation from parents. They existed in a world of anxiety and danger where they had virtually no control over life. They have reported growing up in post-war in families where the adults refused to talk about their wartime experiences. Alternatively, the nightmare of the Holocaust experiences might be repressed, involuntarily wiped from memory, to allow the person to endure, but be acted out in repetitive or ritualistic behaviors. The taboo about questioning, talking, was clear. But those children, now adults, describe eavesdropping or simply catching snatches of frightening, confusing conversations among the adults.

All of this is fertile ground for the child survivors, or the children of parents who grew up during the Holocaust to develop persistent, posttraumatic stress responses. They feel compelled to try to suppress their own anxieties and pervasive sense that something is wrong with them, something bad in the home, to protect the parents from exposure. The pressure to ignore the feelings can overwhelm the child, and break out in substitute expressions of anxiety or symptom patterns seemingly unrelated to the home environment. A recurring specter of impending disaster characterizes many of their family dynamics. This legacy is at the root of Andrea's anxious approach to life. She has adopted several coping mechanisms to manage it, including use of suppression in life and clinical work.

In one exchange, Andrea told me the following, when asked how she perceives herself typically responding to difficult situations, and how others might describe her reactions:

> **Andrea:** Do you mean with patients or in general?
> **P:** In general.
> **Andrea:** I would say in life I worry [*laughs*].
> **P:** You worry? When things get difficult, you worry?
> **Andrea:** Yes. I come from a long line of anxious women [*laughs*]. My grandmother was an incredible worrier. She used to, when I was a child and would come visit her … she would say, "Well you know what, this might not be a good day. Don't come." My grandmother lived through terrible trauma when she was an adolescent in Germany during the war. So she was always very anxious, and my mother too. I think, growing up with an anxious mother. I think these traits are passed on.
> **P:** You think it's passed on, intergenerational?
> **Andrea:** It's hard to know. It's very hard to know. It's an interesting question. I've never thought about that, or how others view me [*laughs*]. I think people know that I am anxious and that I worry. But I also have a lot of, I guess, resilience. I manage to do things that are difficult. I don't know why. That's maybe just a character trait, so…

Andrea's responses were themselves characterized by suppression. Clearly she has thought about how others view her. It's apparent in her demeanor and her self-comments, as you will hear below. I imagine this is one way she has adapted to the pressure of having to constantly monitor herself with her family – choosing to minimize the worry about how she impacts them. She describes herself as a chronic worrier. It is a link to her mother and grandmother, but also another demonstration of suppression. The anxiety helps her step back from the frightening, competing impulses to know and not know, to ask and withdraw. When stepping back she is freed to design a plan of action. She is aware of the conflict, but needs to find a route to appease both sides to carry on. The compartmentalization in anxiety allows that. It offers temporary relief of responsibility for actions and feelings.

Andrea went on to describe a situation where this approach has been helpful in life:

> **Andrea:** Oh, I think, for instance, getting my law degree. You know, it took me nine years in night school, and I couldn't face the bar exam. I think now that's why it took me so long to finish. I dreaded that exam. During that period of time, my Mom became very ill. I was obsessed with caring for her. I felt totally guilty if I couldn't be there, but I also had other responsibilities and was in school.
> **P:** Yes.

Andrea: My mother was fighting so much pain and impairment. One of my twins was going through a terrible time at school, right from the start. They couldn't diagnose the problem so threw a string of alphabet disorders at us. We could take our pick. So [*laughs*] in the midst of all this, I was in law school, and I just, ah ... I just kept going until I finished.

P: With all that going on?

Andrea: I don't know. It was something I wanted for myself, needed at the time, so just was able to somehow ... I don't know how I managed to do it, but I wanted it. I closed my eyes to everything else for chunks of time so I could study.

P: That's impressive. Your mind had the power to recognize where you could get support, reinforcement. You were calling on strong resilience resources even with the life storms.

What was that motivational drive that kept Andrea going in school? Coping with all her historical issues, her mother's illness and needs, demands of her own children and husband, would deplete anyone's resources. Was school a way to channel anxiety into a familiar avenue to comfort? Was it a sublimation tool, combined with suppressing the anxiety and dread she carried, which allowed her to continue? As several other interviewees commented about their own battles to cope with overwhelming demands, "I just put my head down and powered on." There can be great value in compartmentalization.

I asked Andrea about what drew her to law, and then to becoming a therapist:

Andrea: Well, I never wanted to be in a big firm. I wanted to work with people who had struggles in their lives, to make a difference. So I worked in a law clinic, and the Public Defender's office.

P: Ah.

Andrea: I found that the part I enjoyed most was when clients would come see me at the office. They would [*laughs*] talk about their problems.

P: So you're used to hearing stories about terrible situations?

Andrea: Yes, and I liked that part best, just talking with them. Who else was listening? They were usually immigrants. They were the first generation here. Many of them had parents who really didn't speak English, and often they'd have to take time off and go to the welfare office or act as translators for their parents. And they would tell me these stories, and I would be so interested in their stories. I found I didn't really want to talk about how to help them through the bureaucracy or the legal system. It was frustrating because you knew that with the burden of their families and earning an income, they would just get snarled up in another episode once this one was cleared. They needed more help than where to go to file a form. So, I began to think about a different career.

P: That's a powerful resilience tool, being able to step back and recognize something's not good for you, even though you worked hard to get it. Then you figure how to take the good parts to build another option while not just quitting the first one.

Andrea: I get anxious, but I can usually figure things out.

Andrea was first drawn to a field that replicated the losses and hardships of her formative years. Work at the law clinic resonated with stories she heard at home about the old days in Europe, and the hopelessness. Intuitively, as she grew emotionally, Andrea seems to have recognized that trying to manage the system can feel futile, and would never address the depth of compassion or resilience her family, or those she worked with, had needed to survive. Her legal clients, like her family, seemed caught in impenetrable barriers to healthy functioning.

Following her instincts Andrea changed direction, shifted to a profession that more directly addresses underlying maturational impairments that inhibit growth. This is another lovely example of the unconscious working its way through core issues by symbolically repeating, reassessing, and integrating resolution of residual emotional conflicts. Coping with the impact of the intergenerational legacy and the realities of her current life could have been disabling for Andrea. With the capacity for using suppression to resist impulsive action, she could continue.

Recall Andrea's statement that, "It's an interesting question. I've never thought about that, or how others view me." That was from the first interview where we talked about a range of life events and emotional challenges. For me it represented the defense barrier Andrea built to protect her from chilling fears about her parents' critical assessment of her. During that initial time together I alluded to several of her responses, in personal and clinical stories, as demonstrations of resilient functioning. In the beginning of the second interview I asked, "Have you had any thoughts or feelings about our discussion since we last talked?" Andrea responded, "I hate to say this, but not really." She hated to say it, worried that I might think poorly of her. At the same time, she threw a passive aggressive dart implying the conversation was not worth remembering. I said that was fine, silently noting a possible pattern of defense, combined with a subtle jab toward me for triggering the need for defense. Being asked to "remember" is a sensitive point for Andrea.

I then asked if she could think of an imaginary person, someone who knows her very, very well. Perhaps knows her better than any real person, including herself. How might they describe her? This interview technique helps a person think on an object-oriented level, to distance him or herself a bit from ego protection. It can promote a more spontaneous, less defended reply.

Andrea: That's such a hard question. Um...

P: Yes, it is a tough one.

Andrea: Yeah, because I'm thinking about myself, I mean who else really knows me better than myself, right? So I guess I'm my imaginary self.

P: Your imaginary... (*I understood the symbolic communication in Andrea's response. It is essential that no one know her inner self as well as she. She is the curator of her story. Comments like this alerted me to the contradiction in her earlier comment that she never thinks about how others see her*).

Andrea: Imaginary self. It's really me, talking about myself. I remember a friend of mine told me that when he first started his psych doctorate one of his early assignments was to write an obituary about himself. I thought that was really strange and awful, kind of, but then the other day I found myself sort of thinking about my obituary. What would I say, what would I want said about me? So maybe it's a similar thing. How would I describe myself? I guess like most people I think I'm a mix of a lot of things. I'm curious, and I think I have a good heart. I'm insecure. I have a lot of interests. My family is really important to me. I always need to be learning or I get bored and feel unproductive and unfulfilled. I have a need to be with people, and a need to be by myself.

P: Being this kind of person, do you think it's had an impact on your ability to do the work?

Andrea: The clinical practice? Yes, I think it's hard for me cause I have a lot of self-doubt. So that makes anything I do very, very difficult. Again though, I'm always drawn to want to try new things.

P: What is the self-doubt about?

Andrea: I think it's just the way I grew up. I don't know if we talked about my mother, if I mentioned it last time. My mother was a very, very depressed woman. She had a violent temper and was abusive.

P: Physically abusive?

Andrea: Physically, and in all ways. Mostly I don't remember the physical abuse as much. I think I just sort of blocked it out. My older siblings remember it. They got it too. I tried to get them to tell me more, but they didn't want to. It was just too painful cause I think they all suffer a form of PTSD. I do remember coming home early from school one day, when I was about seven. There was an early dismissal because of the snow. She became just enraged that I tracked snow into the foyer. She pushed me outside and was flailing her arm, sort of hitting me, and screaming at the top of her lungs that I had to clean off my boots. I was hopping from foot to foot, terrified of slipping on the ice, and of her, and trying to swat the snow from my boots.

P: That's very scary.

Andrea: It was scary, yes. That I remember. So I think that the history, you know, it's always with us even if not at the top of consciousness.

P: How did that make you doubt yourself?

Andrea: I just think that not growing up in a stable environment, in which I was never mirrored, or if I was mirrored it was a criticism, was damaging. She was crazy, and I didn't want to be. I don't think they ever really had a strong sense of who I was. School sort of became my salvation because it was someplace, it was reliable, you know. I worked, I did well, the teachers didn't yell at me. So that's I think why I liked school so much when I was a kid and still do.

P: That's impressive. Your little girl's mind had the power to recognize where you could get support, reinforcement. You were developing strong resilience resources even then.

A bit later, after Andrea described those intimate, traumatic memories from her childhood, I again brought up the question of thoughts about emotional resilience since we last met. Her reply shifted from the regretful apology that she had not thought about it to the following:

Andrea: In the context of the interview or since the conference?

P: Since we talked and since the conference.

Andrea: Yes, certainly. I'm trying to think how I can explain, how I can talk about it. It seems to me that the notion of resilience, and I don't know if you see this or agree, and I'm not even trying to substantiate it, it seems to have sort of filtered a little bit into, sort of general consciousness. So it's a word I see from time to time. I might see it in the title of a book that has nothing to do with psychology, or people seem to mention it, or it just comes to mind when I'm doing something difficult. It seems to be entering my mental vocabulary, and the culture. I don't know if you agree with that or not.

P: Well, it sounds like you may have a greater awareness of it?

Andrea: That's probably what it is. It's like I'm looking for it, so I see it.

P: Or the world is resonating.

Andrea: Yes, maybe that's what it is.

P: Since you're thinking of it.

Andrea: Yes, I do think about it a lot. You know, it's such an important concept.

P: When you think about it, what comes to mind?

Andrea: What I'm thinking, I'm wondering what makes a person resilient? How does that happen? I think we live in such difficult times. Constantly faced with all kinds of disasters that it seems to, resilience, it seems to be really more and more important to be able to adapt to very stressful circumstances. So I'm always trying now, wondering, how can I bolster my own resist–, resilience? I almost said resistance, that's an interesting Freudian slip. And I think certainly one way is to be in training and analysis, to be able to talk about it.

P: How might other people describe the way you respond to difficult situations?

Andrea: Um, I don't know because I tend to not confide a lot in other people. I think because of the way I grew up, feeling like no one was really going to listen, I don't share a lot of my emotions with other people so it's really important for me to be in therapy to have some place where I can talk openly. I'm not sure if other people ... there's a part of me that I keep hidden from other people I would say.

P: How does that impact you? Being that way?

Andrea: Well, it's stressful. It's stressful. I have serious concerns about my own health and how lifetime stress exposure may have impacted it. I need to really focus on myself now, and I need to learn how to take better care of myself so I think that will affect my relationships. Either people will understand or they won't and, like I said, I don't know exactly what's going happen. How that's going play itself out.

P: You said that they'll either understand or...

Andrea: Or they won't.

P: What would they need to understand?

Andrea: Oh, I don't know. I guess for an example, I was supposed to go to an event tomorrow and I just canceled. I mean I don't particularly like those things where you have to mill around, talk with strangers. For me it's not fun. It's exhausting. And I have an early morning the next day. I just started doing this so it's very new, and I just canceled it cause I don't ... I'm not up for it. So it's sort of an anti-social thing to do maybe but on the other hand I felt that's what I wanted to, to do.

P: It's what you needed to do ... less fearful of what others think – more risk taking.

Andrea: Right. So I'm becoming more ... comfortable? I think it is gradually happening. I think the more I sit with patients and the more I am able to have a relationship that lasts longer than a few sessions, then I start to feel like that I could do this work or that I should do this. I should continue instead of quit.

P: Sometimes it feels like that, quitting?

Andrea: Yeah. That I want to just leave, you know at times.

P: How do you cope with that?

Andrea: So I ask, what is it that I want to do? There's not some other thing calling me and I think that it would be great. As difficult as this is, I'd like to stay with it because I do enjoy being with patients ... I think when we're in our personal therapy and can talk about countertransference in different places it makes a big difference. For me, whatever I would personally want to run away from, I can't. It's always there, ripe for talking. Which I think is excellent training but sometimes it's hard to do … In the training you learn how to become a therapist and you learn how to become a stronger person I think. What else could one want than to be a more developed person?

P: Have you noticed that happening to you?

Andrea: You know, I think so. When I first came here and I heard about aggression, you hear a lot of symptoms come from internalized aggression and this work, encouraging patients, particularly schizophrenic patients, to voice their aggression is terrifying. I was shaking all the time. I thought, ah, my goodness, I'm really in the wrong place. I have to leave now.

P: Get out while you can.

Andrea: Yes, get out while I can but, you know, I didn't leave and so … and, um, I'm sorry, I'm having a lot of trouble focusing. What did you ask me? I'm just like all over the place.

P: [*I wondered whether it was the admission of fear or recognition of her aggression that triggered Andrea's flight*] I asked you if you noticed yourself…

Andrea: Oh, yes, OK. So I think the constant, the, the aggression which I was always so frightened of, I think cause I grew up in a very aggressive household, I guess I'm getting more comfortable with it. And with other people's. In fact when I first came I didn't think I had any aggression at all so you can see how deluded I was. I think listening to all these stories of rampant aggression and trauma made me overall just appreciate what I have in my life, the things that I have. I don't have financial difficulties. I have a stable marriage. My kids, have to knock wood cause my kids are doing well now. Not that I don't have my own issues, I do. But I think it's made me look at my life in a different way or at least understand the emotional resources that I have that other people might not have. I think it's made me more grateful for that.

P: Have you noticed anything new or shifting in your experiences of listening to clients, family, patients, since we last spoke?

Andrea: I think I'm able to listen maybe a little bit more, what's the word, more objectively. In a more … not less compassionately, but not always sort of thinking about myself, although sometimes things do come up that will trigger something. I had a patient say that her boyfriend slipped on the ice and is hospitalized with a serious concussion. Of course I thought about my experience with my mother. But, I am able to think about it now, not have to automatically shut it down. This may be more of a sense of growing into myself as a therapist.

P: To know how to take care of yourself.

Andrea: Right. Yes.

It is encouraging to note the trend in Andrea's sense of self and personal resilience surfacing to awareness with exposure to small doses of resilience interventions in the interviews. Her stories demonstrated many instances of resilient behavior throughout her life, despite overwhelming adversity.

Andrea's experiences in her personal analysis, and with patients, have proven remarkable resources for increasing confident functioning and self-esteem. Interventions in our meetings highlighting the strength and resilience she brings to challenging situations prompted subtle shifts in her perception of competence and self-assessment. This allowed her to entertain letting go of the severe closeting of feelings that drives her anxiety. With the opening of that door, the need for continual defensive alert is decreasing. Andrea gambled, and risked revealing herself in our discussions. In a domino effect, she became more receptive to remembering old wounds without being overcome by her default pattern: the drive to escape, to run away.

There was one obvious moment when the pull to run fought for control. It happened when she said, "Yes, get out while I can but, you know, I didn't leave and so ... and, um, I'm sorry, I'm having a lot of trouble focusing. What did you ask me? I'm just like all over the place." Like a musician fumbling with a piece where they suddenly begin to focus on their movements rather than the music, Andrea's psyche fought to override her spontaneous recollections of moments of aggression or its denial. That was a clue to understanding the most dreaded emotions underlying her anxieties and depression. Sadness, confusion, and longing are acceptable. Awareness of aggression has always carried fear of the consequences of its expression. The time may be approaching when, even though frightening, Andrea may choose to directly express aggression, chancing consequences like a friend's annoyance, and taking care of herself. This is a courageous woman fighting to thwart the shadows that have afflicted the psychic course of her family history, liberating herself, her children, and what her parents might have been had their world been different.

During our time together, Andrea was able to make some quick shifts in perception of her motives and resilience. She described an interesting vignette in our second session, when asked to tell a couple more stories about challenging cases. She told me about a young patient, Mark, whose bombastic father always insisted on coming into the therapy room with them. His aim was to report on all Mark's negative behaviors and, Andrea felt, to check up on her. She was aware of her powerful impulses to either shout the dad down or run from the room herself. Her loyalty to the boy, who often cowered in a corner, helped her to step away from her impulses and figure out an intervention that would satisfy the father and protect Mark at the same time. She chose to calmly suggest that she and the dad schedule a session when they could have the whole time together because he is the expert on his son, and she knew there was much he could share with her. He stopped interrogating, quieted, and agreed to the plan.

Both Andrea and Mark were relieved when the dad left them in the office. Mark talked about how frightening his father is. He described incidents when he hid behind a sofa, or shut himself in a closet to protect him from the violent, verbal torrents unleashed at him. Sobbing, he talked about his older brother who always fights back against the father, inciting worse rants, and scaring Mark even more. He had never talked about these episodes before he witnessed Andrea assert herself and calm his dad.

Andrea told me she was heartbroken hearing the stories; phantoms from her own childhood reared their heads. She felt helpless to do anything but listen, nod, and commiserate. What could she possibly offer this little boy to help him survive in the scary world of unpredictable adults? She told Mark she felt he might be stronger than he realized, that she noticed it in how he was able to respond when his father became critical in her office.

In a following session, Mark talked about an outburst at home. His dad was furious that the dog peed on the carpet, and blamed the boys. Mark said he was shivering, terrified that some horrific punishment was coming, although his father was never physically abusive. It was the noise and waving arms that frightened him. Andrea told me it reminded her of the story about her mother and the snow boots. Mark said he only wanted to run, but knew that could make it worse. So he sat down on the couch and listened until his father ran out of steam. Then they disinfected the rug together. Mark commented he felt stronger after that, but did not know why. He wondered if his dad had always been someone who needs to shout when he gets frustrated.

So the thread of Reciprocal Resilience weaves its way through our encounters: Andrea, Mark, and me. I provided a receptive container to hear and hold Andrea's stories about the conflicts and fear growing up in a home where an undercurrent of dread and aggression broke out in explosive, unpredictable assaults. I experienced her sense of hopelessness and the anxiety used to ward it off. It is much better to be anxious than hopeless. At the same time I noticed incidents of exceptional resilience and adaptive skills. My comments on the latter were met with pleasant surprise. Andrea does not think of herself as a person in whom others see strength. She carries the image of herself as the constantly criticized disappointment her parents rebuked. But Andrea was able to quickly transfer the confidence from my slight reinforcement of her resilience to her work with an angry father. My comments primed her to be aware in the moment when her already existing coping skills could be put into use for therapeutic purpose. Turning the confrontation with the agitated father into one of cooperation bolstered her confidence. It gave her the fortitude needed to sit with Mark, listening with emotional openness to his bleak, painful accounts of life at home.

As agonizing as the sessions had been, Mark was able to walk away intuitively understanding Andrea's messages. She was with him for anything he would throw at her. She modeled a way to be safe with a dad who could strike fear in anyone. Andrea reinforced her recognition of Mark's own adaptive resources on several occasions, identifying moments of strength. All of this enabled him to engage adaptive coping skills under frightening circumstances and return to tell Andrea. The container and the contained operated in sync, each gaining in the reciprocal loop of the therapeutic relationship.

How did I, in the interviewer/supervisor role in the exchange, benefit? Besides the obvious help with my research, I had the privilege of Andrea freely sharing most intimate thoughts and experiences. That feeling, when you have an idea about something, and another person seems to say, "Okay. I'll jump in and trust you," is extraordinary. The process sparks new ideas and associations, leaving you confident to take more risks to reach out and connect.

Chapter 9

Anticipation
There's a gap here

Coping mechanisms, or psychological defenses, are tools to reduce emotional friction. They are generally experienced as involuntary reactions functioning as temporary, psychic painkillers until a threat passes or feels tolerable. These responses to duress can be useful for reinforcing resilience, or potentially dangerous if interfering with adequate assessment of a necessary action.

Even the higher level, adaptive mechanisms can morph into maladaptive patterns while serving momentary respite. Think of a man worried about his tax returns. He dreads putting all the materials together almost as much as the possibility of owing more money to IRS. He starts the project well in advance to get it over with, but bogs down in categorizing his expenses and identifying receipts. A certain amount of time is dedicated daily to complete the task, believing a sense of control will give him perspective on the issue, and prepare him for the possible unpleasant reality to come. This would indicate use of the adaptive defense of anticipation. It allows him to realistically plan for an incidence of genuine distress. He inoculates himself with the painful feelings spread over time while planning to minimize a stress reaction if the worst happens.

Now, imagine the same man toiling over the tax project, writing, collating, and constantly at his calculator assessing potential tax repercussions. Suddenly he realizes that the deadline has passed. He was so focused on getting a total grasp on the situation that he somehow let the date slip by him. This is denial at work. Denial, one of the least adaptive mechanisms, is at the opposite end of the continuum from anticipation, but as with suppression, is related. Blocking out an unpleasant reality may be a person's only means of avoiding overpowering psychic stress in the moment. Denial, the refusal to accept reality, does not provide any resolution to a conflict. It temporarily splits off awareness of threatening events, leaving one open to potentially more damaging effects than the initial fear. In the tax example, denial undermines the more protective mechanism of anticipation. The higher-level defense was not an integrated facet of the man's functioning, or may have failed him at another time, or he may unconsciously be driven to self-sabotage. Denial subtly crept in as higher defenses slunk out, masquerading as anticipation. Momentarily relieving, it ultimately brought about the consciously dreaded consequences.

Each higher level coping tool one uses represents hardiness to weather stress. The more types available for use, the higher a person's resilience quotient. Anticipation involves planning, awareness of a looming negative situation, and the capacity be goal directed even though anxious. Equally important, anticipation involves affect. It requires willingness to pre-experience upcoming uncomfortable feelings, while making plans to minimize negative outcomes to the degree possible. For example, you are scheduled for a job interview you expect will be grueling. You have been told there will be several senior-level staff present and they typically put applicants through the wringer. Plus, you loathe public speaking. But this is a position you really want. It is an important career step and a lot relies on the interview results. How do you tolerate the waiting and the angst about your performance?

Someone using the defense of anticipation might make a list of every question or scenario that could be thrown at her. She could create answers to the questions, review several times, and ask a friend to quiz her on the list. In preparation for the day, she lays out all the clothing to wear at the interview, and has needed materials ready by the door. Importantly, she might review things one more time on the night before the interview, but arrange a relaxing, early evening. Perhaps she would exercise, watch a favorite show, or read a novel. All this would be a message to her brain and psyche that things are under control. She is prepared. None of this would eliminate the anxiety natural to the interview, but could provide an edge of confidence making the discomfort bearable.

A man who does regular public speaking told me he always suffers performance anxiety. One of the tools he uses to calm the stress reaction is to visualize the audience who will be at the event. He thinks about the fact they are there because they need something he has. Imagining the audience as vulnerable, and himself as wanting to help them with their discomfort at a lack of knowledge or skills, allows him to see his job differently. It takes him mentally off center stage and puts the audience's needs up front. Now, he gets immersed in learning more about what they need and how to help them get it. He has anticipated the problem, but allowed himself to experience the feelings before the performance. There is a plan for diluting the anxiety and redistributing the energy in a more productive channel. Anticipation does not guarantee that when the unthinkable happens we will be ready. It does alert us to considering possibilities, and encourages problem-solving actions, while allowing small doses of the negative feelings to bolster a sense we will somehow be able to tolerate the intolerable.

In summer 2017 there was controversy about whether US east coastal areas should be evacuated in preparation for the impending hurricanes. Many people insisted they had been through terrible storms before and intended to ride out these too. Emergency management professionals argued it is better to prepare for the worst, and then be able to laugh at the exercise if disaster does not come. They encouraged residents to follow the advice of the professionals. As it happened, many people stayed and were stranded on coastal islands without electricity. It was not just the lights that went down, but water sources were shut off, sewers backed up, and waste filled streets while residents could not vacate the islands. It is always a balance, deciding whether to choose the discomfort of planning for a disaster, or take a risk that the odds will be with you and another catastrophe sidestepped. Anticipation as a coping skill permits a reasoned, resilience-oriented approach to managing both the threatening issue and the disturbing feelings associated with it.

In their own words...

Greg: A really neat piece of real estate

Think for a second; visualize your image of a hospice nurse. Trait wise we would all probably agree they would need to be compassionate, stoic in the face of hopelessness, and willing to deal with repeated uncomfortable encounters with angry or grieving family members, as well as the patients in their care. If your reflex image is of a kindly woman, speaking softly but firmly to an agitated patient, you are right for 90% of United States nurses. In line with that, about 11% hospice nurses are male, while 30% of military nurses are men. It is not surprising then, that a good proportion of male hospice workers will have previous experience in the military.

Greg, who volunteered to be interviewed, falls into the category of ex-military, male hospice nurses. A burly man, with a well-trimmed salt and pepper beard, sporting Ray Bans and a Yankees cap, brim backwards, ambled into the office for our meeting. It was early spring, but he was tanned and looked like he just came off a playing field. It turned out he had. He is a coach for one of the local Little League teams. Greg is a gregarious conversationalist. He was open to discussing anything about work, life, hospice, or front line war experiences.

After two decades in the service Greg retired, and thought to resume civilian life working as an ER nurse. The ER kept up the adrenalin rush that charged him in the field, but he began to notice being frequently called to help talk people down from overwhelming anxiety reactions when given bad news. He realized that he was good at comforting those with serious illnesses, while still giving them the needed medical treatments. Someone mentioned hospice nursing to him, commenting that he seemed a natural based on what they observed in the ER. Greg investigated and decided to get the additional training. He said it hadn't occurred to him until someone else said it, but immediately he remembered how important the hospice staff was during his mother's final days. He retrained and finds the hospice work even more personally satisfying than his ER days. "It fascinates me," Greg said, "because it would have been wholly my loss. I never would have thought of hospice work. But fortunately life has that way of kismet, taking you by the hand and leading you to your destination unknowingly."

Now Greg is delving further into exploring a career in mental health services, but mainly taking courses to enhance interpersonal skills for dealing with uncomfortable and challenging encounters on the job. He jokes that there are no difficult patients, just impossible families. But he does not fault them, saying that everyone wants the best care for their family member. It is just that they sometimes think they know all the answers and disagree with the professionals. Then it becomes a delicate dance.

Greg is married to a woman, a journalist, he met while in the service. They have three grown children living nearby, and two young grandchildren. Greg's wife was in a hit and run accident a couple of years ago, so life since has had to accommodate her condition. She is wheelchair bound, but always working on the latest technology or therapy to get her independently mobile. Greg reports they have a close relationship. She is his rock.

When I asked Greg what people might say about how he handles tough situations, his response was paradoxical, and contrasted greatly with the affable, all's well image he presented in our meetings.

> **Greg:** High-strung. They'd say I'm high strung.
>
> **P:** High-strung?
>
> **Greg:** Right. That's just in everyday life. That's why it's so funny to me when, when you hear these descriptions from people who work with you but don't really know you and you go, "Who are they talking about? Who is that person? I wish I were him. I would be if I could."
>
> **P:** Has being that dual-person impacted your ability to do the work that you do?
>
> **Greg:** I'm not high-strung about the work. I mean, it's the politics that gets me crazy.
>
> **P:** Right.
>
> **Greg:** The work itself, I think very clearly when I'm in the work situation. That's sort of one of the gifts of the work is you're ... you kind of hyper-focus in your mind. You're responding to a different place you create in your mind, kind of here and it's not all here. And it's clear. But in everyday life there are all these competing anxious thoughts about stupid things that it's not, it's never as clear as when I'm working. Where I think I let it, I trust something a little more, my gut. It's a little more intuitive.
>
> **P:** So at work then you are that person.
>
> **Greg:** Yeah, it's a more natural process. I think I drive people nuts in my real life.
>
> **P:** How so?

Greg: I'm acutely anxious about all kinds of things in real life. Not about big deal things. I mean, like investing in a business set up for my wife. I don't worry about the money or success. It feels like everything will work out because I plan it out. But I get crazy about small details like will the accountant get the papers ready on time? Will the government approve our Subchapter S? Will W.B. Mason bring my wife the right paper goods? Then I think, "I bet they're going to screw it up. I know they can do that. Let me get a back-up plan so things don't fall apart." All that's running through my head.

P: And what if things don't get there?

Greg: What if it's not there? Right. I can do all of that stuff; fight off the anxiety. Right. Unlikely that it's not going to be there. You've paid him. He came recommended by the lawyer. Chances are it's going to be ok. Then, "It's not gonna be there." creeps in.

P: And if it's not? What's the worst case?

Greg: Right. I do worry. I always go to the worst-case scenario. I am a worst-case scenario thinker, that's how I manage myself. That's how you manage that kind of thinking.

P: So what's the worst-case scenario?

Greg: Dwelling on the worst-case? No, by going straight to it, to the question. What's the worst, so what's the worst-case scenario? Things won't get there, and you'll call them and you'll have to drive to pick it up. Right, I mean it's really not the end of the world, but it's always there.

P: Always there, and about. . .

Greg: About these trivial things.

P: Trivial.

Greg: And then someone can be dying in front of you, and the son is kind of angry and feeling not fully satisfied, wondering, is he getting it? Does this nurse know what my dad needs? Or the family does not understand the care, or not clear about what's been explained. And you just know exactly where to go. There's a feel and you barely have to think. You've gone over this in your mind and almost instinctively know what to say to comfort them. It can be anxiety provoking, but then it's in your control. You feel it. Cause you're not dependent on others. I know the difference. Then it's dependent on me. I'm delivering the message. I'm not going to leave them until I get it right.

P: I wonder how you recognized when someone suggested doing hospice work that it could be for you?

Greg: I don't think any of those things are accidents. I mean, I agree with kind of where you're going in your thinking. I don't think, the people who are in the field, and I point it out to them time and time again because it's true for myself. You don't get there by accident. And I don't know what is the force that brings us there, but the people who are good at it, who are gifted at it, are inevitably people who deeply feel the pain of separation. And because of that they are effective at kind of going to that place and connecting to it, family after family after family.

P: How does one know about the pain of separation?

Greg: How does one know?

P: Mm, you said that people who are gifted, are familiar, know. . .

Greg: For some people it's loss experience, but for other people it's quite the opposite. You know, it, just sort of, they are deep attachers, you know? People like me, they don't throw shit out, they don't. Everything is an opportunity because it's attached to a memory, and memories to a person, to an event. They are actors. . .

P: Actors in the field?

Greg: Memories are actors in the field, bring it to life.

What did Greg, a self-defined "attacher", seek to resolve with his constant exposure to inevitable loss and separation? Did the longing to immunize him to the feelings originating in his deployments in Iraq and Afghanistan, or did he bring them with him? Greg is a man who identifies what he wants, recognizes the challenge and possible pitfalls, and then organizes a plan. Using anticipation as a psychological defense he almost superstitiously, and yet quite consciously, worries about the miniscule details he knows he can either control or salvage. Professional life proceeds on a mystical-like course. His descriptions of intuitive functioning feel more an amalgam of life experiences he has melded to transport him from the awful moment to a mental space where he can observe and plan.

When asked to tell a story about a difficult, anxiety producing or moving case, Greg told me about Louie, a man he had visited several times, and knew the end was not far. Louie's house would be the last visit of the day.

> **Greg:** The time before I'd come to see him, and he's talking about some Uncle Max who had come to visit him. He had a dream that Uncle Max and a friend had come to visit him last night. And his wife's sitting behind him in the chair, and he's in the bed. And I said, "What did you tell him Louie?" He said, "I told them go away. I'm not ready for you yet." See, so he knew. He knew Uncle Max was dead. Told him go away, I'm not ready for you. We ended with me saying I'd be back the following day and he could tell me more. Anyhow, so I'm on my way home and the phone rings. And it's the nurse there. She blurted it out with no lead in, just said Louie just died. And I burst into tears and I, of course, yell at her, "Don't you ever do that to me. I'm driving." I pulled over and she didn't expect it. And I didn't expect it. It was the only time I really ever had spontaneous tears connected to the job. Cause usually I really know, I have a really good sense, and am ready for the most

part. People's death doesn't surprise me. I really thought I was going see Louie again. And I hadn't said goodbye. I always say goodbye if I think that I'm not going to see a patient. But I hadn't. I have a standard way of saying good-bye. It feels right. But I never said good-bye.

In another story Greg talked about a feisty older woman, Kathleen, who insisted that either she wanted a lethal dose of morphine, or be taken out to her lake house. She frequently talked about the lake and the feeling of harmony she felt there. Against all odds, Kathleen's condition was ever worsening, the family had made arrangements to take her on one last trip up north. The odds were so far against them, the plan had to be abandoned. Greg came in that day, and hearing the frustrating news he devised a strategy to help Kathleen through what he described for her as the transition to "a really neat piece of real estate waiting for you in the hereafter".

Greg: So then I did this guided imagery. Where she went out on the lake, took the rowboat and rowed it out to the middle of the lake. I don't know if it was a butterfly or a firefly that I had follow her. It was just this, it was a beautiful moment of trying to take her back to, and my image of this place that I knew she loved. And she died that Saturday. That's a good day in hospice. That's a good day. It hurts, but you stay very connected.

In their own words...

Carol: There's a gap here

We met Carol in Chapter Seven, learning about her use of sublimation as a means to tolerate the anxiety generated by her daughter's work that takes her to dangerous and remote areas. Grappling with the conflict over whether to insist her daughter put off the jobs, or to squelch fear and be supportive, Carol came up with the idea of a joint project that would keep their daily lives connected, though far apart. She developed an art gallery to exhibit her daughter's drawings and designs sent back from the villages she visited as an aide worker.

Carol's early youth was checkered by several moves around the country following her father's corporate career path. Knowing this, and meeting Carol, one would think she adapted readily to the disruptions in schools and friends with her optimistic attitude of, "Just give me a puzzle, and I'll work it through." New neighborhoods were viewed as adventures, not problems. The same is true of her adult life where Carol's many moves and careers echo the childhood pattern. She does not appear to recognize any significance in this, and until recently considered herself someone not troubled by separation anxiety. The fear about her daughter's safety appeared to her a reasonable and new feeling. She did mention in a separate discussion about growing up that, mainly as an only child whose mother had several psychiatric hospitalizations, she learned through coping with them and the moves to always plan ahead. She believes this trait has saved her in many tough situations, and helped her become a competent leader.

It is unlikely that a child with Carol's life story of adverse experiences that included an unreliable mother, frequent home and school changes, and an emotionally distant father, did not result in some stress pattern related to separation anxiety. What is apparent is that there was sufficient emotional fueling and connectedness to develop higher level coping mechanisms to sustain her while navigating anxiety. As in Garmezy and Masten's resilience studies results, some children who have multiple early adverse experiences seem to still emerge as resilient, resourceful adults. This difference is attributed, in part, to emotional connectedness in early developmental stages, education, and financial stability (Garmezy, 1993; Masten, 2007).

An interesting phenomenon seen among those I interviewed and have worked with clinically, is the frequency with which people choose adaptive traits that echo the early ordeals they encountered. The biggest challenges are used to transform fragility into strength. Their most frequently, unconsciously employed coping skills are symbolic communications telling us about their life story. We need to support and respect these adaptations while learning more about how they came to define the person's approach to life, and help them develop a still wider variety of tools. Even the best defense will not be sufficient to address all life challenges. People who consistently default to one pattern may be demonstrating resistance to psychically letting go of a traumatic event that was so threatening that they need to keep repeating the feelings in different situations until they master them. Or they may need to repeat in order to keep emotionally connected, unconsciously, to someone involved in the earlier conflict. The more resources and adaptive skills one has access to, the more resilient they are and can grow.

I asked Carol the question, "Could you think about an imaginary person who knows you very, very well? Maybe knows you better than you yourself do. How would they describe you?" she told me the following story:

> **Carol:** I'm thinking of a friend and colleague who, who used to say, "I would follow Carol anywhere because I could trust her. Carol would just lead us safely through whatever, if it was a disaster or, or whatever, she would. She's the one I would follow." Your saying that brought that friend to my mind. Then I guess this imaginary person would say I'm a good leader and someone who can be trusted. Hmm, kind, generous, loving, tough, strong-minded, stubborn, and a detective (*laughs*).
>
> **P:** Has being this kind of person impacted your ability to do your work?

Carol: Sure. I think it's allowed me to be successful at a lot of things because I think in order to do whatever job I'm given or I have worked on, I have to have some level of determination and I have to be able to use whatever skills I have to figure it out. Whether it's I'm curious, curiosity, or intelligence, or strength, or other mental or physical strength, just to get done what I need to get done. I'm not sure, you know, I'm not really sure how I learned how to do things, how to lead people. But I did, and maybe by being the way I'd like to be treated and treating others that way, I managed. But I've always been that way. I can see like, OK, there's a gap here. There's some disorganization, something. Somebody needs to control the situation, just move ahead and get out of the confusion, and it was always easy for me to do that.

This was one of the instances where an interviewee told me the same story in both the first and second interviews without realizing it was a repetition. In the first interview Carol had said, "I have a girlfriend that I work with and she said, I'd follow you anywhere, you could lead us out of anywhere and we would get there and it would be safe." When I asked if she could give me an example of where she had demonstrated this, how the friend might have come to that trusting conclusion she said, "I can't think of one to tell you the truth. But I guess she had that sense of me. We didn't work together, she never worked for me. But we were good friends and saw each other. I remember her saying that." I had responded with a resilience reinforcing comment, "People instinctively recognize you are trustworthy and resilient? They can rely on you?" Clearly her friend's comment had a special meaning for Carol. Out of the universe of stories she could tell, she twice told that one. However, in the second interview version, she expanded a bit. She attributed additional, positive characteristics to the trait, and credited her capacity to be a leader to it.

Carol reported a slightly enhanced version of herself and her impact on those around her after at least one instance where her ability to radiate resilient capacities was highlighted. This is the trend I have observed while studying the phenomena of resilience building, priming, and a possible impact on a person's psychic growth. When demonstrations of existing, inner sources of resilience are brought to attention there is an increase in a sense of worth and value that is transferrable. As soon as the idea is communicated by a respected, outside observer, a frequency bias begins. The individual starts to notice their resilient responses in similar instances or interactions, where they were previously unrecognized. This triggers a pleasure response in the brain, encouraging further exposure to the source: self-awareness of a centered reliance on one's resilience.

We can wonder what the friend's comment represented to the Carol of those many years ago. What was it she needed to hear and believe about herself that had not been communicated before? In psychoanalytic terms, we might think of the friend's words as an anaclitic response. She was intuiting and responding to an unacknowledged part of psychic identity Carol was ignoring, and that had not been responded to when needed for emotional maturation during her early development (Bratt, 2012). The friend had no objective foundation for her assessment of Carol, but over time together that powerful message was allowed to surface in the safe environment of an intimate friendship.

When a therapist is open to experiencing the patient's symbolic communications and feelings attached to them, they can become available in the therapist's conscious response to the patient. These are the clues clinicians follow when trying to understand the patient's roadblocks to psychic growth. They represent what was left behind, traits perhaps thought undesirable since never affirmed, and now buried under years of alternate adaptation.

Carol viewed her capacity to organize, plan, and lead as objective behaviors emerging mysteriously. She said she had no idea how they evolved. Her stories are tales of someone who was forced to take charge of herself much too soon, and who tamped down feelings of anxiety and uncertainty by siphoning off the powerful discomfort and making effective action plans. Anticipation helped her to step away from disabling feelings, to take charge of the world around her. Her friend's comment about safety and trust in a disaster is a key to the feelings of peril confronting Carol in childhood. These are the feelings too overwhelming for the young child to register consciously and keep functioning. Instead, she needed to feel there could be trust and safety in her and her universe. During our session Carol realized communications like that of her friend freed her to assert herself and take risks.

From Wall Street to prisons to political organizing, and now with degrees in mental health, Carol has wandered to a profession that challenges her need to strategize and control her world. She talked about the difficulties she encountered working in a women's prison where the message was that everything is controlled, it was really in emotional chaos. Nearly 100% of the women she treated had been sexually abused. Many had committed violent crimes, were led into drugs and prostitution by the men in their lives. The continuous overstimulation from the women's stories battered Carol. She said she often left feeling she had been beaten.

> **Carol:** I have to say nearly 100% across the board these women had been sexually abused somehow in their life, which is appalling, but true. The women I worked with all had suffered. So, you know, it's disheartening, and as much as I know men suffer as well, a lot in our world, I've dealt a lot with women and it's often times I walk away and no matter what I've lived through, I feel grateful that I haven't suffered that much. It could always be worse. Sure, I dated guys who didn't suit me but I never let them lead me to prison. Or lead me down a path of drug addiction that you can almost never come back from. And prostitution, and all of

it. That women I've been connected to in some way have suffered that much, it's really hard. I feel for them and I hope that whatever work I do with them, maybe it helps them a little or gives them a tool.

That is Carol. She is sometimes bludgeoned by empathic response, but is always looking for new adaptive tools for herself or those with whom she works. In our second interview she mentioned feeling stronger of late. She likes the concept of looking at the world through a resilience lens instead of only pathology. It suits her sense that there is always a solution, you just have to find it. She also recognizes that the hopelessness of situations she encounters at the hospital or prison can be staggering. It makes her feel as though she has entered an alternate universe where any weapons she thought she had might be useless. In the follow-up interview, after telling me about the friend who said she would follow her anywhere, that being with Carol means safety, she told me about Denise.

Carol: At first I thought she was probably the healthiest, and perhaps she is, of the patients I see there. She's allowed to go out on a pass so they've given her some level of trust. She has a husband and children. She thinks that he's moving away. She's not completely sure. So I think, how could you not know what's happening to your kids? But I guess if someone's institutionalized, they may have no say. Maybe she's in denial, I'm not sure. But, she will tell me some of what goes on when she goes out on a pass. And it's calmed down a little. When she first started going out, I was afraid for her. It made me concerned. She would talk about waiting for the bus or a guy drove past and offered her a ride.

"Don't tell me about the car." I'd think. Just those kind of things. It's like bad decisions are being made. And, and there's nothing I can do. She's never said that anything bad has happened. So it would all be just conjecture on my part. My imagination of what might be going on. But, I fear for her and, and for her feeling of being able to go out and do things on her own. But she doesn't have any money. So she talks on about wanting to find another husband, and you know things that all of us, any normal person, would have those same desires. But she's so compromised. She hears voices. They tell her to do all kinds of things that are not good behavior and will get her into trouble. And I sometimes want to say, "Why won't you just take an additional medication that might get rid of the voices? You could do that."

I fear for her, and I get angry at the same time. So I think about it, I plan some possible interventions and go over things before seeing her. I think of any small tools that will help her tolerate whatever is going on inside her head, and maybe eventually help her develop some sense of judgment. And I plan what I'll do for myself after I see her. To lower my own anxiety level. I figure that if I can devise ways to tolerate the awful feelings when I'm with her, and sometimes see through them to some possibility, maybe she'll feel it with me, it'll click.

It was impossible to ignore the similarity in Carol's emotional responses to hearing Denise's stories and her own sudden onset of fear about her daughter's safety. These events did not occur simultaneously, but I believe they represent a current running deep in Carol's psyche that has been layered over with life experiences of mastery in challenging conditions. Perhaps, with these experiences and emotional growth through therapy and positive personal relationships, additional psychic energy is becoming available to deal with the old wounds. With a more integrated sense of true emotional resilience, in contrast to behavioral skills only, she is able to slowly allow the old demons to rise and take their place in proper perspective. This can enhance a sense of inner balance. It will allow her to be available to experience potential, emotional benefits in her work listening to frightening stories of people out of control of their lives. Of course, it can be hypothesized that it is precisely the overwhelming nature of the stories she hears that draws Carol to that aspect of her field. Expanding awareness of her inner resilience can encourage her to make choices about which patients she sees while functioning as the psychic container, a reciprocal reservoir and source within the relationship from which both will benefit.

Survival of the container

The DSM-IV describes anticipation as, "[r]ealistically anticipating or planning for future inner discomfort. The mechanism is goal-directed and implies careful planning or worrying and premature but realistic affective anticipation of dire and potentially dreadful outcomes." (APA, 1994). Greg and Carol were both able to develop the planning skills, and the affective ability to pre-experience feelings expected from looming misfortunes while engaged in the preparation. It can be suspected that this extraordinary capacity for resilient functioning symbolically represents emotional scenarios from early life, though each experienced enough hardship as adults to trigger a need for the hyper-alertness of anticipation. Is it as Greg suggested, that those who can be emotionally available to connect in the therapeutic relationship loop are people who have intensely experienced painful separations in childhood? It gives them psychic leverage if they are willing to be with it? Does a world in chaos, as Carol's youth was, force some children to develop cunning street smarts, or exceptional planning skills? Is the combination in the mechanism of anticipation of foresight, planning, and emotional availability a key to survival of the container, and reciprocal growth in the therapeutic dyad?

References

American Psychiatric Association. (1994). *Diagnostic and Statistical Manual of Mental Disorders*: *4th ed.* Washington, DC: American Psychiatric Press.

Bratt, P. (2012). Consulting the patient: The art of being together: Perspectives on technique and therapeutic field. *Modern Psychoanalysis*, 37, 193–202.

Garmezy, N. (1993). Children in poverty: Resilience despite risk. *Psychiatry*, 56, 127–136.

Masten, A.S. (2007). Resilience in developing systems: Progress and promise as the fourth wave rises. *Development and Psychopathology*, 19, 921–930.

Chapter 10

Humor

Poopy solutions

Are we born with a capacity for humor? An infant can play peek-a-boo endlessly, giggling and laughing with joy. What elements of humor are involved in this preverbal play? The little fingers are clasped, covering the child's eyes, symbolically communicating a primitive awareness of the concepts of separation and individuation. In her world what she does not see is not there. The ball rolls under the blanket, it is gone. An infant must reconstitute a sense of self in the world every time when waking from sleep. Until an awareness of object permanence is consolidated and incorporated into the infant's feelings of ongoingness, the continuous identification and reintegration occurs. It is an evolving process that encompasses weaving multiple threads of growing understanding. Each develops singly, then merges into a conscious awareness at about 6–8 months.

Peek-a-boo helps with that process of grasping object permanence: things are there even if you cannot see them. It is the beginning of cognitive development and symbolic representation, both necessary for learning language. Peek-a-boo also involves the element of surprise that triggers the laughter. The infant is playing at being alone, and happy to discover you are both there. The element of surprise tickles them because it is like having a win. The child does not understand you will be there when the hands are taken away. Progressively the game promotes a predictive capacity. The baby has a sense you will be there. And you are! Additionally, the laughter and smiling is contagious. Your smile says you are happy to see the baby again. Peek-a-boo taps several areas essential for healthy maturation: object permanence, eye-hand coordination, relationship development, the capacity for anticipation and frustration tolerance, and pattern recognition. These are all necessary, foundational components of resilience.

Do play and laughter in games like peek-a-boo indicate we are hard-wired for humor? Another element in the game is potential anxiety management. During this pre-object permanence period separation anxiety emerges. The game, the play, the laughter defuse it. Laughter and smiling are expressions of relief and pleasure. They help the infant distance herself from the fearful notion that the parent is gone, and they are alone. It is through play, the growing capacity for imagination, and the child's ability to find pleasure in the absurd that self-regulation and coping mechanisms arise. Laughter assures the child that all is well. Mutual laughter engages relational connectedness, as well as a sense of safety and release of bound up energy. It is the prototype for reciprocal resilience found in the therapeutic relationship.

Like other adaptational methods, humor can be deviated from its positive nature. There are four types of humor. Two positive are affiliative and self-enhancing styles. Two maladaptive are aggressive humor and self-defeating humor. The first ones assist in healthy adaptations. The positive use of humor enables one to tolerate uncomfortable or threatening situations, without potentially injuring someone else. These forms of humor aim to unite and heal in difficult moments. In contrast, the maladaptive ones use humor at either someone else's expense, or are a distorted attempt to gain approval or acceptance through self-abuse (Kuiper, 2012).

Vaillant says about the coping mechanism of humor, "Humor permits the expression of emotion without individual discomfort and without unpleasant effects on others … Humor always surprises people … Mature humor allows people to look directly at what is painful" (Vaillant, 2000, p. 95). Corresponding resilience traits are: an ability to laugh at oneself and life's absurdities; a sense of humor and realistic optimism under stress; and a concern for the welfare of others and about relationships.

As a defense mechanism, humor was the least demonstrated in stories about their work by the clinicians I interviewed. Several were humorous people, but I have two hypotheses about why use of it in reported scenarios fell in the margins. First, the nature of the interview as a part of a research project, coupled with a mindset to be serious about clinical work, may have triggered an uncharacteristic, constricted use of humor. References to humor were often made more from an intellectual perspective than experiential. At times there were apologies for laughter, despite statements about the essential nature of humor. As with Sam, who said:

> I think it can be helpful, for me it helps me keep things in perspective. Frequently my anxiety, for example, if I find something beyond reasonable proportions … I find humor can help to bring things back into, into proper ratios, but underneath that humor there are tears and maybe I'm not wanting to see them.

This was a realistic description of the use of humor as a defense, without actually using it.

There is concern about the misuse of humor in the clinical setting (Akhtar, 2010), and a long-standing, but shifting idea in psychodynamic therapies that humor should be avoided by clinicians. One problem associated with use of humor in therapy is that there is little predicting how the patient will respond to the therapist's sense of humor and feel either disconnected or misunderstood. Another is that injecting humor may inhibit the patient's ability to talk about, or experience, uncomfortable feelings. These views have been challenged recently with a proviso that humor be used with caution and sufficient experience with the patient to know their style of humor. With that caution, introduction of humor in the clinical setting can be helpful. This refers to the use of humor as a communication tool, not necessarily as a coping mechanism.

There was a significant increase in overall use of humor from Interview I to II in the research, but there was still a 52% difference between it and the next lowest used second interview defense, sublimation. It is likely that respondents were more relaxed during the second interview and felt freer to access humor and relate stories connected to it. There was a high incidence of statements that humor is essential to survive as a therapist, but not evidenced in use in the interviews.

In line with concern that humor can be used to avoid conflicted feelings, Sam also commented that:

> I have found myself, in my initial encounter with you, a little shielded ... Not knowing what to expect ... this time I was a little shielded because of a situation that's going on in my life, I both wanted and didn't want to talk about it here. So I've considered the question of resiliency ... I find myself hoping that my humor wasn't just derailing me from facing something that I didn't want to talk about. I'm half suspicious of it, but know I used humor and detachment to avoid thinking about that situation while we've been talking."

So one can be conscious of utilizing humor as a means to manage stress or anxiety, but that awareness itself can be a source of conflict.

In their own words...

Margo: Poopy solutions

Parents often demand that Margo, an art therapist, change their child's disruptive behavior at once. A young boy comes in making fart sounds, talking about poopy jokes, just as he does in school where he is met with rebuke. Margo understands these acts of defiance are symbolic communications of conflict so embraces them through joining and humor, rather than inhibitions. She reports that as her own ability to loosen up grows, regardless of the parental demands, she notices less conflict and more accepting emotional communication with her own family members.

Margo worked for some time in a special needs school. As bureaucratic demands and restrictions increasingly stifled her ability to use creative treatment approaches, she decided to leave teaching and open her own practice. It has grown rapidly because of her reputation for skill at working with difficult, oppositional children. Margo is a small, playful woman who dresses in a style destined to make children smile. There is an almost magical or fantasy-like air about her colorful outfits. Bright oranges, spangles, and sneakers with toes she has painted, as if real toenails, defuse the seriousness with which she approaches working with challenging children and their families. As most clinicians who work with children say, Margo contends that one of the hardest parts of the work is that one client really means about three, when parents are included. Each of them may have different ideas and demands about the therapeutic process. Still, she is much happier than in the old days working in the school.

When asked to tell me a story about some incident, two, three, that have had a profound, deep emotional impact on her, Margo instantly started laughing. She described a young boy whom she had known when in the school system, and his parents brought him to see her in her private practice. He had severe reading and symbol processing issues, so was relieved to share the experience of freedom that the art therapy provided. In school he was either angrily silent or openly oppositional. Margo said he was a frequent flier at the principal's office.

> **Margo:** Suddenly Tim walked over to my bookcase and pulled out a book. It was a picture book, much younger than where he was supposed to be reading. He said, "You read it to me and I'll draw about it." We did that for a few sessions, a couple of books, and I noticed that gradually Tim was looking over my shoulder, trying to read along, as much as he was drawing. I asked if we should both be going through the book, and he just sat next to me. Everything started to change then. Like he was reading it, he was able to. And having a blast, you know. And would come in and make fart jokes, and he talks about poopy and he does all, all his regressive stuff. It's alive in the room and he laughs his big belly laughs, and he pulls out a book for us to read. If he makes a poopy joke in school the teacher's going to yell at him. And then he can't read. It's so obvious. So I just laugh and make a poopy joke back with him. He thinks that's the greatest thing ever and he reads. You know, it's so cool.
>
> **P:** It's the poopy solution.
>
> **Margo:** Yeah, yeah, exactly. Exactly. Again, it's very satisfying. It can be a frustration because this could be happening elsewhere. It's also frustrating to me that it's not happening elsewhere.

Margo commented that just allowing the kids "to be where they are" without having to say things the "proper" way has an amazing impact. The schools, with all the tests and requirements for achievement, "It's like it's an emotional killing field. Your odds of escaping without psychic injury are getting worse …Children need to discharge energy, to laugh and be absurd, to be free to create," Margo said. She told me another story about a little girl who came from a family of respected, professional artists.

Margo: I had another girl, she's younger, had just completed second grade. She comes from a family of very, very talented artists. That's an interesting flag for me because she started out taking art lessons and was really into it. Wanted to do it, really into it from the first lesson, according to the parents. I know the teacher, a great teacher. But the girl, Lara, she stopped doing anything in the studio. Would just sit and stare. Wouldn't touch, everything was either too scratchy or gooey. She didn't like the smells. Now, nothing had really changed in the studio from when she first started the class. So they knew something was up, plus the school problems were escalating. Difficult behavior. What I learned about her before she even came in was that was a pattern. She starts something, is real enthusiastic about the idea of doing it, starts, a bunch of meetings or whatever it is, then becomes completely resistant. She's only eight, so how many things could it have been?

So, red flag being, I wondered does she feel like she has to measure up all the time, to do something creative with me? They brought her to me to try to figure out the emotional issues, my friend just dealt with art lessons, not art therapy. I wondered, is there pressure to be like that, to perform? So I set out several different media and she could choose anything at all. We could even just listen to music or stories. It was all up to her.

For about six months, we played Candyland. She found it in my games cabinet. She would stack the art media, or put it away, and we just played. We hung out on the floor playing Candyland. There was no art going on whatsoever, no lessons. At first there wasn't even any talking. Just play therapy, every week, and I just waited. She started giving the pieces names and making up stories about them. Really talking out loud to herself. Then she found the dollhouses and they became part of the Candyland stories. She would set up the furniture all different ways. We would put on shows and she was the student of the day, principal of the day, that's what she called it. She'd get to become principal of the day at school, something they have in school. And she would enact the whole thing, all these fantasies she would enact them. And I would act them out with her. We played and played and played. They became comedy sketches, making fun of the teachers, kids, herself. I was the frequent butt of mocking. I simply couldn't get anything right, and we laughed so hard.

Lara's mother was looking at me, about ready to go crazy, you know. No art was coming out of these sessions, very little change at school, and nothing at home. She would come to pick up Lara and there was such intense concern. "Is she being polite, is she doing what she's supposed to be doing?" Every time it was the same thing. They were so worried because of her defiance, her school refusal. I said to her, trust me. Please trust me. It's going, she's going to come around.

And it regressed more, terrifyingly. It became all about anal-related stuff. Bowel movements and all that stuff again. She got really deeply into that. And when she would say it, and realize that it was OK, she couldn't believe it. She was beside herself with joy. Laughing, regressing.

I had the idea with what little the mother heard she said to Lara, "You can't say that there." So life, exuberance, it's very restricted. Lara had a fixation there, about the control and excretions. A few months of that kind of play therapy and talking about all that stuff and vomiting and all this. It was all about bodily-functions. She'd talk about that and I'd feel exhausted by the end of it.

Then one day she sat down at the table and opened a case of pastels. "What's your favorite?" she asked, as if this was an everyday thing. Once that happened she became a demon with paints, pastels, coloring, clay. It was a lovely, gooey mess. Gradually the playtime got shorter, and then we started zeroing in on what she wanted to do with the media. Sometimes she would look at it and burst out laughing, like she had just pulled off the best trick. In a way she had.

Eventually Lara decided to show some of her work to her parents. Some was a smeared mess! She asked if we could do one of our plays for them. We did the one where she was the principal scolding people for the funniest things, and all of us were howling. It was like she released something in the parents with her goofy behavior, and they discovered their daughter. It was fantastic.

Margo is a creative, patient, and devilish soul. In her own life she struggles between wanting to do the right thing and longing to act up, break loose. Leaving the school was a courageous leap into unknown prospects, but she brought her reputation for connecting with kids in difficulty with her. That smoothed the way to a thriving practice.

What had Margo done with Tim and Lara? What was the therapeutic function of humor? In each case her own ability to appreciate life's absurdities, even her own, filtered into the therapeutic relationship. She has a deep belief in the importance of meeting children where they are emotionally. She understands that no matter how vile, frustrating, or illogical their communications, they are the child's tool for symbolically sharing inner life. Margo instinctively, and through training and experience, recognizes that eruptions of silliness can make the scary less frightening. She happily encourages the child to expand on even the most outrageous things that spontaneously spill out to her, their rapt audience.

With children we may never know what the exact trigger was for a fixation or maladaptive functioning. Could Tim really always read? Had something shifted, grown in his processing capacity through the session, or just maturation? Had permission to wallow in his poopiness reassured him that even when a mess, he could be lovable? Often children develop behaviors that explain why they are not feeling loved in the way that they would like. Not being able to read, and being the person most likely to be found in the principal's office are good enough explanations for a child believing, "If only I behaved, or did my homework, they'd really love me." It's a lot easier than the notion that "I'm disgusting and no matter what I do, they'll never love me." We don't know that about Tim, but it's an hypothesis. We do know that his time with Margo enabled him to feel free to be his naughtiest, his funniest, and that shared laughter and acceptance catalyzed a shift in his willingness to risk reading.

For Tim, and for Lara, wielding humor like armor in sessions allowed them to face the dragons of internal conflict that otherwise would be too painful or frightening. Laughter is magic. Lara's parents, artists themselves, seemed rule bound in their worries about propriety for her. One wonders if this is an expression of a need to rein in their impulses to run free. According to Margo, they seemed to lighten and loosen visibly when they recognized what looked like Lara's outrageous behavior could be her way of exercising creativity unfettered, and was met with such approval by the therapist.

In their own words...

Lisa: Slipping on a banana

Lisa, another therapist who is a career changer, told me an interesting story about the use of humor as a coping device in a difficult situation. I mention the career change aspect because it is striking how many people start out in other fields and gradually decide to either retrain or extend their education to become psychotherapists. They seem to have launched into careers that felt compatible or pragmatic, and then some exposure to mental health treatment or the study of the mind intrigues them. These are people who want to make a difference in lives and have a keen sense that happens through relationships. It may also be that maturational experiences, combined with unforeseen frustrations in the original career, pushes them to explore new alternatives. Lisa is one of those. Technology and profit margin innovations changed the nature of the work she once loved.

> **P:** There's someone, a stranger, but for some reason they know you better than anybody knows you.
> **Lisa:** Better than anybody knows me.
> **P:** And if somebody said tell me about her, what's she like?
> **Lisa:** Oh OK. Well, I would think that they would say I have a good sense of humor cause I think that, and that I don't mince words if I have something that I feel strongly about. I'm tenacious, kind of stick to whatever it is that I'm going to be doing. Reliable, you can depend on me. I'm very curious; I ask a lot of questions.

P: You mentioned humor.

Lisa: Yes.

P: Is that an important component in your work?

Lisa: Oh, it's important. It's a very important component of working with any patient. Did I tell you the last time the story about humor in the clinical area with students?

P: Does it sound familiar?

Lisa: There was this student evaluation, we would do evaluations at the end of the semester, and they do evaluations of the faculty. And it's like fifteen items to rate them on, supposed to give feedback, all that stuff. Number seven was: displays a sense of humor.

P: Ha.

Lisa: The other faculty members thought that shouldn't be there because it … maybe they'll be making jokes just to get high ratings, or they're going to rate some faculty higher than the other because of their sense of humor. And this other faculty member and I said are you kidding me? We were just laughing and dumbfounded. At first I even thought they were joking. I said, "If you don't have a sense of humor teaching ten students in the clinical area, you couldn't survive all that trauma." We're a trauma center, teaching students to work with some of the most serious and strange situations. It can go from horrifying to absurd. So we decided, my friend and I, we think that humor should be here as a requirement. There's a relationship between humor and ability to function in traumatic situations. I told them we'll get to the bottom of this, what this could be related to, you know, academically. There had to be some research on it. So we looked up humor, did some investigating, and we wrote this little, two-page paper that documented having a sense of humor's related to critical thinking. That if you see something that's funny, you identify it as funny because there's an inconsistency, an incongruity that you notice. Someone slips on a banana, that's a silly example but what makes it funny is that it doesn't make any sense. There's something happening that shouldn't be happening. And so, one of the traits you need to have in order to exercise critical thinking is humor. And we all know a capacity for critical thinking is crucial for the work. So we presented our little paper and the item stayed in the questionnaire. And we all laughed.

P: Very good!

Lisa: I thought that was a triumph. We humored them about their academic rigidity by operating like they wanted. We told them that we wanted to take them, their opinion about humor very seriously. But it turns out we'd rather risk somebody faking humor to get a good rating, than give up our standards about critical thinking on the job. That got a few of them snickering. In the end, we gave everyone a good laugh.

P: How about then, humor in sessions. Is there a, a role that you see there?

Lisa: I think so. I mean I do think so. You know the patient that I mentioned before, who I've seen for some time, we laugh together. She'll say something kind of offbeat, and I'll join her or expand on it, and she'll agree and she'll laugh. I mean, it's not necessarily about some serious things in her life, but other things that are happening, and relationships with people, and that kind of thing. I do think it's important. I think a sense of humor is what makes us human. It helps you connect in ways because you kind of share a secret surprise.

Taking humor seriously

Aristotle said, "The secret to humor is surprise." Although in ancient Greek times there was a dismissal of the value of humor. Humor seemed a betrayal of the virtues espoused by thinking, serious men. It was also thought potentially damaging, hurtful or insulting. In laughing one could create a distance from the other person, cause them to feel you were mocking them, or feeling superior. Over the centuries there has been much discussion about the merits or negative aspects of humor. On the element of surprise, of incongruity as a necessary component, all agree. It is exactly the anomaly, or the disruption in our expectations, that startles and tickles us.

Humor is also a part of play. Children signal to each other that they want to connect or are relaxed, not in an aggressive mode, with laughter and playfulness. When genuine, laughter reduces aggressive impulses. One cannot be frankly laughing and smiling and aggressive at the same time unless there is a pathological issue. Like sleep, humor and laughter involve muscle relaxation and the release of hormones that trigger feelings of safety, satisfaction, and happiness. Humor defies our expectations. It sets us up to think one way, holds us there, and then unexpectedly turns things around. As Lisa commented, tongue-in-cheek, when lobbying about the importance of humor, they took it seriously.

Humor challenges our mind to auto-correct or adapt to the idea or image presented, to the absurdity. Mae West, a natural with witticisms, said, "Marriage is a great institution, but I'm not ready for an institution." You are set up to hear something about the wonders of marriage, when instead the punch line is a pun on the meaning of institution. The disjunction makes you laugh. Oscar Wilde is said to have commented from his deathbed, "This wallpaper is atrocious. One of us has to go." The set-up is to expect a rant about the wallpaper. Wilde was really using a form of self-deprecating humor about his imminent mortality.

Magicians understand that the way to connect, to hold an audience entranced, relies on a basic concept that the big, dramatic move obscures the smaller one that drives the trick. We love illusions, tricks that make us question whether we can believe what we are seeing or hearing. They charm us because of their power to transport us back to youthful, trusting days when we could believe in magic. Humor and the capacity to suspend belief for the illusion of magic are components of resilient functioning. As seen in Lisa's work with her faculty board, helping them see both the absurdity in their resistance about humor, and revealing the science behind the assertion, helped them become more flexible. Lisa transformed their opposition with humor. At the same time, she used it to defend herself from being overwhelmed by feelings of anger at them. It freed her to find an alternate way to satisfy the committee and herself. In this example she employed humor as sublimation.

Working with Lara's oppositionalism, by joining it and encouraging free expression of anything from silence to raucous play, Margo was Houdini: using the big move to mask the small one. The big move was support of the defiance. The small one was her consistent commitment to whatever relationship Lara defined. She followed Lara's lead, giving her for the first time a sense that she could have an impact over her life, and that it would be accepted. She followed Lara's contacts, leaving all interactions up to her direction.

The same was true with Tim. His poopy ramblings could have triggered annoyance or rejection. Instead Margo worked to understand more about the meaning behind the words. She did not take them as simple, throwaway potty mouth barrages. She understood that from the universe of things Tim could be saying, he chose these words, these actions for a reason. Margo's persistence to accept and understand created the holding container Tim needed to experience himself safely.

While these talented therapists were working their special magic with patients and with staff, they were also feeding themselves through the process of Reciprocal Resilience. Margo gained increased confidence in her ability to be the person, the holding environment that was strong enough to withstand pressure from both Tim and Lara's parents, and develop a trusting relationship. She had doubted her skill at working with such complex cases, but experienced a new sense of competence working with these families. Lisa described a victory. She was empowered and gratified by the response from her colleagues, and they felt understood by her.

References

Akhtar, S. (2010). Happiness: Origins, forms, and technical relevance. *American Journal of Psychoanalysis*, 70(3), 219–244.

Kuiper, N. (2012). Humor and resiliency: Towards a process model of coping and growth. *Europe's Journal of Psychology,* 8(3), 475–491.

Vaillant, G.E. (2000). Adaptive mental mechanisms: Their role in a positive psychology. *American Psychology,* 55(1), 89–98.

Epilogue

Chapter 11

Pulling everything together

Introduction: The big move, the small move (or just magic)

This book is about magic, illusion, and slight of mind, as well as about Reciprocal Resilience. What I have learned from some of the greatest, and the funniest, magicians is that all magic acts begin with serious research. The beginnings of their performances involve rigorous study of how the desired effect has been understood in the past, or might be achieved now. We would never imagine that by the time it reaches the stage, endless hours of preparation, practice, study, and reworking have occurred to bring what looks effortless to dazzle, fool, and entrance us. Few disciplines tend to the details of innovation, imagination, investigation, emotional responses, interpersonal cues, or pattern recognition like magicians and psychoanalysts. Spies, detectives, mothers, and computer geeks incorporate some of these tools. But magicians and analysts blend them to weave the fabric subtly cloaking their intent, while draping you in a gauzy reverie.

Magicians transport you to a space where you willingly believe in the impossible, no matter how skeptical you attempt to be. Analysts create a similar, brief suspension from the demands of reality, encouraging you to take them to a space where they can be with you in any scenario, memory, or feelings you share.

How many people have asked me over the years if I can read their mind? Or have insisted I can? In social settings it gets laughed off. In the office, there is some truth in it. Analytic listening involves a willingness to give up being the person who knows. You have to welcome understanding patients are the expert on themselves. To travel successfully with them on their psychic journey you must be willing to be the container for all the good and the ugly feelings, and the fears that will emerge in the psychic field the two of you create. The job, as with all magic acts, includes the big move to focus you, and the small move to introduce the delicate, transformative emotional communication the patient can tolerate, without them realizing. That is the small move. The big one is that you are not just listening, but hearing.

Mutual Growth in the Psychotherapeutic Relationship is about stories, story-tellers, and listeners, and the magic that can be drawn from even the darkest moment. It explores the possibility of benefit to clinicians exposed to narrations of crushing experiences, while demonstrating a method of research compatible with the way clinicians actually think. You have heard the stories from therapists here revealing in their own words, generally unaware they were doing so, the enormous challenges most face in life, and the defenses developed to cope with them. You have also learned the benefits from their clinical work discovered in telling their own stories. Where was the big move and the small as *Mutual Growth in the Psychotherapeutic Relationship* unfolded?

Turning lead into gold: Early relationships matter

Vaillant (2011) commented that defenses can "turn lead into gold" (p. 89). Our psyches, and the clinicians who strive to understand and help them grow, are masters of illusion no less than Houdini.

While Vaillant likes to refer to defenses as mechanisms of deception (Vaillant, 2000), I prefer to embrace them as magical expressions of fragile, developing egos exercising sleight of hand to help the individual navigate rocky shoals in life. By ego, here, I mean that part of the human psyche that struggles from conception onward to define a person in the world. This ego enables them to understand ever more complex conditions that interfere with actualizing a coherent identity, and protects the developing self. It is the mediator between our impulses and rules of reality or social imperatives, helping us identify what we need, and how to get it in order to live satisfying lives. Freud described the ego as the reality principle forever caught in a struggle to reduce the conflict between the superego's demands and the id's impulses (Freud, 1990). In *Mutual Growth in the Psychotherapeutic Relationship* the concept of ego is expanded to encompass a focus on its role in the process of developing self-identity, executive function, healthy need satisfaction, and emotional resilience.

The maturing self is faced constantly with challenges in all domains: physical, neurobiological, psychic, interpersonal, environmental, cognitive, and emotional, throughout development. If a child continued growing at the same rate it does during the first couple of years, it would reach 39.3701 feet, or twelve meters, by age twenty. Something called the Square-Cube Law in physics saves us from that (What if? https://what-if.xkcd.com/77/). This gives an idea of the enormous growth stressors that occur naturally as the infant grows, even before adding all the environmental, emotional, and relational elements. Then throw in adversity. Nearly twenty years of Adverse Childhood Experiences Studies (ACEs) (https://www.cdc.gov/violenceprevention/acestudy), originating at Kaiser-Permanente, have demonstrated that increased numbers of adverse childhood experiences can derail healthy maturation, and negatively impact the incidence of chronic illness, emotional disorders, and life failures. Even early mortality surges exponentially with just four ACEs (Felitti & Anda, 2009). How does anyone actually survive, let alone thrive?

Answers to that question lie in understanding the power of early interpersonal attachments, the drive to survive, and the mind's capacity to fool itself in ways that get it through hardship and growing beyond. That is, as several of the theorists and researchers mentioned in this book assert, the degree to which a child's coping skills mature, and the availability of interpersonal resources present the key adaptational tools (Wright, Masten, & Nurayan, 2013; Masten (2007); Garmezy (1970). The group in the seventy-five year Harvard Grant Study (Vaillant, 2000, 2012) represented a fairly socio-economically diverse, Caucasian, well-educated male cohort. Study results indicated the most important factor contributing to general well-being over the course of life is close relationships, particularly early warm ones. This was found regardless of socio-economic status, intelligence, or career success. Interpersonal connections in life and work were the strongest predictors of life satisfaction. This finding affirms the research of Masten (2007), Garmezy (1970), and Luthar and Cicchetti (2000) about critical protective factors in the development of resilience. The short answer to how does anyone actually survive, let alone thrive, is resilience.

Resilience

Martin-Breen and Anderies conclude from their research:

> Resilience is then defined as an ongoing process of continual positive adaptive changes to adversity, which changes enable future, positive adaptive changes. Such definition assumes bidirectional interactions as well as recognition that the history, including previous adaptations, determine (positive) adaptive outcomes.
>
> (Martin-Breen & Anderies, 2011, p. 45)

The coping tools we develop in the interactions with the environment, close relationships, and our internal processes allow us to find alternatives and solutions to conflict while enabling growth to continue. Is it any wonder we need some form of magic to master the triad of challenges hurtling toward us, internal, interpersonal, and environmental, especially in childhood when neurobiological changes occur at such rapid speed while the world makes its own demands?

Defenses are the brilliant illusions that power us through to resilient functioning. In the therapist's office, as with our own self-awareness, we see the many ways these involuntary emissaries of our psyche can save the child in the moment, but evolve into less adaptive resources over time. After all, the growing child can only interpret the world from his or her minute breadth of experience. Judgment and problem-solving skills are drawn from interpretation and intuition based on limited exposure to complex issues. Children do the best they can with the tools available. Growth and resilience are dependent on multiple factors. Once a threatening situation is averted, the method used for overcoming it becomes the first line of defense when a similar issue arises. But the earliest choice may have been simply a primitive survival tool not adequate to cope with later conflict. Thus, psychic resources can become either crippled, or rerouted to successful problem-solving approaches, dependent on many factors in a person's life. What is consistent is that mechanisms chosen will echo the early conflicts, and continually reflect how they resurface in various disguises. These solutions of the moment begin to define personality style while holding the answer to the riddle of what psychic conflict stands in the way of the person moving forward.

Reciprocal Resilience: A study

The results of the research project discussed in *Mutual Growth in the Psychotherapeutic Relationship* demonstrate that a phenomenon of Reciprocal Resilience occurs in the emotional loop of the therapeutic relationship. Therapists may benefit in personal and professional life from the work they do listening to stories of distress and trauma, particularly in respect to the experience of personal resilience.

A goal of this volume has been to introduce clinical practitioners who tend to steer away from conducting research to a form they may not realize exists. The method used in the study discussed in the book is syntonic with how clinicians think and process meaning, and with the analytic process itself. One difference is that the researcher's intent is to learn more about certain phenomena, not to function exclusively in a therapeutic mode. It may incidentally overlap, for example, the study may involve comparative outcome effects. But the organization and study of clinical material in conducting qualitative investigations echoes the psychodynamic, analytic process. There is certainly more research control involved, detailed study of data, and work done that is exclusive of contact with subjects, unlike what happens in the therapeutic relationship. I would encourage anyone who is curious to learn new ways to use your clinical skills, and would like to contribute to a body of literature that will continue telling us more about the meaning and transformational validity of the therapeutic relationship, to come on board: think about doing research. It can be an exciting, meaningful adventure. The professional community, and those whose care is entrusted to us, need as much input as possible to understand and implement psychic growth.

While every volunteer immediately provided descriptions of, and discussed, the exceptional stressors they manage in their work, they were able to reflect further when asked to consider their experience of any benefits. The

notion of benefits was a surprising concept for them. Benefits reported fall
into two subtypes: enhanced well-being and increased professional skills.
Additionally, enhanced well-being could be subdivided into comparative
positive assessment and personal growth. Participants described a strong
desire to be heard, to be known. Two other emergent themes were the desire
to be part of a community of like-minded people who appreciate what it is
like to listen to painful stories, and the capacity for emotional connection as
a life and identity-affirming need. The fourth theme to surface was the wish
to make a difference, to have a positive impact on the world.

Ten out of the fourteen volunteers showed an increase in Mature Adaptive
Defenses, the correlates of resilience, in their story descriptions from the first
to second interviews. Not only was there frequent use of higher level adaptive
tools for conflict resolution and anxiety reduction among these volunteers,
but some defenses were noted more often than others. Healthy altruism was
by far the most used coping style, followed by sublimation. These two mechanisms are especially valuable when used in the clinical setting. They promote
a dynamic involving continuous reciprocal communication between both
parties, and are resilience reinforcing for each. Healthy altruism requires an
emotional understanding of the needs of another and oneself, combined with
an ability to recognize that choosing to take action for another may meet
a similar need of one's own. Through sublimation the therapist can even
achieve enthusiasm about a challenging task at hand, which has a reinforcing
impact on his or her inner sense of well-being and competence.

One factor has become clear in my studies of resilience in the therapeutic
setting: mental health professionals have not been oriented toward considering any personal benefits their work might include. There are several reasons
this may have become the norm. The simplest one is tied to an unarticulated
belief in the profession that it is wrong to profit from another's crisis or bad
fortune. This is an issue unaddressed in colleges, universities, or psychoanalytic training institutes. To state that a person in a mental health profession
might routinely consider intangible, and internal, personal gain part of the
compensation for their work, would be considered perverse thinking and
unprofessional by many. Another reason for ignoring benefits is our natural
inclination to look first at the negative threat (Dijksterhuis & Aarts, 2003).
Humans are innately survivors so attend first to threats to that powerful
drive. A third reason to unconsciously ignore benefits may be the consensus
of a culture that focuses on eliminating or reducing negative impacts.

When given the freedom to look three dimensionally at the experience
of their clinical work, encompassing all the negatives and considering any
benefits, participants' attitudes, statements, even their demeanor, changed.
I began to hear comments like, "At the time, if you had advertised for a
hospice nurse, I don't think I even would have applied, and it would have
been wholly my loss. But I love the work, it's very humbling. It's identity
validating and self-affirming."

Another therapist commented, " I'm getting something out of every inter-action ... I'm getting personal growth and knowledge. Out of every interac-tion, I learn something about myself."

Still another said:

> I love the work I do, it's an extremely fulfilling job, it's a fulfillment. When I first started in analysis I got this feeling of being heard, that I've never had before. So it was such a new experience, and I guess I'd like to ... I always wanted to give back to other people, being really listened to. I hadn't been listened to all my life. The feeling of knowing that I am available to hear these people and nobody else might've done that, knowing that's a relief to them because of what I've experienced being a patient, it's big.

Participants described a sense of deep satisfaction at doing something mean-ingful, when asked to consider any positive professional or personal impact of their work. They talked about improvement in their personal relationships and frustration tolerance, and deeper appreciation for family. They spoke of gaining a better perspective on their life situations and what they considered problematic. Interviewees often mentioned developing a different sense of optimism about working through problems and increased confidence in the effectiveness and importance of their work. They said that the severity of the life issues they witnessed and the need for healing connectedness gave them a feeling that there is more in the work than the immediate problem. Each person they were able to help represented an ever-widening circle, a spiritual sense of being in the world. Many expressed gratitude, describing it a privilege to be able to be the person chosen to provide a healing container and witness the patient's recovery and growth. Growth as a person, through the experience of their work, was a common theme.

Benefits from clinical work described in this study are similar to those reported by others investigating the question of benefits mental health professionals may experience (Hernandez, Gangsei, & Engstrom, 2007, Hernandez-Wolfe, Engstrom, & Gangsei 2010; Engstrom, Hernandez, & Gangsei, 2008; Berthold & Deutsch, 2011; Hunter, 2012). As in the responses from therapists in the aforementioned investigations, participants here reported a meaning-making aspect of their work that has a beneficial impact on the clinical practice as well as on personal relationships.

Surprising benefits: A paradigm shift

Hernandez et al. (2007) first proposed a concept of vicarious resilience, which I expanded to Reciprocal Resilience, a more active integration of re-silience resources. Engstrom & Okamura (2004) began to look at the possi-bility that clinicians may have a type of transformative experience during the course of working with trauma victims. This notion arose out of interviews with trauma therapists who remarked about not only the difficulties, but the positive effects they noticed doing the work, listening to the stories. Further investigators found that participants reported having deeply moving and life-altering experiences in the course of their work. These included a resurgence of feelings of hopefulness, an increased awareness of the human capacity for resilience, an appreciation for the resources and people in their own lives, a sense of something more important – a communal, spiritual sense – of humanity, a value of community resources, a sense of privilege at being allowed to accompany the patient on an intimate and painful emotional journey, and increased frustration tolerance (Hernandez-Wolfe et al., 2010; Hunter, 2012; Berthold & Deutsch, 2011).

Hernandez et al. (2007) concluded that a clear resilience process transpires in the clinical working together of clinician and patient when dealing with overwhelming experiences:

> The themes emerging from this qualitative study indicate to us that therapists who work in extremely traumatic social contexts learn about coping with adversity from their clients, that their work does have a positive effect on therapists, and that this effect can be strengthened by bringing conscious attention to it.
>
> (Hernandez et al., 2007, p. 237)

It seems this reservoir of positive identity factors, arising from engagement in the therapeutic relationship, is an untapped resource for enhancing the mental health professional's conscious and unconscious relationship with resilience and sense of self in the world. Langer comments on our bias to focus on, and tendency to believe, what we have heard repeated by multiple sources, and to ignore what is off stage:

> Not only do we as individuals get locked into single-minded views, but we also reinforce these views for each other until the culture itself suffers … There is an awareness of this in science. Scientists proceed along a path gathering data that builds on accepted wisdom. At some point someone turns everyone's attention to a very different view of the previously acknowledged truth. This phenomenon happens frequently enough that scientists are generally not surprised by what is called a paradigm shift.
>
> (Langer, 1997, p. 97)

Thomas Kuhn brought attention to the "paradigm shift" concept in *The Structure of Scientific Revolutions* (Kuhn, 1962). As a physics student studying Aristotle's *Physics*, Kuhn suddenly realized that the master's theories were inaccurate. He was baffled to think how much of contemporary science was based on erroneous concepts. The struggle to understand this folly eventually led Kuhn to postulate his idea of paradigm shifts. That is, ideas established, replicated, and used without question to solve new questions encountering anomalies along the way that require reconsidering phenomena. These incongruities are not taken seriously unless a sufficient number occur to demand attention, or when someone is subjectively struck by the existence of an anomaly and spurred to question the basic premises behind the theory or idea. This stepping back, or thinking-out-of-the-box, to re-examine the issue in its full context is the first step in a potential paradigm shift (Kuhn, 1962). When such a change occurs, it can create scientific and political upheaval because foundational tenets are being questioned, as are the findings based on them. In the case of the current research, the outcome of such a shift may enrich observation of a phenomenon, the therapist's experience, increasing understanding of the impact of interactions between clinician and client on the professional listener. Awareness of the possibility of benefit, and introducing the concept of resilience, and the process of Reciprocal Resilience, into the professional vocabulary, can act as a paradigm shift tool for strengthening the clinician's experience of resilience.

Reciprocal Resilience in the therapeutic relationship

Exploration: The pleasure of not knowing

This book evolved from an inquiry centered on understanding the conscious and unconscious experience of personal and professional resilience of clinicians whose work involves therapeutic listening to stories of horrible, overwhelming life situations. As I studied the phenomenon of the clinicians' experience of self in the world, it became increasingly clear that their well-being is rarely considered. Their patients and clients are universally treated as more important from the perspective of the therapeutic world. When therapist well-being is addressed it is generally in the context of 1) advice about self-care so that the job will be effectively accomplished; or 2) from a view of recovery from inevitable, negative effects of the work they do (Hernandez et al., 2010).

Such a skewed outlook augurs a dismal perspective on potential job and personal satisfaction for the profession. Salaries are generally low compared to other fields requiring the same, or less, education and training. Work conditions are often physically uncomfortable or even dangerous. Clients range in extremes of pathology, life situations, and maturation. Little, if anything, is done to create a comfortable work environment for clinicians. We have an entire population of mental health professionals whom we trust to be mindful of the well-being of others, and whose health, well-being, and professional satisfaction, as related to the clinician without reference to the clients, we as a culture largely ignore. It became my goal to understand more about this social glitch and to explore ways to ameliorate it.

Psychoanalysts are researchers, detectives of the mind. We are accustomed to the pleasure of not knowing an answer and exploring a mystery, a hidden agenda; the reason someone behaves in ways that clearly lead to their own painful dissatisfaction. We also find satisfaction in observing how the human mind can creatively right itself, exercise flexibility in considering problems from different perspectives, and demonstrate a powerful capacity for emotional connectedness. These are important components of emotional resilience as well as of a therapeutic alliance. In addition to being vulnerable to potential negative effects, it is possible for therapists to benefit from listening to stories of distress while engaged in clinical work. It is also vital for those training clinicians to recognize possible benefit from the work and learn ways to reinforce and facilitate it.

Among those I studied, the notion that someone was interested in simply knowing about his or her experiences, and not in a therapeutic context, was a persuasive induction for a positive transference. Levin asserts that transference, within and external to the psychoanalytic setting, can be used as a powerful learning tool. Transference responses are activated at a primitive emotional level, primed by a perception that echoes or resonates with an earlier, emotionally charged experience (Levin, 2011).

Once the priming value of the interviews in the project became clear, I began to study them as vehicles for development of transference that could promote feelings of safety and facilitate learning integration. I was curious whether a clinician exposed to examples of his or her own resilience traits, demonstrated through stories of working with overwhelming feelings of their own and clients', or in personal life, could use them to fuel further resilience. Could a therapist be primed to recognize the expression of personal resilience in difficult clinical encounters and understand it as both generative of a process of Reciprocal Resilience and a benefit of the work?

Resonating with the patient

In my role as an attentive, curious listener during interviews, I noticed I was using typical Modern Analytic interventions, such as joining or reflecting, in order to encourage further exploration (Margolis, 1986). Joining is a technique, a communication from the therapist to the patient, that signals agreement with what is being said on several levels. It resonates with what the patient is consciously saying, but is directed toward the unconscious, emotional message that may be different from the overt statement. When the clinician is attuned to the emotional meaning of what is being said, the unconscious content being protected by the defense becomes accessible. Joining as a therapeutic intervention is only used as a means to resolve resistances to continued communication. For example, after some time working with a young woman who had been severely sexually abused as a child, we had the following exchange:

> **Patient:** I want to ask you for something. That's why I'm talking about this. I want you to help me not be promiscuous. It feels out of my control. I want you to help me stop feeling bad about my sexual needs, and stop the promiscuity. Can you do that?
>
> **Therapist:** I need to know more about what's meant here by promiscuous. In the meantime, would it be all right if we just helped you enjoy sex when you choose it, while we figure out if it's a good idea to give up anything?
>
> **Patient:** You don't talk a whole lot, maybe like me as a kid, but when you do, you come up with the most outrageous ideas! Sure I'll agree to like the sex I have until we decide whether it's a good idea or not. I was so afraid you'd tell me to just stop!

In this case what was being protected was the patient's fear that I would reject her impulses, the conflicted feelings she harbored about her sexuality and herself. She believed I would insist she stop the sexual acting out, and was not sure she could. She wanted my acceptance. I responded in the language of her overt statement, a desire to end promiscuity, but addressed it in terms of the importance of her feelings and capabilities rather than the right or wrong of it. This resonated with her ambivalence and insecurity, reassuring her she was more important than the behavior.

Joining can be ego syntonic or dystonic, felt pleasurably or as jarring. Ego dystonic joining comes as a surprise, is potentially experienced as abrasive, but can serve the same purpose as syntonic joining, facilitating resolution of resistances to talking freely.

> **Patient:** I don't want to have to tell you everything.
>
> **Therapist:** You should be very careful of what you say to anyone.
>
> **Patient:** But how are you going to help me if I'm not completely honest?
>
> **Therapist:** That's my job to figure out. You should do whatever you need to feel safe, and I should do my job.

The patient expected me to insist on full disclosure. This oppositional attitude early in the treatment represents a type of resistance that could be a lethal, treatment destructive resistance. The intervention took the wind out of that sail by asserting that the patient should do everything to protect herself. While supporting the unconscious defenses of defiance and secrecy, it laid the groundwork for me to take responsibility for progress while indicating it was a collaborative process in which the patient had direct input.

These examples of joining as an exploratory therapeutic tool are what are referred to as maturational interpretations.

> The therapist does not intervene to reduce maturational needs directly; nor does he address himself to maladaptations (defenses) that do not interfere with maturation. Rather, he intervenes to lay the foundation for new growth by freeing the patient from the stranglehold of pathological maladaptations.
>
> (Spotnitz, 2013, p. 585).

In working with the participants in my study, maturational interpretations, syntonic communications, were generally used as the priming actions to address the person's resistance to awareness of existing resilient functioning and to encourage further elaboration. The end goal was to promote integration of a sense of personal resilience, if possible. Ways they demonstrated resilient behavior were highlighted in this process. For example, when someone said, "I was confused, but figured I needed to step up and make a plan," I replied, "Even in the chaos, you knew a solution could be organized." Then the person agreed that was what happened and told me how the conflict got resolved. I noted this as priming behavior on my part: calling attention to the useful, resilient actions in the face of the individual not recognizing that strength (Dijksterhuis, 2004; Dijksterhuis, Chartrand, & Aarts, 2007; Levin, 2011; Molden, 2014). Once it was reframed they were able to incorporate the notion into their "world view" of the story. The feelings attached to the original memories were often ones of anxiety, fear, panic or incompetence. When I introduced a potentially different outlook on their responsive behavior during the conflict-laden situation, the door was open to examine the story from other perspectives (Langer, 1997). The negative emotional charge tied to the story when previously stored silently in the therapists' memory vaults was lessened by introduction of a benign alternative. This was especially noticeable during second interviews when several subjects re-told the same stories without consciously recalling that they had reported them in the first one, and the representation of their role was altered. It was not so much rewriting history but an emphasis change in describing a formerly unidentified strength.

Reframing the therapeutic encounter

Seeing the influence of the interview process on the volunteers' perception of their own resilience, I also began to understand that priming with attention to the frequency effect amplified the opportunity to impact their experience of personal resilience. Hasher and Zacks (1984) described the impact of the frequency effect on attitudes, motivation, and decision-making. When a phenomenon is brought to attention, and reinforced through repetition or authority, it becomes more and more likely that the individual will begin to believe that phenomenon is true or real. The influence of the Frequency Illusion, sometimes referred to as the Baader-Meinhof Phenomenon (Bellows, 2006), accounts for many decisions that people make based on experiences they cannot explain, but that are stored as existing facts. For example, Bellows mentions that when buying a home, people tend to incorporate what they have heard from others about values and neighborhood rather than acquire actual research data. The likelihood something is believed increases the more often it has been said. When the Frequency and Recency Effects are combined they become a powerful prompt for conscious and unconscious response to the phenomena, and this frequency of repetition reinforces the individual's often unspoken belief in its validity. It is plausible that my interventions, supportively and casually highlighting resilient behaviors and identifying them as such, could trigger a shift in recognition of resilience-based functioning and enhance awareness of current resilience resources (Dijksterhuis, 2004; Levin, 2011).

I found that by shining the light on both the clinician's resilience and the question of any benefit from listening to repeated stories of disaster and terror, a new pattern of looking at the therapeutic encounter as a situation enabling reciprocity could be introduced. Therapists began to consider therapeutic relationships with patients as potentially beneficial to their own well-being, and reported stories of when that was their experience. A simple reframing of events, temporarily short-circuiting the therapist's self-evaluation and the cultural imperative to be self-denying as a clinician, prompted conscious and/or unconscious enhancement of the experience of personal resilience.

Therapists were more open about their inner lives during the second interview. There were many courageous moments when histories of perceived personal traumas or abuse in their past were revealed, or difficult self-reflection and disclosures of personal or professional anxieties and concerns were shared. I understood this as a relaxed sense of security after the safe feeling of the first interview, even though dimly remembered. It was an expression of a positive transference toward a listener who only wanted to understand their lived experience, and an unconscious responsiveness to the subtle, resilience reinforcement experienced in the initial meeting. Their openness and willingness to share such in depth reflections on their sense of self and how they think the world views them was deeply moving. It was not done with a conscious wish to have a curative experience, but with a trust that allowing vulnerability with me would lead to something worthwhile, somehow. I experienced the challenge of listening raptly and encouraging their often painful self-revelations as emotionally charged, connecting, and as a gift. There was a feeling of giving to each other that I understood as a model for Reciprocal Resilience. We were engaged in an emotional loop that was having a potentially transformative effect on each.

Reciprocal Resilience in clinical supervision

The interview process in this project was not intended as a therapeutic intervention. What it did was to highlight how Reciprocal Resilience can be fostered in brief encounters where a therapeutic listener is actively and empathically engaged, and is resilience-building minded. For example, in the case of a training or supervisory session, more direct engagement, some personal sharing, and intentional resilience-reinforcing interventions can be beneficial and model a collaborative relationship (Levin, 2011; Bratt, 2012). This reinforces the emotional connection, leaving the way open for a reciprocal interaction in a secure feeling environment. While the existence of reciprocity is generally unconscious on the supervisee's part, it would be helpful for supervisors or clinicians if they were able to recognize the strength and growth their resilience resources induce and support. This would fuel appreciation of the existence and importance of the supervisor's own capacities, and have a resilience generative impact on both. The reciprocity process can occur similarly, be bi-directional in the therapist-patient relationship, but for now the focus is on ways to promote the experience of personal resilience for clinicians, and an awareness of Reciprocal Resilience as a benefit of their work.

A shift in attitudes and skills in dealing with conflict situations was evidenced and demonstrated through the increased use of Higher Adaptive Defenses in the study's second interview stories. It could be asked whether participants were attempting to describe a change in order to please me. Their general comfort with revealing how little they had thought about the research, combined with the spontaneous statements throughout the second interview about changes and shifts, reinforce the idea that they were at least unconsciously experienced. Finally, participants also reported in the second interview more definitively and freely about benefits they got from their work. Their responses resonate with the findings of Engstrom et al. (2008), Hernandez et al. (2007), Hernandez-Wolfe et al. (2010), Hunter (2012), and Berthold & Deutsch (2011). Those authors suggest that "[v]icarious [*reciprocal*] resilience is a process characterized by a unique and positive effect that transforms therapists in response to client trauma survivors' own resiliency" (Hernandez, Gangsei, & Engstrom, 2007, p. 237).

Reciprocal Resilience strategies in clinical supervision: Four pillars of therapist education and personal/professional satisfaction

Increased interdisciplinary focus in research on the special nature of the reciprocal quality of the therapeutic relationship is important. It could provide the basis for a paradigm shift in understanding and assessing the impact of their work for current and future mental health professionals. Academic and clinical training should routinely include attention to characteristics of resilient functioning, methods for enhancing it, and the benefits of clinical work, as well as warnings of known hazards and the need for self-care. Recognizing that priming can speak to the unconscious, that perception can travel faster than cognition, and that interpersonal connectedness can trigger motivation, provides a basis for developing tools for well-being among mental health professionals.

Any organization or institution intending to train and educate mental health professionals should be mindful of the expressed needs for healthy functioning and burnout prevention described by the clinicians who participated in *Mutual Growth in the Psychotherapeutic Relationship*. It is essential to provide a milieu in which therapists will learn to be the welcoming, emotional holding container for the soul-bending stories they hear, while retaining mental acuity, if an optimal clinical environment is to be achieved. The following are the four pillars, foundational socio-emotional, interpersonal and psychic needs on which successful therapist education and long term professional sustainment rely, as described by participants in the *Mutual Growth in the Psychotherapeutic Relationship* project.

1. To be heard, to be known

Classes and supervision are best taught in an experiential, not didactic manner. Students are encouraged to share, to drive the conversation, and bring in material from their life and professional experience. They learn best when given the opportunity to integrate theoretical and emotional material, especially when generated from within the group. The instructor provides the boundaries and reading material, facilitates the discussion, and strives to find instances in the group interaction that relates to assignments. Sometimes people think the experiential method means the instructor comes in like an empty slate, with no preparation. On the contrary, assignments have been read, reflections from students studied, and a general outline of objectives for the class developed. This is the mental roadmap with which the instructor navigates the class. The approach gives each person an opportunity to be heard, and to listen.

Personal therapy is also an important avenue to help the student feel free and safe to externalize the painful, distraught, frustrating experiences from their work, and to learn about their own countertransference triggers. The capacity to recognize what generates from within one's own history, what the patient induces, and how to use these feelings is the core of the clinician's resilience and effective functioning. It is surprising that psychoanalytic training is the only discipline that universally requires a personal therapy experience. Without it, clinicians are more vulnerable to emotional distress, somatic complaints, and frustration with their work.

2. To be part of a community of like-minded people

This element cannot be over-emphasized. Every therapist with whom I have spoken, either in the course of working on *Mutual Growth in the Psycho-therapeutic Relationship* or in other contexts, has proclaimed that without an available community of peers, who appreciate what it is like to listen to painful stories, with whom they can interact in an informal way, their work and personal lives suffer. People have lamented that after leaving a job or area where that was available, and moving to one where it is not, has been devastating. Therapists say they cannot take their jobs home, but it is there with them. When someone asks, "What did you do today?", who wants to hear about the abused children, the suicidal teen, or the battling couple? It is impossible to communicate some of the bizarre stories one hears, or behaviors witnessed, without sometimes sounding critical or demeaning, even though that is not the case. Therapists have said that the opportunity to share a kind of gallows humor with peers, to shuck off the constraint of having to "be on" all the time for patients and just chat back and forth about difficult cases is invaluable. One man told me that without that outlet, he would be divorced. While most people have several resources for discharge and processing, the communal aspect of shared experiences is essential for these professionals whose entire life is based on refueling by relationships.

3. To emotionally connect

The model of training described above, the experiential method, offers therapists an opportunity to develop the connectedness capacities they believe are essential. One person said, "I learned things and made connections and that was probably the most important thing. Every seminar I sat in, you got this feeling that, you know, people want to connect." Another reported that he wondered to himself, "Why are you feeling good? He just told you this terrible thing last night. What I realized was that I made a connection with somebody, that I could make a connection with somebody. It's important."

One can be part of a like-minded community, sharing experiences but connecting, relies on the ability to mirror someone's internal experience of the world with them. When a child says that they are frightened of something on the patio and the parent says, "Don't be afraid. See, there's nothing there," as they nudge the little one outdoors, they are not emotionally connecting. That parent should get down on hands and knees, and try to see the world through the child's eyes. It is quite different than from a vantage point several feet higher. We do not need to always have the same experiences as those with whom we want to connect. We do have to be willing to let go of our own predetermined responses and be open to glimpsing things from the inner eye of the other person. This is the empathy factor, important for all, but essential to enhance in mental health professionals. Empathy is the divining rod for discovering the wonders of psychic treasures in our patients.

The opportunity for intensive clinical experience, along with interactive classes, supervision, and an informal common meeting place, provide graduated practice in ways to emotionally bond. When therapists are provided with them they develop a conscious capacity to choose to be connected or not. They learn about their own triggers and resistances to attaching. Through careful mentoring they develop the keen skills necessary for successfully connecting in their work and personal lives, as well as ways to buffer and insulate when needed.

4. To make a difference

Who does not want to view themselves as impacting the world, making a difference? With mental health practitioners this need is a driving force: to achieve change in a most personal and intimate context. One of the tenets of *Mutual Growth in the Psychotherapeutic Relationship* is that emotional resilience provides the foundation for growth. The emergence of the concept of Reciprocal Resilience as a factor in clinical effectiveness, and as a phenomenon providing personal benefit to therapists, reveals a little explored avenue for inspiring psychic growth. When resilience and psychic faculties are enhanced, transformative shifts are possible regardless of the daunting challenges one faces.

Therapists, particularly newer ones, need reinforcement and encouragement about their capacity to grow. They are often charged with the most difficult, impossible-seeming and disheartening cases when they, themselves, have little confidence in their skills. They need supportive mentors and supervisors who are mindful of the clinician's tendency to altruistically pretzel brains and emotions in their effort to make a difference in their patients' lives (Kernberg, 2016). These mentors and supervisors will be doing a kindness, and making a difference, if they can take time to learn about their supervisees as individuals, not just as therapists. This probably happens routinely in many clinical or academic settings, but I am suggesting a concerted focus on the therapist without reference to their role as a clinician. The work of supervision is the task of helping the therapist understand and resolve patients' resistances to healthy functioning (Kernberg, 2016, Marshall, 1997). This will be greatly helped if some of the supervisory encounter involves connecting by getting to know the supervisee through brief stories from their own lives. If the therapist feels heard and resilient functioning is highlighted, the tendency to self-attack and withdraw, so common among newly minted professionals, can be averted and their ability to persevere with challenging cases much enhanced.

"Reciprocity opens the possibility of appreciating, attending to, and making meaning out of the process [*of therapy*] whereby therapists themselves may heal, learn, and change with clients" (Hernandez et al., 2010, p. 74). Hernandez et al. developed a training process to improve clinicians' awareness of the reciprocity that can exist in the therapeutic relationship, and exercises to encourage resilience-building attitudes. Their program is designed for mental health professionals specifically engaged in trauma work. It includes segments on identifying the positive and negative consequences of the work, reflection on therapists' perception of themselves, as well as that of their patients' assessments of them, and group discussions sharing experiences from the work. The idea of reciprocity is gradually introduced in the context of the therapist learning from witnessing the patient's struggles to cope effectively with adversity. Hernandez et al. emphasize exploration of the socio-cultural context of clinician and patient, the integration of the multiple identities each party brings to the therapeutic dyad, and how these influence the meaning made of the trauma experience (Hernandez et al., 2010).

I am suggesting a process for increasing clinicians' experience of personal resilience that shares some similarities with the Hernandez method, but is intended for all mental health professionals whose work involves therapeutic listening to stories of hardship and overwhelming experiences. It represents an approach that can potentially have an immediate impact on the clinician's experience, as well as be developed as part of the curriculum for training therapists. This model takes advantage of the power of unconscious motivation, the use of object-oriented interventions to preserve ego functioning (Margolis, 1994), respect of current defenses, and the reciprocal nature of the therapeutic relationship. Like Hernandez et al., I incorporate development of awareness of possible benefits from clinical work, but emphasize the interactive, interpersonal field generated by therapist and patient, and likewise by clinician and supervisor as the sources of reciprocity. Hernandez et al. view the experience of reciprocity as a vicarious one emerging from the therapist witnessing the client's efforts to adapt. My observation is that the therapeutic relationship is itself the tool for reciprocity and resilience enrichment. I propose, for initial or short-term resilience building, a process in which the clinician is first encouraged, by an attentive supervisor or instructor, to reflect on challenging cases and how they were managed. The supervisor uses an active listening model that includes exploratory, object-oriented questions to reflect, or highlight, resilience-oriented techniques the therapist demonstrates in coping with the difficult feelings and conflicts raised by the case material. This approach reinforces responses that are ego syntonic for the therapist. It makes use of the transference alive in the supervisory relationship in parallel with the therapeutic one, creating a modeling experience for the therapist. I also suggest that the supervisor introduce the notion of the reciprocal potential in the therapeutic dyad and its usefulness for both parties.

This micro-intervention can be expanded and incorporated as an intrinsic component in training mental health professionals. It is important to provide for those charged with the emotional well-being of the fragile or injured, an awareness of the possible benefits of their work as well as negative effects. A clinician's professional equity rests on the ability for emotional connection. The value of this should not be understated. It is evidence of a form of emotional resilience not easy to achieve, and not found in most people. Good therapists are a type of emotional savants willing to accept, feel, and hold the intolerable feelings induced by their patients while helping them sort through resistances that interfere with life satisfaction. Like a painter's well-cared for and valued brushes, the clinicians' capacity for emotional reciprocity is their tool for creative thriving.

Understanding the phenomena of Reciprocal Resilience can have a reassuring and motivating effect on the practitioner. It adds a new dimension to the value of the work done, as well as a safety net for clinicians routinely facing challenges to the breadth of their emotional grit and intellectual, analytic thinking. The therapist's capacity to remain centered and open, as the holding container for all that will transpire, is the ballast for the patient's fears. Together they bridge the relational gap, generating the emotional charge to fuel the therapeutic encounter, and through the Reciprocal Resilience process offer psychic growth for each.

References

Adverse Childhood Experiences Study. Centers for Disease Control and Prevention Website. Retrieved from: https://www.cdc.gov/violenceprevention/acestudy.

Bellows, A. (2006). The Baader Meinhof Phenomenon. Retrieved from: http://www.damninteresting.com/the-baader-meinhof-phenomenon.

Berthold, S.M., & Deutsch, A. (2011). Serving survivors of torture: Attending to vicarious trauma and enhancing vicarious resilience. Retrieved from: http://www.healtorture.org/sites/healtorture.org/files/PowerPoint%20Vicarious%20Trauma%20and%20Vicarious%20Resilience%20webinar.pdf.

Bratt, P. (2012). Consulting the patient: The art of being together: Perspectives on technique and therapeutic field. *Modern Psychoanalysis*, 37, 193–202.

Dijksterhuis, A., & Aarts, H. (2003). On wildebeests and humans: The preferential detection of negative stimuli. *Psychological Science, 14,* 14–18.

Dijksterhuis, A. (2004). Think different: The merits of unconscious thought in preference development and decision-making. *Journal of Personality and Social Psychology,* 87(5), 586–598.

Dijksterhuis A, Chartrand T.L., & Aarts H. (2007). Effects of priming and perception on social behavior and goal pursuit. In: J.A. Bargh (Ed.), *Social psychology and the unconscious: The automaticity of higher mental processes* (pp. 51–132). Philadelphia, Pa: Psychology Press.

Engstrom, D.W., & Okamura, A. (2004). A plague of our era: Torture, human rights, and social work. *Families in Society,* 85(3), 291–300.

Engstrom, D., Hernandez, P., & Gangsei, D. (2008). Vicarious resilience: A qualitative investigation into its description. *Traumatology,* 3, 13–21.

Felitti, V.J., & Anda, R.F. (2009). The relationship of adverse childhood experiences to adult health, well-being, social function, and healthcare. In: R. Lanius,

E. Vermetten, & C. Pain (Eds.), *The hidden epidemic: The impact of early life trauma on health and disease* (pp. 77–87). Cambridge, UK: Cambridge University Press.

Freud, S. (1990). *The ego and the id.* New York: Norton.

Garmezy, N. (1970). Process and reactive schizophrenia: Some conceptions and issues. *Schizophrenia Bulletin, 2,* 30–74.

Hasher, L., & Zacks, R. (1984). Automatic processing of fundamental information: The case of frequency of occurrence. *American Psychology, 39*(12), 1372–1388.

Hernandez, P., Gangsei, D., & Engstrom, D. (2007). Vicarious resilience: A new concept in work with those who survive trauma. *Family Process, 46*(2), 229–241.

Hernandez-Wolfe, P., Engstrom, D., & Gangsei, D. (2010). Exploring the impact of trauma on therapists: Vicarious resilience and related concepts in training. *Journal of Systemic Therapies, 29*(1), 67–83.

Hunter, S.V. (2012). Walking in sacred spaces in the therapeutic bond: Therapists' experiences of compassion satisfaction coupled with the potential for vicarious traumatization. *Journal of Advanced Nursing, 60*(1), 1–9.

Kernberg, O.F. (2016). *Psychoanalytic education at the crossroads: Reformation, change and the future of psychoanalytic training.* New York, NY: Routledge.

Kuhn, T. (1962). *The structure of scientific revolutions.* Chicago: University of Chicago Press.

Langer, E. (1997). *The power of mindful learning.* Cambridge, Ma: DeCapo Press.

Levin, F. (2011). *Psyche and brain: The biology of talking cures.* London: Karnac.

Luthar, S., & Cicchetti D. (2000). The construct of resilience: Implications for interventions and social policies. *Developmental Psychopathology, 12*(4), 857–885.

Margolis, B. (1986). Joining, mirroring, psychological reflection: Terminology, definitions, theoretical considerations. *Modern Psychoanalysis, 11,* 19–35.

Margolis, B.D. (1994). The object-oriented question: A contribution to treatment technique. *Modern Psychoanalysis, 19,* 187–198.

Marshall, R.J. (1997). A dynamic and structural model of the triad in supervision. *Modern Psychoanalysis, 22*(1), 41–57.

Martin-Breen, P., & Anderies, J.M. (2011). *Resilience: A literature review.* New York, NY: The Rockefeller Foundation.

Masten, A.S. (2007). Resilience in developing systems: Progress and promise as the fourth wave rises. *Development and Psychopathology, 19,* 921–930.

Molden, D. (2014). Understanding priming effects in social psychology: What is "social priming" and how does it occur? *Social Cognition, 32,* Special Issue, 1–11.

Spotnitz, H. (2013). The maturational interpretation. *Psychoanalytic Review,* 100(4), 583–587.

Vaillant, G.E. (2000). Adaptive mental mechanisms: Their role in a positive psychology. *American Psychology, 55*(1), 89–98.

Vallaint, G.E. (2011). Involuntary coping mechanisms: A psychodynamic perspective. *Dialogues in Clinical Neuroscience, 13*(3), 366–370.

Vaillant, G.E. (2012). *Triumph of experience.* Boston: Harvard University Press.

What if? Retrieved from: https://what-if.xkcd.com/77/.

Wright, M.O.D., Masten, A. S., & Narayan, A. J. (2013). Resilience processes in development: Four waves of research on positive adaptation in the context of adversity. In: S. Goldstein & R.B. Brooks (Eds.), *Handbook of resilience in children, 2nd Edition* (pp. 15–38). New York, NY: Springer.

Bibliography

Adverse Childhood Experiences Study. Centers for Disease Control and Prevention Website. Retrieved from: https://www.cdc.gov/violenceprevention/acestudy.

Akhtar, S. (2010). Happiness: Origins, forms, and technical relevance. *American Journal of Psychoanalysis*, 70(3),219–244.

Akhtar, S. (2013). *Psychoanalytic listening: Methods, limits, and innovations.* New York, NY: Karnac.

Akhtar, S. (2014). *Good Stuff.* New York, NY: Rowman & Littlefield.

Akhtar, S., & O'Neil, M.K. (2015). *Hopelessness.* London: Karnac.

Almond, R. (2003). The holding function of theory. *Journal of the American Psychoanalytic Association,* 51, 131–153.

American Psychiatric Association. (1994). *Diagnostic and Statistical Manual of Mental Disorders: 4th ed.* Washington, DC: American Psychiatric Press.

American Psychological Association. (2017). Ethical principles of psychologists and code of conduct (2002, Amended June 1, 2010 and January 1, 2017). Retrieved from http://www.apa.org/ethics/code/index.aspx

Anthony, E.J. (1974). The syndrome of the psychologically invulnerable. In: E.J. Anthony & C. Koupernik (Eds.), *The child in his family: Children at psychiatric risk* (pp. 3–10). Oxford: John Wiley & Sons.

Anthony, E.J., & Cohler, B.J. (1987). *The Invulnerable Child.* New York, NY: The Guilford Press.

Baranger, M. (2012). The intrapsychic and the intersubjective in contemporary psychoanalysis. *International Forum for Psychoanalysis,* 21, 130–135.

Bargh, J.A., & Morsella, E. (2008). The unconscious mind. *Perspectives in Psychological Science,* 3(1), 73–79.

Barnett, J.E., Baker, E.K., Elman, N.S., & Schoener, G.R. (2007). In pursuit of wellness: The self-care imperative. *Professional Psychology: Research and Practice,* 38, 603–612.

Bartlett, D.W. (1994). On resilience: Questions of validity. In: M.C. Wang & E.W. Gordon (Eds.), *Educational resilience in inner-city America: Challenges and prospects* (pp. 97– 108). Hillsdale, NJ: Erlbaum.

Bauwens, J., & Tosone, C. (2014). The influence of clinicians' trauma histories and primary and secondary traumatic stress. *Traumatology,* (3), 209–218.

Beck, S.M., & Perry, J.C. (2008). The definition and function of interview structure in psychiatric and psychotherapeutic interviews. *Psychiatry,* Spring, 71(1): 1–12.

Bellows, A. (2006). The Baader Meinhof Phenomenon. Retrieved from: http://www. damninteresting.com/the-baader-meinhof-phenomenon.

Benjamin, J. (2010). Where's the gap and what's the difference? *Contemporary Psychoanalysis*, 46(1), 112–119.

Bernauer, J., Lichtman, M., Jacobs, C., & Robertson, S. (2013). Blending the old and the new: Qualitative data analysis as critical thinking and using NVivo with a generic approach. *The Qualitative Report,* 18(2), 1–10.

Berthold, S.M., & Deutsch, A. (2011). Serving survivors of torture: Attending to vicarious trauma and enhancing vicarious resilience. Retrieved from: http:// www.healtorture.org/sites/healtorture.org/files/PowerPoint%20Vicarious%20 Trauma%20and%20Vicarious%20Resilience%20webinar.pdf.

Bion, W.R. (1963). *Elements of psycho-analysis.* London: Heinemann.

Bion, W.R. (1970). *Attention and interpretation.* London: Tavistock.

Bonanno, G. (2004). Loss, trauma, and human resilience: Have we underestimated the human capacity to thrive after extremely aversive events? *American Psychologist,* 59, 20–28.

Bond, M., & Perry, J.C. (2004). Long-term changes in defense styles with psychodynamic psychotherapy for depressive, anxiety, and personality disorders. *American Journal of Psychiatry,* 161(9), 1665–1671.

Bota, R., Munro, S., Nugyen, C., & Preda, A. (2011). Course of schizophrenia: What has been learned from longitudinal studies? In: M.S. Ritsner (Ed.), *Handbook of schizophrenia spectrum disorders: Volume II* (pp. 281–300). New York, NY: Springer.

Boulanger, G. (2013). Fearful symmetry: Shared trauma in New Orleans after Hurricane Katrina. *Psychoanalytic Dialogues,* 23, 31–44.

Bratt, P. (2002). The impact of strategic emotional communication on memory and identity development. Communication in the 3rd International Neuropsychoanalysis Congress, Stockholm, September 1–3.

Bratt, P. (2012). Consulting the patient: The art of being together: Perspectives on technique and therapeutic field. *Modern Psychoanalysis*, 37, 193–202.

Brockhouse, R., Msetfi, R., Cohen, K., & Joseph, S. (2011). Vicarious exposure to trauma and growth in therapists: The moderating effects of sense of coherence, organizational support, and empathy. *Journal of Traumatic Stress,* 24(6), 735–742.

Brown, L. J. (2012). Bion's discovery of alpha function: Thinking under fire on the battlefield and in the consulting room. *International Journal of Psychoanalysis,* 93(5), 1191–1214.

Busch, F. (2001). Are we losing our mind? *Journal of the American Psychoanalytic Association*, 49(3), 739–751.

Calhoun, L.G., & Tedeschi, R.G. (2012). *Posttraumatic growth in clinical practice.* New York, NY: Routledge.

Cicchetti, D. (2007). The construct of resilience: A critical evaluation and guidelines for future research. *Child Development*, 71(3), 543–562.

Cicchetti, D., & Curtis, W.J. (2006). The developing brain and neural plasticity: Implications for normality, psychopathology, and resilience. In: D. Ciccheti, & D. Cohen (Eds.), *Developmental psychopathology: Vol 2: Developmental neurosciences* (pp. 1–64). New York, NY: Wiley.

Cicchetti D., & Garmezy N. (1993). Prospects and promises in the study of resilience. *Developmental Psychopathology,* 5, 497–502.

Cohen, K., & Collins, P. (2012). The impact of trauma work on trauma workers: A metasynthesis on vicarious trauma and vicarious posttraumatic growth. *Psychological Trauma: Theory, Research, Practice and Policy*, 5(6), 570–580.

Cowen, E. L., Wyman, P. A.,Work, W. C., Kim, J., Fagen, D. B., & Magnus, K. B. (1997). Followup study of young stress affected and stress resilient urban children. *Development and Psychopathology*, 9, 565–577.

Cramer, P. (2000). Defense mechanisms in psychology today: Further processes for adaptation. *The American Psychologist*, 55(6), 637–646.

Cramer, P., & Blatt, S.J. (1993). Change in defense mechanisms follow intensive treatment, as related to personality organization and gender. In: U. Hentschel, G.J.W. Smith, W. Ehlers, & J.G. Draguus (Eds.), *The concept of defense mechanisms in contemporary psychology* (pp. 310–320). New York: Springer-Verlag.

Damasio, A. (1999). *The feeling of what happens: Body and emotion in the making of consciousness.* New York, NY: Harcourt Brace.

Dijksterhuis, A. (2004). Think different: The merits of unconscious thought in preference development and decision-making. *Journal of Personality and Social Psychology*, 87(5), 586–598.

Dijksterhuis, A., & Aarts, H. (2003). On wildebeests and humans: The preferential detection of negative stimuli. *Psychological Science*, 14, 14–18.

Dijksterhuis A, Chartrand T.L., & Aarts H. (2007). Effects of priming and perception on social behavior and goal pursuit. In: J.A. Bargh (Ed.), *Social psychology and the unconscious: The automaticity of higher mental processes* (pp. 51–132). Philadelphia, Pa: Psychology Press.

Docherty, N.M., St-Hilaire, A., Aakre, M.A., & Seghers, J.P. (2009). Life events and high-trait reactivity together predict psychotic symptom increases in schizophrenia. *Schizophrenia Bulletin,* 35(3), 638–645.

Egeland, B., Carlson, E., & Sroufe, L.A (1993). Resilience as process. *Development and Psychopathology*, 5(4), 517–528.

Engstrom, D., Hernandez, P., & Gangsei, D. (2008). Vicarious resilience: A qualitative investigation into its description. *Traumatology*, 3, 13–21.

Engstrom, D.W., & Okamura, A. (2004). A plague of our era: Torture, human rights, and social work. *Families in Society,* 85(3), 291–300.

Epstein, L. (2008). Some implications of conducting psychoanalysis as a talking cure. *Contemporary Psychoanalysis*, 44, 377–399.

Ernsberger, C. (1979). The concept of countertransference as therapeutic instrument: Its early history. *Modern Psychoanaly*sis, 4, 141–164.

Felitti, V.J., & Anda, R.F. (2009). The relationship of adverse childhood experiences to adult health, well-being, social function, and healthcare. In: R. Lanius, E. Vermetten, & C. Pain (Eds.), *The hidden epidemic: The impact of early life trauma on health and disease* (pp. 77–87). Cambridge, UK: Cambridge University Press.

Figley, C.R. (2002). Compassion fatigue: Psychotherapists' chronic lack of self care. *JCLP/In Session Psychotherapy*, 58(11), 1433–1441.

Fletcher, D., & Sarkar, M. (2013). Psychological resilience. *European Psychologist*, 18(1), 12–23.

Freud, A. (1979). *The ego and the mechanisms of defense.* New York, NY: International University Press.

Freud, S. (1894). The neuro-psychoses of defence. *The complete psychological works of Sigmund Freud* (Vol. 3, Standard Ed.) (pp. 43–61). London: Hogarth Press.

Freud, S. (1990). *The ego and the id.* New York: Norton.

Freudenberger, H.J. (1974). Staff burnout. *Journal of Social Issues,* 30(1), 159–165.

Gabbard, G. O. (1999). *Countertransference issues in psychiatric treatment.* Washington, DC: American Psychiatric Press.

Gabbard, G.O. (2001). A contemporary psychoanalytic model of countertransference. *Journal of Clinical Psychology,* 57, 983–991.

Galletta, A. (2013). *Mastering the semi-structured interview and beyond.* New York, NY: NYU Press.

Garmezy, N. (1970). Process and reactive schizophrenia: Some conceptions and issues. *Schizophrenia Bulletin,* 2, 30–74.

Garmezy, N. (1971). Vulnerability research and the issue of primary prevention. *American Journal of Orthopsychiatry,* 41, 101–116.

Garmezy, N. (1974). The study of competence in children at risk for severe psychopathology. In: E.J. Anthony & C. Koupernik (Eds.), *The child in his family: Children at psychiatric risk* (Vol. 3, pp. 77–97). New York: Wiley.

Garmezy, N. (1985). Stress-resistant children: The search for protective factors. In J. E. Stevenson (Ed.), *Recent research in developmental psychopathology: Journal of Child Psychology and Psychiatry Book Supplement 4* (pp. 213–233). Oxford, UK: Pergamon Press.

Garmezy, N. (1987). Stress, competence, and development: Continuities in the study of schizophrenic adults, children vulnerable to psychopathology, and the search for stress-resistant children. *American Journal of Orthopsychiatry,* 159–174.

Garmezy, N. (1991). Resiliency and vulnerability to adverse developmental outcomes associated with poverty. *American Behavioral Scientist,* 34(4), 416–430.

Garmezy, N. (1993). Children in poverty: Resilience despite risk. *Psychiatry,* 56, 127–136.

Garmezy, N., Masten, A.S., & Tellegen, A. (1984). The study of stress and competence in children: A building block for developmental psychopathology. *Child Development,* 55, 97–111.

Geltner, P. (2013). *Emotional communication: Countertransference analysis and the use of feeling in psychoanalytic technique.* New York, NY: Routledge.

Gladwell, M. (2005). *Blink: The power of thinking without thinking.* New York, NY: Little Brown and Company.

Glaser, B., & Strauss, A. (1967). *The discovery of grounded theory: Strategies for qualitative research.* London: Weiderfeld and Nicolson.

Gordon, E.W. & Song, L.D. (1994). Variations in the experience of resilience. In M.C. Wang & E.W. Gordon (Eds.), *Educational resilience in inner-city America: Challenges and prospects* (pp. 27–43). Hillsdale, NJ: Lawrence Erlbaum Associates.

Gottlieb, G. (2007). Probabilistic epigenetics. *Developmental Science,* 10, 1–11.

Grossmark, R. (2012). The flow of enactive engagement. *Contemporary Psychoanalysis,* 48: 287–300.

Harris, M., Martin, M., & Martin, D. (2013). The relationship between psychological well-being and perceived wellness in graduate-level counseling students. *Higher Learning Research Communications,* 3(2), 14–31.

Hasher, L., & Zacks, R. (1984). Automatic processing of fundamental information: The case of frequency of occurrence. *American Psychology,* 39(12), 1372–1388.

Helgeson, V.S., Reynolds, K.A, & Tomich, P.L. (2006). A meta-analytic review of benefit finding and growth. *Journal of Consulting and Clinical Psychology,* 74(5), 797–816.

Hernandez, P., Engstrom, D., & Gangsei, D. (2010). Exploring the impact of trauma on therapists: Vicarious resilience and related concepts in training. *Journal of Systemic Therapies*, 29(1), 67–83.

Hernandez, P., Gangsei, D., & Engstrom, D. (2007). Vicarious resilience: A new concept in work with those who survive trauma. *Family Process*, *46*(2), 229–41.

Hernandez-Wolfe, P., Killian, K., Engstrom, D., & Gangsei, D. (2014). Vicarious resilience, vicarious trauma, and awareness of equity in trauma work. *Journal of Humanistic Psychology*, 56(2), 153–172.

Herrman, H., Stewart, D.E., Diaz-Granados, N., Berger, E.L., Jackson, B., & Yuen, T. (2011). What is resilience? *Canadian Journal of Psychiatry*, 56, 258–265.

Hunter, S.V. (2012). Walking in sacred spaces in the therapeutic bond: Therapists' experiences of compassion satisfaction coupled with the potential for vicarious traumatization. *Journal of Advanced Nursing*, 60(1), 1–9.

Kahneman, D. (2012). *Thinking, fast and slow.* New York, NY: Macmillan.

Katz, S.M. (2013). General psychoanalytic field theory: Its structure and applications to psychoanalytic perspectives. *Psychoanalytic Inquiry*, 33, 277–292.

Kernberg, O.F. (1986), Countertransference, transference, regression, and the incapacity to defend. In *Between Analyst and Patient: New Dimensions in Countertransference*. (Ed.) H.C. Hayes. Hillsdale, NJ: Analytic Press.

Kernberg, O.F. (2011). Divergent contemporary trends in psychoanalytic theory. *Psychoanalytic Rev*iew, 98, 633–664.

Kernberg, O.F. (2016). *Psychoanalytic education at the crossroads: Reformation, change and the future of psychoanalytic training.* New York, NY: Routledge.

Kuhn, T. (1962). *The structure of scientific revolutions.* Chicago: University of Chicago Press.

Kuiper, N. (2012). Humor and resiliency: Towards a process model of coping and growth. *Europe's Journal of Psychology*, 8(3), 475–491.

Langer, E. (1997). *The power of mindful learning.* Cambridge, Ma: DeCapo Press.

LeDoux, J. (2003). *The synaptic self.* New York, NY: Penguin.

Leipold, B., & Greve, W. (2009). Resilience: A conceptual bridge between coping and development. *European Psychologist*, 14, 40–50.

Leiter, M.P., Harvie, P., & Frizzell, C. (1998). The correspondence of patient satisfaction and nurse burnout. *Social Science and Medicine*, 47, 1611–1617.

Leiter, M.P., & Maslach, C. (2004). Areas of worklife: A structured approach to organizational predictors of job burnout. In: P. Perrewé & D.C. Ganster (Eds.), *Research in occupational stress and well being* (Vol. 3, pp. 91–134). Oxford, UK: Elsevier.

Levin, F. (2011). *Psyche and brain: The biology of talking cures.* London: Karnac.

Liegner, E. (2003). Countertransference: Resistance and therapeutic leverage. *Modern Psychoanalysis*, 28, 7–13.

Ligiero, D.P., & Gelso, C.J. (2002). Countertransference, attachment, and the working alliance: The therapist's contribution. *Psychotherapy: Theory, Research, Practice, Training*, *39*, 3–11.

Luthar, S., & Cicchetti D. (2000). The construct of resilience: Implications for interventions and social policies. *Developmental Psychopathol*ogy, 12(4), 857–885.

Margolis, B. (1986). Joining, mirroring, psychological reflection: Terminology, definitions, theoretical considerations. *Modern Psychoanalysis*, 11, 19–35.

Margolis, B.D. (1994). The object-oriented question: A contribution to treatment technique. *Modern Psychoanalysis,* 19, 187–198.

Maroda, K.J. (2005). Legitimate gratification of the analyst's needs. *Contemporary Psychoanalysis,* 41, 371–388.

Marshall, R.J. (1997). A dynamic and structural model of the triad in supervision. *Modern Psychoanalysis,* 22(1), 41–57.

Marshall, R.J. (2006). Suppose there were no mirrors: Converging concepts of mirroring. *Modern Psychoanalysis,* 31, 289–312.

Marshall, R.J. & Marshall, S. (1988). *The transference-countertransference matrix: The emotional-cognitive dialogue in psychotherapy, psychoanalysis and supervision.* New York, NY: Columbia University Press.

Martin-Breen, P., & Anderies, J.M. (2011). *Resilience: A literature review.* New York, NY: The Rockefeller Foundation.

Maslach, C., & Leiter, M.P. (1997). The truth about burnout: How organizations cause personal stress and what to do about it. San Francisco, CA: Jossey-Bass.

Masten, A.S. (1994). Resilience in individual development: Successful adaptation despite risk and adversity. In: M.C. Wang & E.W. Gordon (Eds.), *Educational resilience in inner-city America: Challenges and prospects* (pp. 3– 25). Hillsdale, NJ: Lawrence Erlbaum.

Masten, A.S. (2001). Ordinary magic: Resilience processes in development. *American Psychologist,* 56(3), 227–238.

Masten, A.S. (2007). Resilience in developing systems: Progress and promise as the fourth wave rises. *Development and Psychopathology,* 19, 921–930.

Masten, A.S., Garmezy N., Tellegen, A., Pellegrini, D.S., Larkin, K., & Larsen, A. (1988). Competence and stress in school children: The moderating effects of in-dividual and family qualities. *Journal for Child Psychiatry and Psychology,* 28, 745–764.

McCann, I.L., & Pearlman, L.A. (1990). Vicarious traumatization: A framework for understanding the psychological effects of working with victims. *Journal of Traumatic Stress,* 3, 131–149.

Metzger, J.A. (2014). Adaptive defense mechanisms: Function and transcendence. *Journal of Clinical Psychology,* 70(5), 478–488.

Molden, D. (2014). Understanding priming effects in social psychology: What is "social priming" and how does it occur? *Social Cognition,* 32, Special Issue, 1–11.

Norcross, J. C. (2010). The therapeutic relationship. In B. L. Duncan, S. D. Miller, B. E. Wampold & M. A. Hubble (Eds.), *The heart and soul of change: Delivering what works in therapy* (pp. 113–141). Washington, DC: American Psychological Association.

Pearlman, L.A., & MacIan, P.S. (1995). Vicarious traumatization: An empirical study of the effects of trauma work on trauma therapists. *Professional Psychology: Research and Practice,* 26(6), 558–565.

Perry, J.C. (2014). Anomalies and specific functions in the clinical identification of defense mechanisms. *Journal of Clinical Psychology,* 70(5), 405–488.

Perry J.C., & Bond, M. (2000). Empirical studies of psychotherapy for personality disorders. In: J.G. Gunderson & G.O. Gabbard (Eds.), *Psychotherapy for personality disorders* (pp. 1–31). Washington, DC: American Psychiatric Press.

Perry J.C., & Bond, M. (2012). Change in defense mechanisms during long-term dynamic five-year outcome. *American Journal of Psychiatry,* 169(9), 916–925.

Perry, J.C., & Cooper, S.H. (1986). A preliminary report on defenses and conflicts associated with borderline personality disorder. *Journal of American Psychoanalytic Association*, 34(4), 863–893.

Perry, J.C., Hoglend, P., Shear, K., Vaillant, G.E., Horowitz, M.J., Kardos, M.E., & Bille, H. (1998). Field trial of a diagnostic axis for defense mechanisms for DSM-IV. *Journal of Personality Disorders,* 12, 56–68.

Peterson, C., Park, N., Pole, N., D'Andrea, W., & Seligman, M.E.P. (2008). Strengths of character and posttraumatic growth. *Journal of Traumatic Stress,* 21(2), 214–217.

Phelps, A., Lloyd, D., Creamer, M. & Forbes, D. (2009). Caring for carers in the aftermath of trauma. *Journal of Aggression, Maltreatment & Trauma,* 18, 313–330.

Power, D. (2014). Hoodwinked: The use of the analyst as autistic shape. Retrieved from: *http://www.frances-tustin-autism.org/eng/pal_pdfs/DolanPower.pdf.*

Ray, S.L., Wong, C., White, D., & Heaslip, K. (2013). Compassion satisfaction, compassion fatigue, work life conditions, and burnout among frontline mental health care professionals. *Traumatology,* 19(4), 255–267.

Richardson, G.E. (2002). The metatheory of resilience and resiliency. *Journal of Clinical Psychology,* 58, 307–321.

Richardson, G.E., Neiger, B., Jensen, S., & Kumfer, K. (1990). The resiliency model. *Health Education,* 21, 33–39.

Rolf, J.E. (1999). An interview with Norman Garmezy. In: M. Glantz & J. Johnson (Eds.), *Resilience and development: Positive life adaptations* (pp. 5–14). New York, NY: Kluwer Academic/Plenum Publishers.

Roth, A., & Fonagy, P. (1999). *What works for whom? A critical review of psychotherapy research.* NY: Guilford Press.

Rutter, M. (1987). Psychosocial resilience and protective mechanisms. *American Journal of Orthopsychiatry,* 57, 316–331.

Rutter, M. (2012). Resilience as a dynamic concept. *Development and Psychopathology,* 24, 335–344.

Saakvitne, K.W. (2002). Shared trauma: The therapist's increased vulnerability. *Psychoanalytic Dialogues,* 12, 443–449.

Schmale, A.H. (1964). A genetic view of affects with special reference to the genesis of helplessness and hopelessness. *Psychoanalytic Study of the Child,* 19, 287–310.

Seidman, I. (2006). *Interviewing as qualitative research.* New York, NY: Teachers College Press.

Simon, C.E., Pryce, J.G., Roff, L.L., & Klemmack, D. (2006). Secondary traumatic stress and oncology social work: Protecting compassion from fatigue and compromising the worker's worldview. *Journal of Psychosocial Oncology,* 23(4), 1–14.

Spotnitz, H. (1969). *Modern psychoanalysis of the schizophrenic patient.* New York, NY: Grune & Stratton.

Spotnitz, H. (1979). Narcissistic countertransference. *Contemporary Psychoanalysis,* 15, 545–559.

Spotnitz, H. (1985). *Modern psychoanalysis of the schizophrenic patient* (Second Edition). New York, NY: Human Sciences Press.

Spotnitz, H. (1995). The need for insulation. In: *The Psychotherapy of Preoedipal Conditions* (pp. 117–136). New York, NY: Jason Aronson.

Spotnitz, H. (2013). The maturational interpretation. *Psychoanalytic Review,* 100(4), 583–587.

Stamm, B.H. (2005). The ProQOL manual. The professional quality of life scale: Compassion satisfaction, burnout & compassion fatigue/secondary trauma scales. Retrieved from: http://www.compassionfatigue.org/pages/ProQOLManualOct05.pdf.

Stamm, B.H. (2012). Helping the helpers : Compassion satisfaction and compassion fatigue in self-care, management, and policy. *Resources for Community Suicide Prevention*, 1–4.

Tabachnick, B., Keith-Spiegel, K.G., Pope, P., & Kenneth, S. (1991). Ethics of teaching: Beliefs and behaviors of psychologists as educators. *American Psychologist*, 46(5), 506–515.

Thomas, D. (2006). A general inductive approach for analyzing qualitative evaluation data. *American Journal of Evaluation*, 27(2), 237–246.

Thomas, G., & James, D. (2013). Re-inventing grounded theory: Some questions about theory, ground and discovery. *British Educational Research Journal*, 32 (6), 767–795.

Tusaie, K., & Dyer, J. (2004). Resilience: A historical review. *Holistic Nursing Practice*, 18, 3–10.

Vaillant, G.E. (1977). *Adaptation to life*. Boston: Little, Brown and Company.

Vaillant, G.E. (1992). *Ego mechanisms of defense: A guide for clinicians and researchers*. Washington, DC: American Psychiatric Association Press.

Vaillant G.E. (1993). *The wisdom of ego*. Cambridge, MA: Harvard University Press.

Vaillant, G.E. (1998). Where do we go from here? *Journal of Personality*, 66, 1147–1157.

Vaillant, G.E. (2000). Adaptive mental mechanisms: Their role in a positive psychology. *American Psychology*, 55(1), 89–98.

Vaillant, G. (2002). *Aging well*. Boston: Little, Brown and Company.

Vallaint, G.E. (2011). Involuntary coping mechanisms: A psychodynamic perspective. *Dialogues in Clinical Neuroscience*, 13(3), 366–370.

Vaillant, G. E. (2012). *Triumph of experience*. Boston: Harvard University Press.

van Breda, A. (2001). Resilience theory: A literature review. Retrieved from: *http://www.vanbreda.org/adrian/resilience/resilience_theory_review.pdf*.

Werner, E.E. (1993). Risk, resilience, and recovery: Perspectives from the Kauai longitudinal study. *Development and Psychopathology*, 5, 503–515.

Werner, E.E, & Smith, R. (1992). *Overcoming the odds: High risk children from birth to adulthood*. Ithaca, NY: Cornell University Press.

What if? Retrieved from: https://what-if.xkcd.com/77/.

Wilson, T.D. (2002). *Strangers to ourselves: Discovering the adaptive unconscious*. Boston: Belknap Press.

Windle, G. (2011). What is resilience? A review and concept analysis. *Reviews in Clinical Gerontology*, 21(2), 152–169.

Winnicott, D.W. (1949). Hate in the counter-transference. *International Journal Psychoanalysis*, 30, 69–74.

Wright, M.O.D., Masten, A.S., & Narayan, A.J. (2013). Resilience processes in development: Four waves of research on positive adaptation in the context of adversity. In S. Goldstein & R.B. Brooks (Eds.), *Handbook of resilience in children* (pp. 15–38). New York, NY: Springer.

Yates, T.M., & Masten, A.S. (2004). Fostering the future: Resilience theory and the practice of positive psychology. In: P.A. Linley & S. Joseph (Eds.), *Positive psychology in practice* (pp. 521–539). Hoboken, NJ: John Wiley and Sons.

Index

childhood trauma of interviewees
108–10; suppression and childhood
trauma of interviewees 122, 125–6,
129–30, 134
Cicchetti, D. 54
clinical supervision: active listening
model 177; Mature Adaptive Defenses
and the role of supervision 78;
Reciprocal Resilience building through
7, 11, 173, 176, 177; transference in
the supervisory relationship 177; and
the well-being of the clinician 12–13,
44; *see also* training
clinicians *see* therapists
cognitive psychology 31
compassion fatigue 45–6
compassion satisfaction 46
coping mechanisms 136; *see also* Mature
Adaptive Defenses
countertransference: and the clinician-
client relationship 12; co-creative
therapeutic loops 40–1, 42–3;
definition 34; Empathic Listening 39;
Intersubjective Listening 39; objective
countertransference 39–40; within
the research interviews 23; subjective
countertransference 40; transference
in the supervisory relationship 177
countertransference resistance 40
Cramer, P. 54
Creamer, M, 46

denial 124, 136–8
Department of Child Protection and
Permanency (DCPP) 11

ego: defense mechanisms and 52–3;
and the development of self 162;
helplessness and 4; hopelessness and 4;
object-oriented interventions and 7; of
the therapist 7, 85
ego resiliency 36
ego syntonic joining 170, 177
empathy 39, 99–103, 146
Engstrom, D. 8, 41–3, 44, 166–7, 176–7

fawn responses 6
feeling-impulse-action thread 124
fight-flight-freeze 6, 92, 124
Figley, C.R. 45
Forbes, D. 46
Frequency Illusion 172
Freud, Anna 53

Freud, Sigmund 52, 53, 162
Freudenberger, H. 46

Galletta, A. 24, 28
Gangsei, D. 8, 41–3, 44, 166, 167, 176–7
Garmezy, Norman 34–5, 38, 39, 54, 143
Generic Qualitative Research Method
26–7
Gladwell, M. 31
Gordon, E.W. 36
Grossmark, R. 7–8, 41
Grounded Theory protocol 27

Harris, M. 3–4
Harris, T. 114
Harvard Grant Study 53–4, 163
Hasher, L. 171
Helgeson, V.S. 47
helplessness 2, 14
Hernandez, P. 8, 41–3, 44, 166, 167,
176–7
hierarchy of adaptive defenses (Vaillant):
high-adaptive defences 56, 57;
overview of 30, 56; self-deception and
52, 55, 162; *see also* Mature Adaptive
Defenses
Holocaust survivors 125
hopelessness 4–5, 14–15, 128, 134, 146
humor: to alleviate anxiety 65, 149–50,
151; in the clinical setting 150–1;
corresponding resilience traits 64, 150;
and the data analysis of the interviews
30–1; definition 64, 150; within
the hierarchy of adaptive defenses
(Vaillant) 30, 57; as least used defense
mechanism 150; merits of 157–8;
peek-a-boo games 149; within the
research process 20; resilient use of by
research participants 65, 76–9, 150,
151–7, 158, 175; as sublimation 156,
157–8; and the suspension of disbelief
158; types of 150
Hunter, S.V. 43–4

interpersonal relationships 39,
53–4, 163

Jacobs, C. 27–8
James, D. 27, 28
Johnson, J. 45
joining: in the clinical setting 169–70;
defined 169; ego syntonic joining 170;
maturational interpretations 171